CYPRUS

THE TRAGEDY AND THE CHALLENGE

POLYVIOS G. POLYVIOU

Fellow of Lincoln College
Lecturer in Law at the University of Oxford

CYPRUS
THE TRAGEDY AND
THE CHALLENGE

American Hellenic Institute
Washington, D.C.

Published 1975 by
The American Hellenic Institute, Inc.
1730 K Street, N.W.
Washington, D.C. 20006

TO

MY PARENTS AND GRANDPARENTS

PREFACE

N O book should ever be written like this. "Cyprus, The Tragedy and the Challenge" was written with undue haste. An outline of it was written in Cyprus during the hostilities, an atmosphere hardly conducive to clear thought or objective and dispassionate scholarship. The rest of the work was prepared in Oxford, in the middle of a very hectic term of tutoring and lecturing, without much time for thorough research or sustained thought. But one could not wait longer. The niceties of academic presentation must, on occasion, give way to more pressing needs, and such is the case here. For a catastrophe of biblical dimensions has struck Cyprus. Its people, once prosperous, are now fighting for survival in their ancestral land. Most of them have been reduced overnight to the miserable condition of refugees; their homes have gone, their sons have vanished, their life rendered empty and futile. Almost half of Cyprus is still under foreign occupation. And the memory of the world is short. The drama of Cyprus seems to have been already forgotten. Yet, the tragedy continues, and it is one of the purposes of this study to bring the problem of Cyprus to the attention of politicians, constitutional lawyers, other specialists and international public opinion at large.

In the first two chapters I briefly delve into English Colonial policy on Cyprus and analyse the 1960 Constitution and the events that followed upon its collapse. In the third Chapter I discuss the Turkish invasion of Cyprus, its consequences, legal aspects and international implications, and I then put forward specific proposals and suggestions concerning the Island's political and Constitutional reconstruction.

It is earnestly hoped that this study will not only renew interest in the affairs and fate of Cyprus but will also make some small contribution to efforts for finding a peaceful and just solution to the problem of Cyprus. I must, of course, acknowledge the obvious. As someone who is both a Greek Cypriot and has had the honour of serving under Mr. Clerides at Geneva and elsewhere, I cannot, primarily in so far as relates to interpreting the past, claim an attitude of complete detachment and, again, I realise, principally with regard to English Colonial policy, that strong disagreement may be expressed with my historical analysis. It is hoped, however, that my specific proposals concerning Cyprus' constitutional and political future will not be dismissed out of hand as a manifestation of partisanship falsely pretending to the respectable cloak of disinterested scholarship. They are nothing more, it is believed, than the dictates of common sense constitutionally elaborated, and a conscious effort has been made to discover common ground in the apparently hopelessly conflicting positions of the parties. At least the purpose of my proposals, to bring about a sovereign, independent and peaceful state with full security for all its people, should surely incur neither the condemnation of partiality nor the reproach of irrelevance. I hope that my suggestions will be judged on their merits and that fruitful discussion will be initiated.

I want gratefully to acknowledge the help and assistance of: Dr. George Georghallides, who took the trouble to send me an excellent paper on Anglo-Cypriot relations which I freely drew from; Mr. Zenon Stavrinides, who sent me a paper full of perceptive comments on a great variety of matters; Dr. Kypros Chrysostomides, for many interesting and helpful discussions when I was last in Cyprus; Mr. N. Mitropoulos who put me in touch with Senator Kennedy's office and who kindly provided me with materials relating to American policy; and Mr. Z. S. Eliades, for help throughout.

I also want to thank all those who sent me notes and letters concerning my previous pamphlet on "The Cyprus problem".

Mr. Tornaritis, Attorney-General of the Republic of Cyprus, and Mr. Triantafyllides, President of the Supreme Court, have contributed decisively to my understanding of the Cyprus problem. Both combine profound legal erudition with great knowledge of the developments analysed in this book, and I have derived much from discussions with them.

I owe a very special debt of gratitude to Mr. Clerides for his unfailing kindness and generosity to me. Mr. Clerides assumed the Presidency in accordance with the relevant Constitutional provisions after the fall from power of those who assumed positions of authority after the coup of the 15th July, and exercised the duties of the Presidency and discharged its functions through some of the most tragic and difficult moments of Cypriot history with great dignity and courage. Through his decisive leadership and unsparing efforts in the interests of peace and justice, Mr. Clerides has earned the gratitude and admiration of all Cyprus.

Finally, I wish to acknowledge my indebtedness to Mr. Ashiotis, Cyprus High Commissioner, and Mr. Erotokritos, Commercial Counsellor in London, for kindly providing special facilities for the preparation of this book. In this connexion, the typing skills, patience and helpfulness of Miss M. Kyriazi and Mrs. N. Pieridou proved invaluable.

None of the above should be held responsible for any statements or errors contained in this book. The views put forward are my own. I alone am accountable for them.

CONTENTS

CYPRUS

THE TRAGEDY AND THE CHALLENGE

I

INTRODUCTION

CYPRUS,[1] the third largest island in the Mediterranean, of an extent of 3584 square miles, is inhabited by 80% Greeks and 18% Turks, the rest consisting of other minorities. At present, land ownership by area is 80.6% by Greeks, 16.6% by Turks and 2.8% by others. Land ownership by value is 86.5% by Greeks, 13.1% by Turks and 0.4% by others. The holding of agricultural land by number of holders is 84.2% by Greeks, 15.1% by Turks and 0.7% by others; and, by area, it is 78.3% by Greeks, 20.4% by Turks and 1.3% by others. The irrigated land ownership is 80.6% by Greeks, 16.2% by Turks and 3.2% by others. The importance of such statistics will appear later.

Owing to its privileged geographical position, the riches of its soil and subsoil and the variety of its products, Cyprus has, since antiquity, been coveted by the great powers of the day. As observed by the German archaeologist Hirschfeld, "he who would become and remain a great power in the East must hold Cyprus in his hands". For this reason one conqueror succeeded another.

Cyprus was conquered by the Turks in 1571. The present Turks of Cyprus are descendants of those who came and settled in the island during the Ottoman Occupation — but, it must be emphasised, the crushing majority of the people of Cyprus always were, and, of course, still are, Greeks. The last rulers of the island were the British. Cyprus passed to Britain by Treaty in 1878, though still continuing to be under the suzerainty of the Turkish Sultans. In 1914, when Turkey entered the First World War against the allies, Cyprus was annexed by Britain. By the Treaty of Lausanne, signed in 1923, Turkey recognised, internationally and without any reservation, that it had no right or claim on Cyprus. Throughout the years of Colonialism, the Greeks of Cyprus, being over 80% of the population, never wavered in their demand for freedom. Finally, in April 1955, after all efforts to attain freedom by peaceful means had failed, the Greek Cypriots revolted against the British Colonial regime; and after a four year struggle, Cyprus was proclaimed an independent State. And, one might sadly add, our real troubles began.

Both the pattern of Cypriot politics since independence and the development of the Cyprus problem itself have, in certain important ways, been prescribed on the one hand by events which took place during Britain's administration of Cyprus between 1878 and 1960 and, on the other, by the more general policies pursued by the British Government, particularly after 1950. It must be, of course, immediately admitted that the tasks which Britain faced in Cyprus were of an unusual nature. Unlike the great majority of its imperial possessions, Cyprus was situated in the Eastern Mediterranean — not far from the European heartland. Unlike England's Asian and African colonies, Cyprus had a European population of whom about 80% were Greek by nationality and Orthodox Christian by religion. They naturally looked back with pride to the 3,000 years of their history and the achievements of Greek civilization. For them the British acquisition of Cyprus, coming after 300 years of oppressive Turkish rule, was felicitous and a liberation. But they could not accept it as an end in itself. The Greeks felt intensely — and with the passage of time their nationalist fervour increased — the bonds which united them with the Hellenic kingdom. They were willing to co-operate with the British authorities for the island's welfare. Yet, even during the liberal phase of the British administration, from 1882 to 1931, when Cyprus had a Legislative Council with an elected majority, they refused to sacrifice the struggle for eventual union with Greece for the sake of local liberties. Faced with the Greeks' early rejection of the British imperial system and the subservient role which it gave to native peoples, Britain resorted to policies which have had lasting, as well as profoundly unfortunate, results on Cyprus.

Since it had no hope of altering the outlook of the Greeks, the British Government gave its attention to the 18% Turkish minority whom it made its ally in Cyprus. Far from initiating policies which might in time have led to the gradual disappearance of the historic divisions between Greek and Turk, the British Government actually galvanised Turkish fears and suspicions of the Greeks. This it did largely because the Turkish minority offered itself as the almost ideal medium for the enforcement of British policies on Cyprus. During the declining years of the Ottoman Empire and the First World War, the authorities at Constantinople showed little interest in Cyprus or the Turkish Cypriots. This detachment from the island's life continued under the Turkish Republic. Kemal Ataturk himself did not consider it worth his while to include Cyprus among the territories which he claimed for Turkey in the 1919 National Pact. By the Treaty of Lausanne he cheerfully acknowledged Britain's 1914 annexation of Cyprus and divested Turkey of all rights and claims over the island. Ataturk's lack of interest in Cyprus was expressed by the Turkish Government's encouragement of a project for the emigration and settlement of the Moslem population of Cyprus in Anatolia. The patron of the Turkish Cypriots until the emergence of interest for Cyprus in Turkey in the late 1940s and early 1950s was undoubtedly Great Britain. The attraction of the cause of the Turks of Cyprus lay in the fact that until the last decade of British rule the Turks appeared to be generally free of the nationalism which animated the Greek Cypriots. They sought no extension of democratic rights, obediently supporting Britain in all the spheres of Government action. In return for their collaboration Britain rewarded the Turks: it never attempted to instruct them that as a minority they should come to terms with the inevitability of some sort of political evolution in Cyprus which would be likely to place them under the preponderant influence of the more numerous Greek community. Furthermore, by repeatedly justifying, particularly in later times, its stereotyped rejections of the Greek Cypriot demand for the union of Cyprus with Greece not on the real grounds of the potential strategic importance attached to the possession of Cyprus but on the grounds that the Turkish Cypriots needed protection from future Greek domination, Britain pre-empted any possibility for the achievement of a political understanding between Greeks and Turks. In the actual administration of the island, Britain fostered separate Turkish institutions and indeed a substantial measure of segregation for the Turkish population which was encouraged to close ranks against its Greek neighbours and to rely on the Government's good-will.

It has been well said that "one of the characteristic features of the British Colonial regime was that (until very late) it never seriously envisaged its own ending"[2]. Even when limited proposals for self-government were being put forward, the British Government was never very specific concerning such arrangements; and, invariably, such proposals were coupled with the proviso that the British Government could not "contemplate a change of sovereignty in Cyprus". Particularly instructive, for instance, is the statement of Mr. Hopkinson, Minister of State for

Colonial Affairs, in a speech before the House of Commons:
"...It has always been understood and agreed that there are
certain territories in the Commonwealth which owing to their
particular circumstances can never expect to be fully
independent". And the Minister made it clear that Cyprus was one
of such territories. "The question of the abrogation of British
Sovereignty cannot arise ...British Sovereignty will remain"[3]. As
a result of such refusal even to contemplate a change of
sovereignty in the case of Cyprus, the authorities in London never
made any genuine attempt to encourage the development of the
political and social conditions which would be necessary for the
government of Cyprus in a framework other than that of a British
Colony.

Owing to the 1955 rebellion against British rule, Britain's
possession of Cyprus became very costly in money and blood. In
its hour of need, the British Government threw away all pretence
that it was the impartial arbitrator between Greeks and Turks. It
expressed full support for the Turkish Cypriot objections to the
self determination of Cyprus and skilfully mobilised both the
Turkish Cypriots and the Ankara Government in an effort to
frustrate the Greek Cypriot campaign for the liberation of Cyprus.
The very concept of partition, as will be immediately made
apparent, owed a great deal to the 1956-57 anti-Greek Cypriot
plans of the Colonial office and of the island's Government.

Considering British policy regarding Cyprus between 1954-60,
we can clearly see that there were three main issues of
fundamental importance on which the British Government, to
begin with and for a substantial period thereafter, had no coherent
policy and in connection with which, as a result, many shifts of
view and numerous variations both in doctrine and presentation
appeared. These three questions were: (a) How should one state
the Cyprus problem? Was it an internal problem or an
international question? (b) What were the strategic considerations
in connection with Cyprus? Whose defence was Cyprus most
important for? And how could such defence considerations be
most appropriately provided for? And (c) Was self-determination
relevant to the case of Cyprus? How would one apply such a
concept to Cyprus?

(a) That the British Government was, for a long period, not able
to make up its mind as to "what the problem (was)" was pointed
out by Mr. Aneurin Bevan in a speech before the House of
Commons on the 14th March, 1956[4]. "There has been confusion

as to whether the affair is a purely Cypriot-British affair or whether it is an international affair". Indeed, this appears from a consideration both of Parliamentary Debates and of statements by British Representatives before the UN.

Thus, the Marquess of Salisbury, on the 15th December, 1955, said:[5] "If Cyprus today is not an international question which might have incalculable effects on the relations of other nations in the Eastern Mediterranean, in my view that is simply because we British are there". The noble Lord also said: "So long as that situation continues, so long as we remain there, while the international position is as it is — however unpleasant it may be for us; and it is extremely unpleasant and extremely expensive — it will be the direct concern only of Britain and Cyprus". And this was said after a tripartite Conference had been called, including Turkey and Greece. Further, the Colonial Secretary himself, on the 21st December, did not seem to see eye to eye with Lord Salisbury. He had said: "I can say that were it not for the fact that Turkish interests were involved, and that this was more an international than a colonial problem, a way out of this difficulty could have been found long ago"[6]. There was similar ambiguity of position in the International forum of the UN. It has been well said that originally "the British defence of continued control over the island could be summarised in two principles of international law: the sanctity of treaties and the absolute authority inherent in the concept of Sovereignty"[7]. England, so the argument went, acquired sovereignty over Cyprus as a result of the Treaty of Lausanne. This was a solemn and binding International agreement. It could not be revised without the consent of Britain, and the concept of sovereignty meant that the Cyprus question was, primarily, an internal British problem. The artificiality and excessive legalism of such an argument were, from the start, apparent; and it was soon abandoned in favour of an explicit acknowledgment that Cyprus was, indeed, a complex international problem, such an argument being now cleverly used to support Britain's continuing refusal to allow the principle of self-determination, in its traditional form, to apply to the people of Cyprus. How did this come about? Greece and the Greek Cypriots had been urging that the Cyprus question was more than a British internal matter or even a colonial one. For them, it was above all an international issue, in the sense that the established international principle of self determination was the only one that afforded a tenable and principled solution to the problem. But now

Britain, in the best manner of an experienced lawyer, turned this argument on its head. The Cyprus crisis was, indeed, an international problem, but not in the sense that self determination, as traditionally understood, could be accorded to the people of the island — it was an international issue in that three nations were concerned with the problem of Cyprus. "First, the UK: The sovereignty of the island is now vested in us. It is our responsibility to safeguard the peace and well being of the Cypriots . . . A large majority of the population are Greek Cypriots. In addition to their cultural and religious leanings towards Greece, they aspire toward union with Greece. Therefore, Greece has a strong interest in the island. Then there is Turkey. A considerable number of Turkish Cypriots live in the island, people who look to Turkey as their fatherland. The island is of great strategic importance to Turkey, covering its southern ports and has a long association with Turkey in the past. It is a case, therefore, . . .of three countries having an interest in the problem. It is a tripartite problem".[9] We already see that no attempt is made to differentiate the "interests" of Greece and Turkey in the matter. The fact that 80% of the population were Greek Cypriots is simply one of the many factors which should be taken into account, to be counterbalanced by Turkey's geographical "claims" and by the island's strategic importance to Turkey's security. Over and above such considerations, there was also the question of British strategic interests. For example, in the course of the same speech from which the above extract is taken, Mr. Lloyd pointed out that "the island is important to us from a military point of view so that we should be able to fulfil our international obligations"; and, at the same time, mention is already made of the two Communities of Cyprus rather than of the majority and the minority. "Each Community should control its own affairs".[9] We clearly see through such complex strands of argument that British diplomacy, gradually but perhaps inevitably, was, at every turn, outmanoeuvring the Greek efforts to project the Cyprus problem on the agenda of the International organisations and the conscience of the world by, ingeniously, taking advantage of such efforts by first admitting that Cyprus was, indeed, an international problem and then deriving from such admission not the inevitability of unfettered self determination being accorded to the people of Cyprus, but the necessity for some solution to the problem that would provide for, and secure, all the manifold interests involved in the island.

(b) The security aspects of the problem, as already seen, have been very important. For a substantial part of the period we are discussing it was, "very hard to discover whether the (British) Government (were) anxious to have Cyprus as a base or a base on Cyprus";[10] or why Britain's security interests could not be satisfied otherwise than by continuation of British sovereignty in view of the fact that, as Mr. Bevan pointed out in the House of Commons, "it ha(d) been clear from the beginning that if there had been Union with Greece, NATO bases would not have been denied" and that British defence needs would be well provided. Indeed, something else that was not made clear was whether the strategic necessities that were being discussed were those of Britain, of NATO or the Commonwealth. For instance, Sir John Harding in January, 1956, said, with the approval of the Colonial Secretary, that one of the difficulties about Union with Greece "arose from the fact we (the British) might desire to use the base on Cyprus for military operations in the Middle East in which Greece was not directly associated and concerned". Yet, on other occasions, it was stated by the British Government that the relevant strategic interests were those of NATO and the Western World in general (which, of course, included Greece).

More fundamentally, such strategic needs and interests, whether of NATO or Britain, were never fully articulated or subjected to close scrutiny. As Lord Attlee pointed out in a speech before the House of Lords, what was normally said on the general strategic importance of Cyprus seemed to him "to run entirely contrary to . . . (a) thoughtful, broad and wise survey of conditions in the hydrogen bomb age . . .".[11] "We are told", Lord Attlee continued, "that Cyprus is essential for our position. We are told that Cyprus is needed to protect oil fields in Iraq, Persia or Kuwait. This is called 'our' oil — though why, I do not know: we have not yet paid for it, and it is in other countries. But I . . . should like to know exactly how one protects from Cyprus oil fields in Iraq and Iran. I do not quite know how that is to be done". Indeed, one cannot escape the conclusion that the question of Cyprus' strategic importance was "too often considered in an out of date manner".[12] In this area, too, however, there was a conscious shift towards Turkey, the Colonial Office emphasising, as time went on, not so much the strategic significance of Cyprus for Britain but its military value for Turkey. In this connection, there gradually developed a distinct similarity between the positions of England and Turkey. The Turkish Representative, Mr. Sarper, stated before the UN (11th Session) that "Cyprus was of primary importance to the defence of Turkey. If the country which held all the islands to the west of Turkey should also extend its authority to Cyprus, which controlled the routes of communication to the South, that country would encircle Turkey. It was obvious that no country would allow itself to be so completely encircled and . . . leave its entire security at the mercy of another country . . .". And the then British Prime Minister, Sir Anthony Eden, stated the following before the House of Commons (on the 14th March 1956): "Cyprus, in truth, commands the curve of Turkey's southern shore, and if ever the island were in the possession of a country with a system of Government unfriendly to her, the consequences to Turkey would be fatal".[13] For that reason he had never felt, and could not believe now, that Cyprus was an Anglo-Greek question. "To attempt to deny it is to deny the map". It was equally unrealistic "to lecture Turkey as to the view she ought to take about an island no further from her coast than . . . the Isle of Man (from Britain)".[14] It is not surprising that, after such unequivocal support for Turkey's claims, Turkey became more and more insistent on respect for her 'rights' over Cyprus. "Geographically", the Turkish Representative stated before the UN, "Cyprus was an off shore island of Turkey, a part of Asia Minor".[15] Furthermore, Turkish Representatives, encouraged by Britain's unexpectedly strong support, began advancing other lines of argument and hardening their position. Even historically, the most extreme and misconceived of such arguments went on, Turkey should be held entitled to Cyprus, for "from the remotest periods down to 1923, the island had always belonged to the power that ruled over Asia Minor". Again, in view of such developments, one cannot but express serious reservations both with regard to Britain's basic premises and Colonial Office tactics. Lord Attlee himself in his above mentioned House of Lords speech thought that "a quite extraordinary emphasis ha(d) been placed on the Turkish position".[16] It was one of "the most astounding things that a representative of the Foreign Office . . . should say that the possession of an island 40 miles away from another country was a serious menace and naturally 'got up the noses' of other countries".[17] It was not only this, however, that cast doubt on the Foreign Office's strategic thinking. Lord Attlee thought that it was 'utter madness'[18] for any one who wanted to attack Turkey to do it from Cyprus. And who were the potential enemies? Was it the Iron Curtain? But "the Iron Curtain touches other parts of Turkey much more closely". Was it Greece? But Greece was part of NATO, and it was made clear throughout that in the event of Union with Greece or Independence military bases — NATO or British ones, as the case might be — would not be denied.

To sum up, even though the strategic considerations associated with Cyprus were the ones that really mattered and the ones that were instrumental in the formulation of Foreign Office policy, such strategic considerations were never really clearly articulated or coherently presented. It can be seen, however, that a basic community of strategic interests between Great Britain and Turkey gradually developed, and it was this military affinity that made Britain ready to contemplate — or at least put forward — partition as a solution to the Cyprus problem.

(c) This brings us to the third issue — that of self determination. The concept of self determination which can be defined as "the liberty of the peoples to determine on the internal plane their Government without any foreign intervention — internal self determination — and on the external field their fate and international status — external self determination"[19] has always presented acute difficulties with regard to the Cyprus problem. The two major problems have been the following: (1) How would or should the principle of self determination apply to the case of Cyprus? And (2) was the right of self determination (inhering in the Cyprus people) validly and, perhaps, conclusively, exercised when Archbishop Makarios and Dr. Kutchuk (the then Turkish Cypriot leader) agreed to the Zürich and London Settlement?

(1) The Greek position as expressed both before and after Independence was that self determination as a right belonged to the people of Cyprus as a whole. In such presentation, the aspect of territory looms large. "The principle of self determination", Mr. Averoff, the then Greek Foreign Secretary, claimed before the UN, "had always been exercised by the whole body of a population living in a given territory and could be exercised in no other way. Minorities enjoyed that right as elements of the population".[20] The Turkish side, encouraged by English references to 'two Communities',[21] completely rejected such approach. It claimed in the early crucial UN Debates that the Turkish Cypriot people of Cyprus were not a minority but a community, 'a people'. Mr. Zorlu, the then Turkish Foreign Secretary, was of the opinion that the terms 'majority' and 'minority' could only be used "in the case of constituted States".[22] Such terms as 'majority' and 'minority' implied "juridical consequences" and could not be

used in the context of dependent territories. "Since Greece had objected to the present status of the Island, its future was now being discussed . . .". No one, the Turkish side went on, had the right "to prejudge the issue and speak as if his own views were already a reality". If the principle of self determination was to be applied, "it must be applied to both Communities", Mr. Zorlu claimed. "And if independence was to be granted, it must be granted to both".[23]

One cannot escape the conclusion, as Mr. Averoff himself claimed, that the Turkish theory "had . . . been invented to fit the case". There remained the questions, first, of explaining why the Turkish minority should be an exception to the juridical concept of a minority and, secondly and more important, of determining whether a minority could legitimately claim the right of self determination, the right to separate itself from the territorial entity. The Turkish side never made any attempt to answer these two questions. Even though, as is conceded later, different minorities may present different problems and thus necessitate a variety of solutions, such was not, it is thought, the case with Cyprus, a specific territorial unit (if ever there was one), particularly when one considers the totality of the circumstances of the case, historical and other. The fact that at the time Cyprus was not independent is not really material. "People", in the case of Cyprus, can surely only mean all the inhabitants of the territory of the island. The principle of self determination should, as a result, have been accorded to all the people of Cyprus as a whole. Such, unfortunately, has not been the case.

The idea of partitioning the island, the extreme but, perhaps, logical outcome of the "two Communities" concept (itself introduced by the British) also owes much to the machinations of the Colonial Office. Limited self government, according to these plans, would be introduced and then, if all went well, self determination would be recognised, but for both Communities separately. This meant that the island would be partitioned, part of Cyprus becoming sovereign Turkish territory. As has been well observed elsewhere, "it seems most unlikely that the British seriously advanced the partition proposals as a sound solution".[24] It is not only that Cyprus, as has been graphically described, is "an ethnographical fruit-cake in which the Greek and Turkish currants were mixed up in every town and village and often in every street"[25] but, also, a vast compulsory population movement, attended by great complications and immense hardship, would have been necessitated. Despite all these considerations, Turkey, of course, was only too pleased to join in the novel proposal of partition. Yet, no sooner had it done so than the British seemed to realise the implications of what they were proposing. They immediately attempted to dissociate themselves from partition. "The UK", it was now said, "was not in favour of partition, but the fact that partition was a solution advanced by some had to be taken into account".[26]

Such was British policy over Cyprus. One cannot but agree with Lord Attlee that the British Government were not "facing up to the problem". Internal repression and external confusion were not conducive to a correct understanding or satisfactory treatment of the problem. Having thus contributed to the expansion of the conflict; having (by the 1955 London Conference) conferred official recognition to Turkey's novel claim to determine the future of the island; having enrolled Turkish Cypriots as auxiliary policemen — thereby directly bringing them into the conflict; having, in other words, played a leading role in the transformation of the old-standing Greek-British conflict into a Greek-Turkish (British) conflict, in 1958 Britain decided that its key interests in Cyprus — which were then as always strategic — would be adequately served by a British withdrawal to the bases at Akrotiri and Dhekelia. Faced with the British threat (under the Macmillan plan) to give Turkey a share in the administration of Cyprus, Greece (which had only in the 1950s agreed to give diplomatic and limited military support to the Cypriot campaign for enosis) was forced to come to terms with Turkey. The two Powers and Britain agreed that neither enosis nor partition but the setting up of Cyprus as an independent and sovereign State under their guarantee could resolve the crisis.

(2) Talks were held in Zürich between the Greek and Turkish Governments, in the absence of any representatives of the Cypriots, and an agreement was reached there on the 11th February, 1959.[27] Upon agreement having been reached at Zürich, a Conference on Cyprus was called in London with the participation of the Governments of the UK, Greece and Turkey, and of the leaders of the Greek and Turkish Cypriots, Archbishop Makarios and Dr. Kutchuk. The leaders of the Greek and Turkish Cypriots did not have the right of amending any of the decisions reached between the three main powers. Eventually, the Zürich Agreement was endorsed at the London Conference. It is clear that throughout the London Conference Archbishop Makarios

had serious reservations about some of the provisions of the Zürich Agreement, and, at one time, it seemed as if he might reject it altogether. Eventually, he decided to accept. The full story has been recounted elsewhere and will not be repeated here.[28]

The important point is: Were such Agreements imposed upon the people of Cyprus? Or was self determination validly exercised? Archbishop Makarios himself has said (in his Proposals to amend the Cyprus Constitution) that he had raised "a number of objections and expressed strong misgivings regarding certain provisions of the Agreement . . .".[30] He had tried very hard to bring about the change "of at least some provisions of that Agreement". His Beatitude went on to say that he failed in that effort and was, as a result, "faced with the dilemma either of signing the Agreement as it stood or of rejecting it with all the grave consequences which would have ensued".[31] In all the circumstances he had "no alternative but to sign the Agreement".[32] This course, Archbishop Makarios concluded, was dictated to him "by necessity". There can, indeed, be little doubt that, both by reason of events and otherwise, strong pressure was brought to bear on the Greek Cypriot Delegation and that it can, with considerable justification, be said that the leaders of the Greek Cypriot people had no alternative but to accept the Zürich Settlement, since its non acceptance would have meant a denial of independence, possible partitioning of the island and almost certainly continued bloodshed. Do such events, coupled with the undeniable necessity arising from circumstances, suffice to negative self determination and render the Agreements null and void?[33]

This presents a difficult problem. It is, of course, clear that a requirement of absolute or even substantial equality between the signatories to a Treaty cannot be insisted upon; otherwise most Treaties would be invalid. The defects inherent in the Zürich and London set up, however, went beyond this. Greek Cypriots and Turkish Cypriots had no negotiating role at the Zürich Conference where the basic structure of the Cypriot State was agreed upon and at the Lancaster House Conference they could not propose amendments to the Accords reached between Greece and Turkey and accepted by Britain. And the choice offered to the leaders of the Cyprus people was to take the Agreement or reject it. Rejection of the Agreement would have meant catastrophe for the Greek Cypriot community. The island would probably have been partitioned and the issue could never again have been re-opened. Such factors can, on one plausible interpretation, be said to amount to coercion invalidating the Agreements. It must also not be forgotten what the nature of the Agreements was.[34] The Greek Cypriot side has repeatedly declared that these Treaties and, by reference, the structures they brought into existence, not only contained many onerous elements but also attempted decisively to shackle the constitutional and political development of the new born State, and an effort will later be made to prove the truth of such allegations. Finally, the Agreements and the Constitution they gave birth to were never subjected to the free scrutiny of the people of Cyprus. Such considerations, in their totality, can be said to make the doctrine of unequal and inequitable Treaties relevant, and militate against the validity of such Treaties.[35]

On the other hand, it must be frankly admitted, the above position is not without its difficulties. It can be maintained that faithful observance of Treaty obligations is a paramount principle of International law; that the undoubted coercion and pressure that existed at the time of the conclusion of the Treaties were no more than one would expect of any international crisis calling for a Treaty; and that the overall settlement was "a compromise" (as Mr. Averoff called it) necessitated by the many difficulties — political, psychological and emotional — characterising the total situation.[36]

Personally, I incline to the view that the right of self determination was exercised only in so far as concerns the solution of Independence and the barest outlines of such Independence settlement. This formulation tries to distinguish between the basic solution of Sovereign Independence and the minutiae and details of the Zürich Settlement, which, it is believed, could not be held to be forever binding on the people of Cyprus and unalterable in perpetuity. The idea of Independence had been strongly supported before the UN by India's Representative, Mr. Krishna Menon. An independent Cyprus, it was thought, could play a beneficial role in the Eastern Mediterranean and the group of non aligned States. Such conception of Independence was eventually adopted by the Greek Cypriot leadership, not without reservations, it is true, since the original goal had been Enosis — but Independence was adopted none the less. The right of self determination, it is thought, was validly exercised with regard to this choice of Independence. The right of self determination, after all, can be conditioned by the demands of international peace and considerations of world politics which very often, as is well known, transcend even the legitimate rights of the parties.[37] But the precise structuring of the Cypriot State and the unheard of shackles imposed thereon by the Zürich Agreement are in a totally different category. These go beyond the bare outlines of an independent and sovereign State and surely require for constitutional and political legitimation informed consent and conscious choice.

Almost fourteen years have passed since then. Much has happened. The political directions of the two Communities, primarily as a result of the recent Turkish invasion, have pulled further and further apart. The principal point made in this study is that divergent though the two approaches may be, it is still possible — not without some effort — to read into the positions of the two sides not only a common objective but also some agreement on the outlines of a constitutional and political settlement giving expression to such objective. I am speaking, on the one hand, of Security — international and internal, Security, that is, both for the Greek majority and the Turkish minority of Cyprus, and, on the other, of an Independent, Sovereign and integral Cyprus, with vigorous safeguards for the rights, both individual and communal, of all its people, adequate participation of both Communities in the affairs of Government and sufficient local or regional government not endangering the basic unity of the State.

A new settlement will have to be accompanied by fresh international guarantees for the inviolability and territorial integrity of Cyprus.[38] The island must also be demilitarised and such demilitarisation positively secured. The 1960 tripartite Guarantee has proved utterly worthless and therefore other ways of securing Cyprus' Independence have to be explored. Dr. Plaza, in his Report, thought that the UN could, if it was so agreed, play, in this connection, "an invaluable role". The possibility could be explored, he said, of the UN itself acting as "the guarantor of the terms of the settlement". I would go further than this. The UN, by assuming, even at this late stage, an active role in the Cyprus tragedy can still salvage some of its credibility which has been seriously hurt by its inactivity in the face of the vicious dismemberment of Cyprus and the unprecedented drama of its people. Not only should the UN adopt dynamic policies for the purpose of putting an end to Turkish agression and illegal occupation of Cyprus territory; in the reconstituted Cyprus State — at least for a transitional or experimental period — the UN could itself play an active role in the administration of the island

and the superintendence of those agencies which will be entrusted with the enforcement and implementation of individual and minority rights. And UN Commissioners with adequate staffs could be stationed in Cyprus for the above mentioned purpose.

If this be interpreted as somewhat of an abdication of sovereignty, so let it be. The tragedy of Cyprus, in the last analysis, has been brought about because we Cypriots, both Greeks and Turks, have been insufficiently proud of our sovereignty. To limit it now for the purpose of salvaging our long term independence, sovereignty and dignity would be a small price to pay.

A solution and an agreed settlement of the Cyprus problem must be speedily found. Every endeavour must be made to bring this about. But time is of the essence. If there is no quick progress out of the present stalemate, Cyprus will be completely destroyed by the Turks, Britain's strategic and other interests in the area will probably be irreparably damaged and the cause of international peace will suffer a grievous blow. [39]

II

ZÜRICH, ITS AFTERMATH AND THE UNEASY YEARS

CYPRUS became independent on the 16th August, 1960. The legal framework of the Republic of Cyprus consists, on the one hand, of the 1960 Constitution, and, on the other, of three Treaties — the principles of these Treaties having been an essential and integral part of the whole body of the Zürich and London Agreements.[1]

Comprehension of the legal framework of the Republic of Cyprus is essential. Unless we understand the mistakes of the past, we shall no doubt repeat them.

The three Treaties, the Treaty of Establishment, the Treaty of Alliance and the Treaty of Guarantee reflected the uneasy compromise effected at Zürich and London, and effectively shackled the newly born state. The Treaty of Establishment sets up the Republic of Cyprus and provides that the territory of the Republic "shall comprise the island of Cyprus . . ., with the exception of the two areas defined in Annex A of this Treaty, which areas shall remain under the sovereignty of the United Kingdom". This Treaty, of course, secures British military interests in the area, and, in effect, provides for the retention of British influence in the Middle East. It could, perhaps, have been thought that the recognition of British sovereign bases was an additional military guarantee of the integrity of Cyprus and its Constitution. If such was one of the purposes of the Treaty of Establishment, such purpose has, obviously, not been carried out.

The Treaty of Alliance was concluded between Cyprus, Greece and Turkey. By this Treaty the contracting parties undertook to resist any attack or aggression directed against the independence or territorial integrity of Cyprus; and for the purpose of this Alliance, and in order to achieve the objective named above, it was further provided that a Tripartite headquarters should be established and that military contingents should be stationed on the territory of the Republic, the Greek and Turkish contingents to consist of 950 and 650 officers and men respectively.

Finally, by the Treaty of Guarantee, which is extensively

discussed later, the Republic of Cyprus undertook the obligation to maintain the Constitutional order created and to keep it unalterable in perpetuity, and the three Guarantor powers, Great Britain, Greece and Turkey, guaranteed the continuation of the existence and maintenance of such order, as well as the independence and territorial integrity of Cyprus, and reserved to themselves the right to take steps for the restoration of Cyprus' status in case of any change in, or disturbance of, such status.

A convincing case can be made against the legality, initial or continued, of the Treaties of Alliance and Guarantee.[2] Such arguments have been cogently put forward elsewhere. Not only have such Treaties never been ratified by the House of Representatives, even though Article 169 of the Cyprus Constitution states that a Treaty or International Agreement can only be binding on the Republic "when approved by a law made by the House of Representatives"; furthermore, many authorities on international law have argued that Treaties which are meant to be binding "for ever" (as is the case with the Treaties of Alliance and Guarantee) cannot be valid by reason of their inconsistency with the concept of Sovereignty, "especially when such Treaties attempt to establish an alliance between a dwarf and giants (foedus inequale)".[2a] It is also argued below with regard to the Treaty of Guarantee, under which, allegedly, Turkey invaded Cyprus, that some of the provisions of this Treaty are clearly contrary to the provisions of the UN Charter and, as a result, of no validity. Moreover, as the learned Attorney-General of the Republic, Mr. Tornaritis, has pointed out, by these provisions of the Treaty of Guarantee, "the Republic of Cyprus is subjected to the will of the Guaranteeing Powers and is deprived of one of the fundamental requirements of a state as an international person, that of internal independence and territorial supremacy"[3] The Treaty of Guarantee can also be said to offend against the international law principle of abstention in the domestic affairs of a Sovereign state.

In addition to the above, Turkey, since Independence, has repeatedly violated both the Treaties of Alliance and Guarantee, and it is well established that a state can abrogate a Treaty when the other signatories violate their obligations thereunder.[4]

Whatever the legal status of such Treaties, there can be no question that serious fetters were, from the very beginning, imposed on the Republic of Cyprus. Such fetters stifled self determination and prevented any, even necessary, political development. Cyprus was not so much a "reluctant Republic" as a stillborn State.

Even more peculiar was the 1960 Constitution.[5] This Constitution will now be examined in some detail.

Executive.[6] The first Article of the Constitution provides that the State of Cyprus is an independent and Sovereign Republic with a presidential regime, the President being Greek and the Vice President being Turk, the President and the Vice President to be elected by the Greek and Turkish Communities of Cyprus respectively. Art. 36 provides that the President of the Republic is the Head of the State and that the Vice President of the Republic is the Vice-Head of the State, taking precedence over all persons in the Republic with the exception of the President; it is further provided by Art. 36 that in the event of the President's temporary absence or temporary incapacity to perform the duties of his office, such position and such duties shall devolve not upon the Vice President of the Republic but upon the President of the House of Representatives.

Articles 37 and 38 deal mainly with ceremonial matters; according to such provisions, the President of the Republic, as Head of State, represents the Republic in all its official functions; signs the credentials of diplomatic envoys and receives the credentials of foreign diplomatic envoys who shall be accredited to him; confers the honours of the Republic etc. The Vice President of the Republic as Vice-Head of the State has the right (a) to be present at all official functions and at the presentation of the credentials of the foreign diplomatic envoys, and (b) to recommend to the President the conferment of honours on members of the Turkish Community "which recommendation the President shall accept unless there are grave reasons to the contrary".

The exercise of executive power is dealt with in considerable detail. Art. 46 provides that "the executive power is ensured by the President and the Vice President of the Republic" and that, for this purpose, they shall have a Council of Ministers composed of seven Greek ministers and three Turkish ministers. The ministers, according to the same Article, should be designated respectively by the President and the Vice President "who shall appoint them by instrument signed by them both". It is further provided that the decisions of the Council of Ministers shall be taken by absolute majority and shall, unless the right of veto or return is exercised by the President or the Vice President of the Republic, be promulgated immediately by them by publication in the official gazette of the Republic.

The President and the Vice President of the Republic do not exercise any executive power except in the case of specified matters, such matters being dealt with in Articles 47, 48 and 49, and with regard to such matters the President and Vice President can act either conjointly or separately. Art. 47 enumerates a list of executive powers to be exercised by the President and the Vice President conjointly; most of them are of a formal character, relating inter alia, to the design and colour of the flag of the Republic, the creation or establishment of the honours of the Republic, the promulgation by publication of the decisions of the Council of Ministers etc. Each is also invested with enumerated powers exercisable independently. The two lists (the President's list being set out by Art. 48 and the Vice President's one appearing in Art. 49) are similar, with some important differences. Thus, the President designates and may remove the Greek ministers, whereas the Vice President designates and may remove the Turkish ministers. The President has the right of convening the meetings of the Council of Ministers, of preparing the agenda of such meetings and of presiding. In his turn, the Turkish Vice President can ask the President for the convening of the Council — he also has the right to be present and take part in the discussions at all meetings of the Council; furthermore, he can propose to the President subjects for inclusion in the agenda — in such a case the President, according to Art. 56, shall include such subject in the agenda if it can be conveniently dealt with at such meeting; otherwise, such subject "shall be included in the agenda of the meeting next following". It must here be mentioned that neither the President nor the Vice President has the right to vote at meetings of the Council of Ministers.

A matter of great importance is the veto power exercisable, either separately or conjointly, by the President and Vice President of the Republic. According to Articles 47(d) and 48(d), either the President or the Vice President may veto a decision of the Council of Ministers concerning foreign affairs, defence or security, or return any other decision for reconsideration (Art.57); and since it is highly improbable that the President will ever disagree with any important decision these powers are in effect a Vice Presidential prerogative. The executive right of final veto is also extended, by Art. 50, to any law or decision of the House of Representatives or any part thereof concerning foreign affairs, defence or security. Moreover, by Art 51, the President and the

Vice President also have the right, either separately or conjointly, to return any law or decision or any part thereof of the House of Representatives to the House for reconsideration. In such a case, the House of Representatives must pronounce on the matter so returned within fifteen days of such return, and if the House persists in its decision the President and Vice President shall then promulgate the law or decision as the case may be, unless in the meantime they exercise, separately or conjointly, the right of veto as is provided in Art. 50 or their right of reference to the Supreme Constitutional Court (Articles 137, 138, 140, 141) so that the question of constitutionality of such law or decision may be adjudicated upon.

It has been pointed out above that specific powers are vested in the President and Vice President, such powers to be exercised, as the case may be, either separately or conjointly. Art. 54 provides that "in all other matters other than those which, under the express provisions of this Constitution, are within the competence of the Communal Chambers", executive power will be exercised by the Council of Ministers; such matters include (a) the general direction and control of the Government of the Republic and the direction of general policy; (b) foreign affairs; (c) defence and security; (d) the co-ordination and supervision of all public services; (e) the supervision and disposal of property belonging to the Republic; (f) consideration of Bills to be introduced to the House of Representatives by a Minister; (g) consideration of the budget, etc.

Finally, Art. 58 provides for the status and executive powers of the individual Ministers.

The Legislature.[7] The legislative power of the Republic is exercised by the House of Representatives "in all matters except those expressly reserved to the Communal Chambers" (Art. 61) The House of Representatives consists of 50 Representatives, and Art. 62 further provides that 70 per centum of such Representatives, that is to say 35, shall be elected by the Greek Community and 30 per centum, that is to say 15, by the Turkish Community, the elections to take place on the basis of separate electoral rolls.

Art. 72 provides that the President of the House shall be a Greek, and shall be elected by the Representatives elected by the Greek Community, and that the Vice President of the House shall be a Turk and shall be elected by the Representatives elected by the Turkish Community. Similarly with the provisions relating to the Presidency of the Republic, it is provided by Art. 72 that in case of temporary absence etc. of the President of the House, his functions should be performed by the eldest Representative of his community unless the Representatives of such community should otherwise decide.

Art. 73 regulates procedures. In particular, such Article sets up a Committee of Selection, such Committee to consist of the President of the House as chairman, the Vice President of the House as vice chairman and eight other members elected by the House of Representatives, six from amongst the Greek Representatives and two from amongst the Turkish Representatives, the principal functions of such Committee being (a) the setting up of the Standing Committees and any other ad hoc or temporary Committees of the House, and (b) the appointment of Representatives to be members of such Committees — the distribution of seats on such Committees to be in the same proportion as that in which the seats in the House are distributed to the Representatives elected by the Greek and Turkish Communities respectively.

All the laws and decisions of the House of Representatives shall be passed by a simple majority vote of the Representatives present and voting, but there are three classes of legislation which require special procedures (Art. 78). Thus, any modification of the Electoral law and the adoption of any law relating to the Municipalities and of any law imposing duties or taxes require "a separate simple majority of the Representatives elected by the Greek and Turkish Communities respectively taking part in the vote".

It must be noticed that the Constitution recognises and protects the independence of the House in a number of ways, e.g. by not granting the power to dissolve the House either to the President or the Vice President; but, of course, it must not be assumed that some kind of impractical "separation of powers" doctrine is thereby enshrined in the Constitution. For example, by Art. 79, the President or the Vice President of the Republic may address the House by message, or transmit to the House their views; Ministers may make statements to, or inform, the House or any Committee thereof on any subject within their competence; and, of course, the veto power of the President and Vice President in foreign affairs, defence and security imposes important limitations on the powers of the Legislature; the same is true — to a much more limited extent, of course — with the right of the

President and the Vice President to return any law or decision of the House for reconsideration.

Art. 86 provides for the two Communal Chambers, such Communal Chambers, which are set up by the respective Communities, to have exclusive legislative competence with regard, inter alia, to the following matters: all religious matters; all educational, cultural and teaching matters; personal status; the composition of courts dealing with civil disputes relating to personal status and to religious matters; matters "where the interests and Institutions are of purely communal nature such as charitable and sporting foundations, bodies and associations created for the purpose of promoting the well being of the respective Community"; imposition of personal taxes and fees on members of their respective Communities in order to provide for their respective needs and for the needs of bodies and Institutions under their control; etc. The Communal Chambers, in addition to their powers just enumerated, are also declared to have competence to direct policy within their communal laws; to exercise administrative powers in the manner and through such persons as may be provided by a communal law; to exercise control on producers' and consumers' co-operatives and credit establishments created for the purpose of promoting the well being of their respective Communities etc. It is also expressly provided that no law or decision of a Communal Chamber shall contain anything contrary to the interests of the security of the Republic or the Constitutional order or the public safety or anything which is against the fundamental rights and liberties guaranteed by the Constitution.

As must be already apparent, the Communal Chambers, entrusted with communal matters, are special legislative assemblies, their range of competence being of a personal rather than a territorial kind; or, to put it somewhat differently, the legislative competence of the Communal Chambers is limited by reference to two general criteria: the subject matter of legislation and the communal status of the persons to whom their enactments are addressed.

The Judiciary.[8] The judicial powers of the Republic, the 1960 Constitution provides, shall be exercised by the Supreme Constitutional Court (Part IX) and the High Court and its subordinate courts (Part X).

Art. 133 provides that the Supreme Constitutional Court shall be composed of a Greek, a Turkish, and a neutral judge. The neutral judge shall be the President of the Court. Art. 133 (2) provides that the President and the other judges of the Supreme Constitutional Court shall be appointed jointly by the President and Vice President of the Republic, provided that in the case of a vacancy solely in the post of either the Greek or the Turkish judge the proposal of the President or the Vice President of the Republic to whose community the judge to be appointed should belong shall prevail if the President and the Vice President do not agree on such appointment within a week of such proposal.

The jurisdiction of the Court is settled by Articles 137, 138, 139, 140, ... 151. Briefly, the Court is given exclusive jurisdiction to pronounce on the constitutionality of any law or decision of the House of Representatives, and such questions of constitutionality may be brought before the Court either by the President and/or the Vice President, acting either separately or conjointly, or by parties with the requisite locus standi — in particular, regarding such parties, Art. 144 provides that a party to any judicial proceedings, including proceedings on appeal, may, at any stage thereof, raise the question of the unconstitutionality of any law or decision or any provision thereof for determination, and, thereupon, the Court before which such question is raised shall reserve the question for the decision of the Supreme Constitutional Court and stay further proceedings until such question is determined by the Supreme Constitutional Court. In addition, Art. 146 provides that the Supreme Constitutional Court shall have exclusive jurisdiction to adjudicate finally on a recourse made to it on a complaint that a decision, an act or omission of any organ, authority or person, exercising any executive or administrative authority, is contrary to any of the provisions of the Constitution or of any law or is made in excess or in abuse of powers vested in such an organ or authority or person. This, of course, is nothing but a general administrative law jurisdiction which does not have any necessary connection with any question of constitutional validity. Two further points must be made about the jurisdiction of the Supreme Constitutional Court. Art. 139 confers on the Court power to adjudicate finally on a recourse made in connection with any matter relating to any conflict or contest of power or competence arising between the House of Representatives and the Communal Chambers or any one of them and between any organs of, or authorities in, the Republic; and recourse to the Court under the above mentioned provision may be made by the President or the Vice President of the Republic, or the House of Representatives, or one of, or both, the Communal Chambers, or any other organ of, or authority in, the Republic involved in such conflict or contest. Finally, as logically follows from what was said above, it is not only laws or decisions of the House of Representatives that have to be subjected to constitutional scrutiny. Art. 142 states that the President of the Republic with regard to any law or decision of the Greek Communal Chamber and the Vice President of the Republic with regard to any law or decision of the Turkish Communal Chamber may refer to the Supreme Constitutional Court for its opinion the question as to whether such law or decision or any specified provision thereof is repugnant to, or inconsistent with, any provision of the Constitution.

The High Court, consisting of a neutral President, two Greek judges and one Turkish judge, is, under the 1960 Constitution, the Highest appellate Court in the Republic, and is declared to have jurisdiction to hear and determine, subject to the provisions of the Constitution and any Rules of Court made thereunder, all appeals from any court other than the Supreme Constitutional Court. The High Court, according to the 1960 Constitution, shall, in addition to its appellate jurisdiction, also have original and revisional jurisdiction "as is provided by this Constitution or may by provided by a law"; it also has exclusive power to issue orders in the nature of hapeas corpus, mandamus, prohibition, quo warranto and certiorari. In addition, the High Court shall, to the exclusion of any other court, determine the composition of the Courts which are to try cases, or adjudicate upon claims, involving parties from both Communities. Such Courts must be composed of judges belonging to both the Greek and Turkish Communities. This is the effect of Art. 159 which, in greater detail, provides that: (a) a court exercising civil jurisdiction in a case where the plaintiff and the defendant belong to the same Community shall be composed solely of a judge or judges belonging to that Community; (b) a court exercising criminal jurisdiction in a case where the accused and the person injured belong to the same Community, or where there is no person injured, shall be composed of a judge or judges belonging to that Community; (c) where in a civil case the plaintiff and the defendant belong to different Communities, the Court shall be composed of such judges belonging to both Communities as the High Court shall determine; (d) where in a criminal case the accused and the person injured belong to different Communities, the Court shall be composed of such judges belonging to both Communities as the

High Court shall determine; (e) finally, a coroner's inquest where the deceased belonged to the Greek Community shall be conducted by a Greek coroner and where the deceased belonged to the Turkish Community shall be conducted by a Turkish coroner. In case where there are more than one deceased belonging to different Communities, the inquest shall be conducted by such coroner as the High Court may direct.

It must also be borne in mind that Art. 160 provided that a Communal law made by the Communal Chamber concerned should provide for the establishment, composition and jurisdiction of Courts to deal with civil disputes relating to personal status and religious matters which are, by the provisions of the Constitution, reserved for the competence of the Communal Chambers.

The Public Service & the Security Forces. The 1960 Constitution provided that 70% of the Public Service should be composed of Greek Cypriots and that 30% should be composed of Turkish Cypriots. It further provided that this ratio should be applied, as far as practicable, in all grades of the Public Service. The general regulation of the Public Service, the disciplinary control of its officers and the implementation of the 7:3 ratio are declared by the Constitution to be the responsibility of the Public Service Commission, itself chosen by the President and Vice President jointly on a 7:3 basis. The Constitution provided that any decision of the Public Service Commission should be taken by an absolute majority of its members, but this general principle was qualified by other provisions making it necessary that in matters of appointments, promotions, transfers and discipline, such majority had to include a certain minimum number of Greek or Turkish votes depending on whether the decision related to a Greek or a Turk.

The 7:3 ratio is also prescribed for the Security Forces of the Republic (such Security Forces being divided into the Police and the Gendarmerie). In the armed forces, however, the ratio, according to the 1960 Constitution, should be 6:4. Further, the three heads of these Forces are to be appointed by the President and Vice President acting jointly; one of them is to be a Turk, and each is to have a deputy head, who is to be chosen from a different Community from the head of the Force.

Such was the 1960 Constitution.[9]

This Constitution stands out for its rigidity, strong bicommunal character and extreme complication. These features can be observed in all three areas of Government. In the Executive branch, the political arrangements that were set up by the 1960 Constitution have no exact parallel elsewhere. The Constitution supposedly establishes a "Presidential Regime", but this must be viewed rather sceptically. Perhaps, it would be more correct to describe the system established as "a Vice Presidential Regime", so inflated are the powers of the Turkish Vice President and so great the obstructive potential of his prerogatives. The veto, final and unqualified, given to the Turkish Vice President in the three areas delineated above, is the culmination of such unparalleled Constitutional generosity. It is also clear throughout that it is not really a President and Vice President that are envisaged by the Constitution, but rather two more or less independent Chief Executives whose main function is not the smooth functioning of the Governmental machine but the representation and protection of their distinct Communities. It has already been noticed that the executive powers of the President are not general or residual but are specifically enumerated;[10] and that the Constitution also attributes exclusive fields of executive competence to the Vice President and to the Council of Ministers. It could perhaps be thought that since the Council of Ministers is, by Art. 54, entrusted with great executive powers, such Council is in reality the main executive organ of the State. On more careful examination, however, this does not appear to be so. It is not only that the Council's meetings are convened by the President and Vice President or that the agenda of meetings is prepared by the President and suggested by the Vice President. What is more important, the Ministers "shall hold office in the case of the Greek Ministers until their appointment is terminated by the President of the Republic and in the case of the Turkish Ministers until their appointment is terminated by the Vice President of the Republic" (Art. 59.3). As a result of such provision, the Greek Ministers derive their authority from the Greek President and the Turkish Ministers from the Turkish Vice President. Bicommunalism is institutionalised in the Executive branch,[11] collective responsibility cannot develop because of divided loyalties, and unregulated "dualism"[12] becomes in effect the real character of the system established. The main features of such Governmental system, it can be seen, particularly in its higher levels, were divided power and conflicting areas or spheres of competence. But, if these provisions, which organised only conflict and competition and omitted all institutional devices for effecting co-operation, were not enough to doom the experiment in Government embarked upon, it was further provided that there would also be a dualistically structured civil service, separatism and divided loyalties, in this way, to be continued downwards in the Governmental hirarchy.

Moreover, the percentage of participation of the Greeks and Turks in the Public Service as fixed by the Constitution bore or bears no relation to the true ratio of the Greek and Turkish inhabitants of the Island which is 81.14% Greeks and 18.86% Turks. Such constitutional provision, by specifying that 70% of the Public Service should be composed of Greek Cypriots, when in fact the Greek Cypriots constitute more than 81% of the population, and that 30% of the Public Service should be composed of Turkish Cypriots, when in fact the Turkish Cypriots constitute less than 19% of the population, did not and does not afford equal opportunity to the majority of the citizens of the Republic to participate in the Public Service. It was, therefore, clearly discriminatory. The implementation of this provision of the Constitution created serious problems for the State. It made it necessary, in considering appointments and promotions, to use criteria other than those universally accepted, such as qualifications, efficiency and general suitability of the candidate, because, obviously, the appointing authority had to take into consideration communal factors, ethnic origin, etc. It was an inevitable result of the attempted implementation of such provision that the best candidates simply could not be selected. Particular hardship was created in the case of promotions. Public servants who possessed all the required qualifications and experience for promotion to higher grades were overlooked in favour of less qualified public servants solely for the purpose of giving effect to an artificially fixed communal ratio of participation in the Public Service.

The attempted implementation of the 70:30 ratio caused great difficulties and soon became "a major Constitutional tension area".[13] On the one hand, the Turkish Cypriots looked upon this provision as essential for the purpose of securing "for the Turkish community adequate representation in all spheres of Governmental activity".[14] Without such provision, the Turkish side went on, the Greek Cypriots would be enabled to gain complete control of the Government machine. "Past experience and considerations of future progress within the newly born state", the Turks further asserted, "clearly indicated that the Turkish Community would be ill served and discriminated against with a lesser proportion of Turkish officials in the Service". Finally, the Turkish side expressed the belief that such representation in the Public Service would go a long way towards removing the existing suspicions and "would actually lead to cultivation of a closer co-operation between the two Communities". The Greek Cypriots, as stated above, could not accept such statements. They looked upon the provision as causing the Greek Cypriot Community a loss of jobs, and as being clearly discriminatory.[15] Equally, the Greek Cypriot side went on, the organisation of the Public Service Commission itself was open to serious objection. Indeed, it is clear that the intercommunal separatism that is so apparent throughout the Executive branch infects the Public Commission as well. The procedures for taking decisions by such Commission created a situation whereby the Greek and Turkish members felt that their paramount purpose, as members of the Commission, was not so much the improvement of the efficiency of the Service but rather the protection of Greek and Turkish interests respectively. As is not surprising in view of the above, considerable friction developed between the two Communities relating to the Public Service and its composition very soon after Independence. This was one of the main features leading to the functional breakdown of the 1960 Constitution.

Looking back on the Executive set-up of the Republic as a whole, one is not really surprised with such breakdown. The relevant provisions increased rather than reduced tension, did nothing to foster co-operation between the two Communities, created, in effect, a peculiarly structured and difficult to operate diarchy and, as a result, prevented the smooth functioning of the State. The Government of the Republic had to be carried on, but never had so many daunting obstacles been set in the path of those who were to operate the Constitution.[16] A surer recipe for failure "could hardly be imagined".[17]

And the error was compounded by the legislative set-up. To begin with, the Constitutional provisions regarding separate majorities, particularly in the form in which they appear, are contrary to all democratic principles. "(Their) effect is that though a Bill may be unanimously approved by the Council of Ministers and though it may receive the overwhelming majority of votes in the House of Representatives, nevertheless it is defeated if it does not receive a separate majority of the Greek or Turkish Representatives taking part in the vote".[18]

The principle of separate majorities,[19] if it is to be applied at all, must obviously only be introduced by reference to well delineated criteria and only (a) for those classes of legislation which could directly encroach upon the interests of the Communities and (b) where no other effective remedy can be found. This, of course, was not so under the 1960 Constitution. The Turkish side, for its part, often declared its belief in the necessity for such provisions as the only effective barrier against discrimination, but it is thought that if security against discrimination was (as it should be) the paramount object of those concerned with the functioning of the state, then such provisions were not really necessary because there were other clauses in the Constitution affording adequate safeguards and remedies, such other clauses, moreover, being more appropriate for this purpose. Any legislation, for example, which is discriminatory can be challenged before the Constitutional Court by the Vice President. Furthermore, Art. 6 of the Constitution provides that no law or decision of the House of Representatives "shall discriminate against any of the two Communities or any person as a person or as a member of a Community". It would, perhaps, have been different if a separate majority was required only in the case of those Constitutional provisions expressly conferring rights on the Turkish Community, though even in this case different protective devices might easily be developed. But even laws imposing duties and taxes could not be enacted unless there was a separate majority of the Representatives elected by the Greek and Turkish Communities respectively. This was nothing but a further obstructive power given to the minority. Communal minority rights, in this way, were raised to a very exalted status by the 1960 Constitution, and such rights, in effect communal veto rights, posed (and, unfortunately, proved) as menacing a danger to democratic Government as unchallengeable majoritarian power. In such a set-up, there is nothing really to prevent the minority from using its power not for its self protection but for the achievement of collateral purposes. In fact, as a result of the Turkish Members' of the House use of the separate majority provision, the Republic was left without tax legislation and the functioning of the state was seriously impeded.

In so far as the composition of the House of Representatives was concerned, bicommunalism, as can be clearly seen, was again made the basis of the relevant constitutional arrangements; and many other provisions were introduced whose only result, it should have been inevitably perceived, would be the reinforcement of such bicommunalism and the prevention of any possibility of a harmonious working partnership developing between the Greek and Turkish members of the legislature.

But even this degree of dualistic splintering of the legislative power was not deemed adequate. So, in addition, as is explained above, Communal Chambers were organised to be in charge of legislation with regard to religion, education, culture, and family and other personal relations, and such Chambers were given their own separate taxing power in order to provide for their Communities' needs. There can be no question, of course, that in a State like Cyprus, with two distinct ethnic cultures, appropriate institutions and authorities should exist providing for the satisfaction and fulfilment of the Communities' needs. Great care should be taken, however, so that (a) the fulfilment of the Communities' needs in this direction does not lead to the fragmentation of the State and the prevention of the development of a unified and responsible citizenship, and (b) no undue problems are created for the operation of the Government, either by way of the multiplication of stuctures or as a result of the creation of opportunities for disruptive friction between the Communities or the organs of government. Unfortunately, all such mistakes seem to have been committed in the setting up of the two Communal Chambers. Not only could their functions have been assigned, in the interests of economy, to, perhaps, subdivisions of the House of Representatives, such subdivisions, in this case, to consist of the Greek and Turkish members of the House respectively, or distributed in some other way not necessitating the setting up of distinct organisational structures with all that this implies in terms of additional taxation and the increased possibility of duplication of services; since the need to have such extra legislative Assemblies was so debatable and nebulous, and since such Assemblies, when created, had no "clearly assigned Executive Establishment",[20] the Communal Chambers were bound to act as a disruptive element in reinforcing the divisive tendencies in a dualistically-structured Governmental machine. And, most important of all, the existence of the two

Communal Chambers resulted in an absurd dimunition of Governmental power. Education, for instance, was placed entirely outside the sphere of Government economic and social policies. As observed above, one can readily agree that both Communities in Cyprus should have the right to maintain their own educational establishments, at least at the lower levels. Both Communities, understandably, take great pride in their traditions and attachment to such traditions is to be welcomed rather than feared. Education, however, must not be thought of in narrow terms, or exclusively in terms of the transmission of hereditary values. It is that, of course; but it is also much more. The provision of education which seems to be an essential prerequisite to the development of the idea of responsible citizenship should be thought of as an indispensable service to be primarily provided by the State, the Communities performing a secondary or ancillary task in connection thereto. But more will be said on this later.[21]

The narrow point to be made here is that the legislative provisions of the Constitution (no less than the executive ones) organised only conflict and competition, omitted all institutional incentives for co-operation and, in consequence, resulted in the pre-existing Communal dualism becoming a built-in part of the Constitution and, as can be clearly seen, the most important part of such Constitution. Such provisions, moreover, constituted an elaborate scheme of checks and balances,[22] in which the need to organise both Communities for effective co-operation and harmonious co-existence was completely sacrificed to the purpose of preventing abuse of power by one of the two parties to the bargain. At the basis of such labyrinthine constitutional structuring seemed to have been the beliefs (a) that the two Communities would never co-operate unless actually forced to do so by the Constitution and (b) that the main danger to the new State would come from the Greek majority. Both these views seem to have been somewhat mistaken.

If we now return to the nature of the 1960 Constitution, we can see that so erratically divided was the system of distribution of power and so delicately balanced the various Governmental and Communal competencies that what was rather desperately needed was an impartial umpire, in the form of a united and coherently functioning Supreme Court, for the purpose of adjudicating upon the differences that were inevitably to arise regarding the interpretation of the Constitution. Yet, instead of a non separatist and neutral arbitration system, Cyprus was provided with a divided system of Courts which was more obviously infected than other organs of Government with the principle of Communal separation. Not only was the Supreme Constitutional Court composed in a manner that could only accentuate communal differences and present the Greek and Turkish judges as communal protagonists rather than as impartial arbiters, but also the very fact that a Greek had to be tried by a Greek and a Turk by a Turk was a slur on the impartiality of the judges and an insult to the integrity of the Judicial profession. In short, this dichotomy of justice, apart from its practical and administrative drawbacks, undermines the very conception of Justice which should not only be administered but also manifestly and clearly appear to be administered impartially, without fear or favour, and free from communal considerations. For, surely, "the very concept of justice defies separation".[23]

It must be here mentioned that the major features of the 1960 Constitution and much besides are made unalterable. Art. 182 provides that the Articles or parts of the Articles of the Constitution set out in an Annex to the Constitution should be known as the basic Articles of the Constitution. Such Articles, Art. 182 goes on, "cannot in any way be amended, whether by way of variation, addition or repeal". This permanent unalterability of the Constitutional structure is, indeed, unprecedented. A situation had been created as a result of the combined effect of the Constitution and the Treaty of Guarantee whereby the Constitutional and political development of the Republic was arrested in its infancy.

It was not only, however, that, as a result of such imposed rigidity, the Republic of Cyprus had been placed in a strait-jacket which both inhibited development and stifled growth or even that it is very debatable whether a Constituent power can perpetually restrict either its successors or those whom it brings into existence to the narrow constitutional patterns originally devised. A very plausible case can be made that the main provisions of the Constitution are in hopeless conflict themselves. Thus, Art. 1 of the Constitution provides that the State of Cyprus "is an independent and sovereign Republic". As emphasised by Professor Tsatsos, who led the Greek Delegation at the Mixed Consitutional Commission, such provision was not inserted (and at such a prominent place) at random, but advisedly, and was intended to be of primary significance. And, as observed by the Attorney-General of the Republic, "irrespective of its position in the Constitution, (the) contents (of such provision) are of such fundamental importance as to guide the approach to the whole Constitutional structure".[24] Indeed, the character of Cyprus as an independent and sovereign State has been repeatedly recognised and acknowledged, both by the admission of Cyprus to the UN and, inter alia, by numerous Resolutions and decisions of the Security Council. It does seem incongruous and contradictory, to say the least, that a State is created which is declared to be sovereign and independent and yet, at the same time, the Constitution of such State is proclaimed to be unalterable in perpetuity, a fetter upon such sovereignty.

The lesson of the 1960 experiment — "and it is an important one"[25] — is that a Governmental system requires for its effective functioning adequate machinery for continuous readjustment.[26] There must exist workable institutional devices for re-assessing the position and for "allowing the partners to negotiate further bargains to implement the existing one". No such machinery, adequate or otherwise, was provided in the 1960 Constitution. There was no room for manoeuvre and no way of resolving deadlocks. Constitutional life was condemned to linger for ever in the constricting confines of artificial and legalistic arrangements, such arrangements, according to the Constitution, to be for ever binding and non negotiable.

Given such a Constitutional Structure, the wonder is not that the system eventually broke down but that it only did so in 1963. The Constitution, it is believed, was doomed from the beginning.[27] Not only was the smooth functioning and development of the country thwarted and seriously prejudiced but also, a very important point, as has been already stressed, was that no "correction" mechanisms were provided. As a result of such an omission, disagreements could only become deadlocks. There was no way of their being resolved short of one side or the other giving way, and such was the Constitutional structure that this could not be done gracefully or in an atmosphere of give and take, but could only appear as a capitulation. Once the Communities, that is, had committed themselves to diverse positions, there could really be no possibility of meaningful negotiation for the purpose of arriving at a solution in the best interests of Cyprus as a whole. The right to compromise was blocked. Tension could only accumulate.

We have already mentioned the requirement of separate majorities as a major constitutional tension area. Another issue causing great difficulties was the attempted implementation of the 70:30 ratio in the Public Service and the gross iniquities arising as a result. A somewhat different source of tension was the proposed creation of a Cyprus army. The important question was whether such an Army (whose formation was envisaged in the Constitution) was to be formed on a separate or a mixed basis. The Turkish side insisted on separation, namely that soldiers of Greek and Turkish origins respectively could not be quartered together on account of linguistic and religious differences. The Council of Ministers, however, decided that there should be no separation, but that the Army should be completely integrated. Such decision was vetoed by the Turkish Vice President. As a result of such developments, the plan to form a Cyprus Army was abandoned. The issue, however, which above all others led to the breakdown of the Government and proved to be the most volatile of all was the separation of the Municipalities.[28]

Art. 173 of the 1960 Constitution provided that separate Municipalities were to be created in the five largest towns of the Republic — "provided that the President and Vice President of the Republic shall within four years of the day of the going into operation of this Constitution examine the question whether or not this separation of Municipalities . . . shall continue". And, Art. 177 provided that each municipality should exercise its jurisdiction within a region (of the relevant town) the limits of which should be fixed for each municipality by agreement of the President and Vice President of the Republic. Apparently, Mr. Averoff, the then Greek Foreign Secretary, considered this a dangerous provision and the most objectionable separatist measure in the Agreements, on account of its giving the Turks administrative control of territory rather than functions. His fears were justified.

If one were now to examine Art. 173 in isolation, one could perhaps say that its application would be simple since it clearly declares in imperative language that separate municipalities should be established. "The difficulty arises, however, from the fact that in none of the towns concerned the population lives exclusively in areas inhabited by Greeks or Turks and that there are areas in which the population is mixed".[29] The President and Vice President, acting under Art. 177, appointed Committees consisting of Greeks and Turks in each town, which Committees met and tried to reach agreement on defining the areas of the Municipal Councils, but without success. This remained an unsolved issue. Therefore, the President of the Republic, for the purpose of resolving the deadlock that had developed, on the 19th March, 1962, made certain proposals to the Vice President which were designed to by-pass the difficulty of defining regions for the separate Greek and Turkish Municipal Councils which had, as already stated, proved an impossible task, and which proposals were at the same time intended to fully safeguard the Turkish interests. Archbishop Makarios expressed the view that the geographical separation of the Municipalities was difficult to bring about without severe detriment to both Communities. His Beatitude suggested the establishment of a united municipal authority and the proportional representation of Greeks and Turks thereon (in proportion, that is, to the population in each town). With a view to safeguarding the rights of the Turkish citizens, his Beatitude suggested that: (1) The staff to be employed by the Municipal authorities should be in proportion to the Greek and Turkish populations in each town; (2) a percentage of the annual budget of each Municipality, to be fixed in advance, should be made available for the needs of the Turkish citizens in a way to be suggested by the Turkish members of the Municipal Council; and, (3) in each of the five towns where the mayor was a Greek the deputy mayor should be a Turk, if this was justified by the proportion of the Turkish population. On the 20th March, 1962, the President of the Turkish Communal Chamber, Mr. Denktash, commenting on the Archbishop's proposals, described President Makarios' statement as an "unrealistic" approach to the question. During subsequent negotiations and meetings regarding this problem, Mr. Clerides, President of the House of Representatives, expressed the view that in his opinion there was a duty on the President and the Vice President acting under the provision of Art. 173 of the Constitution to consider whether separate Municipalities should exist or not. He advised that it might be an opportune moment for both sides to solve the problem by first carrying on an experiment for a limited period and then proceed accordingly, depending, that is, on whether the results of the experiment were satisfactory. In Mr. Clerides' view the right approach was to set up Mixed Councils to administer the Municipal affairs of each of the five towns with proportionate representation on such Councils based on the Communal population of each of the said towns, giving at the same time all the necessary legal safeguards to assure the Turkish side, which would be numerically smaller, that no discrimination whatsoever could be practised by the majority against them, and leaving entirely for the Turkish members of each Municipal Council to decide the manner in which a certain percentage of the estimates of the Joint Committee, fixed by law, would be disposed of for the Turkish inhabitants of each of the said towns. Apparently, the President of the Turkish Communal Chamber, Mr. Denktash, on hearing the proposal of Mr. Clerides, replied that it was an interesting proposition. Thereafter, a paper was prepared by Mr. Clerides and the Attorney-General, Mr. Tornaritis, expounding further such proposals. Such proposals, it can be seen, had many advantages. They would have reduced financial expenditure with regard to the burden of maintaining separate Municipalities. They would have avoided the "thorny problem of geographical division". They would have safeguarded the interests of the Turkish community. And, perhaps most important of all, there would have been if such proposals were finally accepted and implemented, an important indication that the two Communities were at last prepared to work together in the interests of a more efficient performance of essential Governmental functions. The Turkish side, indeed, initially, accepted such proposals and an announcement was made to the press that "common ground" had been found paving the way for eventual agreement on the subject. Yet, not long afterwards, the Turkish side reverted to its old position, demanding geographical separation of the towns. A great opportunity for a decisive breakthrough in intercommunal relations was lost.[30]

This episode has been described at some length because it illustrates many of the points that have been made above. Strong bicommunalism — not only recognised but also enshrined in the Constituent Documents as the foundation of all the Constitutional arrangements set up —, artificial fragmentation of functions, unprecedented constitutional rigidity, the facility with which the Constitution lent itself to being used not as a formula for harmonious integration but as an inviolate charter of separatism — such were the main features of the 1960 Constitution. And though Constitutions and legal machinery, however skilfully contrived, cannot provide the necessary solutions if not supported by a determined will to make such arrangements work, Constitutions and machinery, it is fervently believed, can make an important contribution in their own right and can serve effectively both in providing the framework within which the necessary Governmental processes can go forward and in facilitating — particularly in a bicommunal state — the readjustment of positions and the continuous reassessment of functions, both necessary prerequisites for the success of the democratic experiment. So divisive, unfortunately, was the 1960 Constitution that not only could it not provide the focus for a concerted effort at achieving unity but itself became a fertile ground for friction. So, calamitously, separation became an end in itself. Community leaders could not withdraw from, or abandon, entrenched positions without at least the appearance of compromising or even betraying the narrow communal interests which the Constitution had made them representatives of. Even where the possibility of the Constitution's modified application was apparently envisaged in the Constitution itself, as was the case with the possibility of abolishing separate Municipalities, blind communal prestige was allowed to overrule public interest. The unification of the Municipalities, as described above, was rejected at a last minute turnabout of the Turkish leadership because, though adequate guarantees relating to feared discrimination against Turkish townsmen had been proposed and virtually accepted, and, furthermore, even though the functioning of separate Municipalities had proved financially disastrous for the Turks themselves, the unifications of the Municipalities would have dealt a serious blow to separatism and would have been an important landmark towards the unification of the State.

As a result of the deadlocks that had actually occurred and the difficulties that had been encountered in the attempted operation of the Constitution, on the 30th November, 1963, the President of the Republic, Archbishop Makarios, made proposals to the Turkish Vice President for the revision of "at least some of those provisions of the Constitution" which impeded the smooth functioning of the State.[31] His Beatitude pointed out in a preamble to his proposals that one of the consequences of the difficulties created by certain provisions of the Constitution was "to prevent the Greeks and Turks of Cyprus from co-operating in a spirit of understanding and friendship, to undermine the relation between them and cause them to draw further apart instead of closer together, to the detriment of the wellbeing of the people of Cyprus as a whole". The proposals of Archbishop Makarios were the following: (1) The right of veto to be abandoned. (2) The Vice President to deputise for the President in case of his temporary absence or incapacity to perform his duties. (3) The Greek President of the House of Representatives and the Turkish Vice

President to be elected by the House as a whole and not as under the Constitution. (4) The Vice President of the House of Representatives to deputise for the President of the House. (5) The constitutional provisions regarding separate majorities to be abolished. (6) Unified Municipalities to be established. (7) The administration of justice to be unified. (8) The division of the Security Forces into Police and Gendarmerie to be abolished. (9) The numerical strength of the Security Forces and of the Defence Forces to be determined by a Law. (10) The proportion of participation of Greek Cypriots and Turkish Cypriots in the composition of the Public Service and the Forces of the Republic to be modified in proportion to the ratio of the population of Greek and Turkish Cypriots. (11) The number of the members of the Public Service Commission to be reduced from 10 to 5. (12) All decisions of the Public Service Commission to be taken by simple majority. (13) The Communal Chambers should be abolished and a new system should be devised. Should the Turkish Community, however, desire to retain its Chamber, such a course is open to it.

From what has been said above, it can be easily gathered that the writer is of the view that the 1960 Constitution was doomed to failure. It is not only that the 1960 constitutional arrangements are incredibly complex and detailed, contradictory and unworkable, or that "a Constitution requiring the ethnic origin of the coroner in a coroner's inquest to be that of the deceased could only fail".[32] The documents of the 1960 Settlement, in their utter rigidity, unprecedented unamendability and complete disregard both of the dangers of an alienated majority denied the prerogatives normally belonging to majorities and the hazards posed to the democratic process by the allocation of unchallangeable and obstructive powers to minorities — particularly when exercise of such powers need not be accounted for —, represented anything but "an imaginative resolution of many difficult problems".[33] The 1960 Settlement could never have worked, whatever the patience or the spirit of compromise of either or both sides. Indeed, such qualities as patience or the spirit of compromise could not manifest themselves in the context of the 1960 Constitution, having been, in effect, rendered redundant and impossible as a result of extremely detailed draftsmanship and the continuous reinforcement at every turn of communal suspicion and distrust. There was no room in the 1960 constitutional framework for living law to develop and no room, in the communally infested arrangements set up, for the notion of a responsible citizenship totally independent of ethnic origin to assert itself. Amendment of the Constitution was, therefore, essential.

The writer's personal view, however, is that putting forward all 13 proposals simultaneously may have been a mistake and a tactical miscalculation. It would have been preferable, given the climate of distrust, for a gradual process of amendment to have been embarked upon. It seems, for instance, that the suggestion of Mr. Clerides concerning the Municipalities issue was an admirable one, not only because of its substance but, particularly, because such proposal was for an experimental period, the whole venture to be re-examined at the end of a specified period of time. It is a great pity that such suggestion was not acted upon, both because, in all likelihood, the operation of unified Municipalities would have proved satisfactory to the Turkish Community and could have opened the way towards further unification, and also because introducing amendments to, or modifications of, the Constitution for an experimental period would have both afforded added safeguards to the Turkish Cypriots and allowed the Government, at the end of the period fixed, to review such modifications and their effect, if any, on the communal balance of interests. Piecemeal amendment, coupled, moreover, with time limits at the end of which the changes and modifications effected would be reconsidered, would, perhaps, have proved acceptable to all parties concerned. This, unfortunately, was not done. And as things stood at the time, it was virtually impossible to persuade the Turkish Community, or, rather, its leadership, that the Makarios proposals were anything but an attempt to abrogate the Constitutional Order. Distrust and misunderstanding had reached such a stage that even a limited dialogue concerning such measures was impossible. In fact, the Makarios proposals were first of all rejected by Turkey and not by the Turkish Cypriots. Shortly thereafter, the Turkish Cypriot leadership issued its reply to the President's memorandum. Such proposals, Dr. Kutchuk asserted, were "of a sweeping nature"[34] and attacked the very roots which gave life to the Republic; their "ulterior intention was to leave the Turks at the absolute mercy of the Greeks". As a result, they were "completely unacceptable". Dr. Kutchuk could not agree that "an honest and sincere attempt" had been made to apply the Constitution; and he knew "as a fact" that "this request for a change" emanated from Greek political motives. In his reply to the President's memorandum, Dr. Kutchuk insisted that Cyprus should be thought of as a state comprising two distinct and separate communities; and he absolutely refused to take any steps or measures which would bring about greater unity among the people of Cyprus as a whole. "Cyprus . . . is a state brought about by settlement reached between the Greek and Turkish communities". This, the then Turkish Vice President insisted time after time, was "the ruling factor" which should never be forgotten in approaching constitutional problems. Given this intransigently separatist attitude on the part of the Turkish leadership, it is not really surprising that there could be no settlement and no resolution of the difficulties that were admittedly facing the operation of the Government. It must be mentioned that international opinion sympathised with the Archbishop's attempt to remove, by Constitutional amendment, the sources of anomaly and conflict that have been analysed above; and the proposals put forward were moderate enough to attract the support of Sir Arthur Clarke, the then British High Commissioner in Cyprus. Further, that even moderate Turks accept some of the blame for the Constitutional breakdown is borne out by a considerable amount of evidence. Particularly interesting is a letter to the Istanbul 'Daily Milliyet' by a former Turkish Ambassador to Cyprus, Mr. Dirvana. He accused Mr. Denktash of having been uninterested in the economic, social and cultural development of the Turkish Community despite the existence of ample funds and the Independence of the Turkish Chambers. "For months I tried in vain to persuade Denktash to concentrate on this area . . . But Mr. Denktash did not care about such things. He was only interested in quarrelling with the Greek Cypriots, often purposelessly".

Violent disturbances broke out between the two Communities on the 23rd December, 1964. Normality never really returned to the island again. Four issues will be briefly touched upon here. The UN's involvement with Cyprus;[35] the Intercommunal talks;[36] the internationalisation of the Cyprus problem; and the anomalous legal situation that was created as a result of the policy of self segregation followed by the Turkish Community after December 1963.[37] This last issue will be dealt with later in the context of an attempt to show that the 1960 Constitution still exists despite its incomplete implementation and I do not propose to say much about it here. Suffice it to observe that this "abnormal situation" was created as a result of the Turkish officers' refusal to turn up and assume their functions under the Constitution. "But the life of the State and its Government could not be wrecked and had to be carried out".[38] Consequently, those acts of the Government of the Republic of Cyprus which did not and do not conform to the procedures set out in the Constitution can be justified by reference to the principle of necessity, i.e. that the framework of the Constitutional order still survives, but that deviations from its norms, in carefully circumscribed cases and in truly exceptional circumstances, can be justified on grounds of necessity.

As soon as violence erupted between the two Communities, Turkey began adopting an aggressive stance. On the 25th December, Turkish war planes (which in 1964 were to bomb defenceless villages in Cyprus), in an effort to intimidate the Government of Cyprus, flew at tree level over the island, and the Turkish Government, that same evening, announced that they were about to invade Cyprus. This, in fact, became the usual pattern of events. Threats, intense pressures, intimidation — such have been the tactics of Turkey throughout the period 1963-1974. In fact, the Turkish invasion of Cyprus, carefully planned over many years, can be seen as the culmination of such aggressive policies. The Republic of Cyprus, under the pressure of Turkish threats about an imminent invasion of the island, took the matter to the UN since the Cyprus question, or so the Government thought, was and is primarily a question concerning the application of universally accepted principles of the UN Charter. The UN dealt with the Cyprus problem both in the Security Council and in the General Assembly.[39] Under its decision of the 4th March, 1964, the Security Council, recognising in no uncertain terms that the responsibility for the maintenance of law and order belonged to the Government of the Republic, recommended "the creation, with the consent of the Government of Cyprus, of a UN peace keeping force in Cyprus". The function of the Force was "to use its best efforts to prevent a recurrence of fighting and, as necessary, to contribute to the maintenance and restoration of law and order and return to normal conditions". The UN Force in Cyprus became operational on the 27th March, 1964, and, until the recent Turkish invasion of Cyprus, did its best to contribute to the cause of peace in the island. Furthermore, the Security Council, by paragraph 7 of its 4th March Resolution, recommended that the Secretary-General "designate, in agreement with the Government of Cyprus and the Governments of Greece, Turkey and the U.K., a Mediator", who was to use his best endeavours with the representatives of both Communities and also with the aforesaid four Governments "for the purpose of promoting a peaceful solution and an agreed settlement of the problem confronting Cyprus, in accordance with the Charter of the UN". The late Finnish diplomat, Sakari Tuomioja, was appointed as first Mediator. He was succeeded by Dr. Galo Plaza. Dr. Plaza's report, essential reading for all those interested in the Cyprus problem, was submitted to the Secretary-General on the 26th March, 1965. Dr. Plaza described the 1960 Constitution as a "constitutional oddity" and could not help wondering whether "the physical division of the minority from the majority", which was sought by the Turkish side, was not "a desperate step in the wrong direction". He was, moreover, reluctant to believe, as the Turkish Cypriot leadership claimed, in the "impossibility" of Greek Cypriots and Turkish Cypriots learning to live together in peace. Dr. Plaza was clearly in favour of an independent and unitary Cyprus, with effective protection of individual and minority rights, and expressed his satisfaction with the assurances which Archbishop Makarios had given concerning such protection. Both the Governments of Cyprus and Greece considered the Mediator's findings as constituting a constructive approach to the problem and, in conformity with the wishes of the UN, wished his mediation to continue. This, however, proved impossible on account of the Turkish Government's attitude. Both the Turkish Government and the Turkish Cypriot leadership asserted that the report went beyond the Mediator's terms of reference and stated that they considered Dr. Plaza's functions as Mediator to have come to an end. It must be noted that the Secretary-General rejected Turkey's assertion regarding Dr. Plaza's alleged excess of his mandate and stressed that he found nothing in the Mediator's report which he could consider as incompatible with his terms of reference; also, in a letter to Dr. Plaza, which was circulated as a Security Council Document, the Secretary-General referred to the report as "a most important contribution to the search for a just and lasting solution to the Cyprus problem".

In view of the fact that owing to the declared intransigent position of Turkey, the prospects for an agreed settlement of the Cyprus problem did not appear encouraging, and also on account of Turkey's continuous threats and intimidation — the Turkish Government often seriously contemplating an invasion of Cyprus, and openly doing so —, the Government of Cyprus decided to place the question of Cyprus on the agenda of the 19th session of the General Assembly. The General Assembly, on the 18th December, 1965, by 47 votes against 5, after taking cognizance of the fact that "the Republic of Cyprus, as an equal member of the UN, is, in accordance with the Charter, entitled to and should enjoy full sovereignty and complete independence without any foreign intervention or interference", called upon all states, "in conformity with their obligations under the Charter", and in particular, Art. 2, paragraphs 1 and 4, "to respect the sovereignty, unity, independence and territorial integrity of the Republic of Cyprus and to refrain from any intervention directed against it". Nothing, of course, could be more explicit. The real importance of this Resolution was that it recognised clearly and unambiguously that Cyprus, "as an equal Member State of the UN", was entitled to and should enjoy sovereignty and independence, not by virtue of or by the grace of certain Agreements and Treaties but by virtue of internationally recognised principles. Equally, nothing, perhaps, was more predictable than Turkey's failure to honour such Resolution. Indeed, as is suggested elsewhere, Turkey's actions over the years have done nothing but undermine the UN's prestige and effectiveness. Turkey, in effect, has been permitted to force the UN Mediator's resignation simply because his views were not to its liking, and repeated UN resolutions concerning the Cyprus problem have been openly ignored. In such circumstances, one, indeed, doubts the UN's continued usefulness.

The local Intercommunal talks which, until recently, held out the major hope for an agreed and lasting settlement of the Cyprus problem, must now be briefly dealt with. After the crisis of November-December, 1967, the Security Council, in its effort to find a peaceful solution to the problem, adopted, by its Resolution of 22nd December, 1967, the procedure "of the good offices of the Secretary-General" on the basis of the appeals that had been made by the Secretary-General himself. The Secretary-General, having made various soundings, put forward at the beginning of 1968 the suggestion for the commencement of local talks in Cyprus under the aegis of his Special Representative in Cyprus. As a result, Intercommunal talks started between the Representatives of the Greek and Turkish Communities, Mr. Clerides and Mr. Denktash, and such talks, in time, were enlarged by virtue of the participation therein, in an advisory capacity, of two constitutional experts, one from Greece and one from Turkey. From the very beginning, it was mutually agreed that the aim of the local talks would be the exploration of various possibilities for the solution of the constitutional problem on the basis of an independent, unitary and sovereign state. It must also be mentioned that in this connection, the Cyprus Government, in its desire to create a suitable climate for the success of the talks, took unilaterally, in June 1968, measures aiming at the normalisation of the situation. Such measures, regrettably, were not followed by reciprocal gestures on the part of the Turkish leadership.

The intercommunal talks have gone through various phases, but by 1970 or 1971 the outlines of a compromise settlement had clearly emerged. It seems that the Turks agreed to relinquish many of their special rights obtained under the Zürich Settlement, such as the veto right and the 70:30 ratio — this last to be replaced by one nearer the actual composition of the population — and that substantial agreement was reached on the composition of the new legislature and about the powers and functions of the Executive and Judiciary. But as the quid pro quo for relinquishing their rights at the top, the Turks wanted broader powers at the bottom, so to speak. Hence, their emphasis on regional autonomy. The demands of the Turkish Cypriot side on the issue of local Government were, as formulated, clearly unacceptable because they conflicted with the principles of a unitary state and the accepted forms and underlying philosophy of Local Administration. In addition, the Turkish Cypriot proposals — aiming at the creation of a state within a State and the setting up of two completely separate regional administrations — failed to safeguard the economic viability of the local areas to be created and their effective administration, would have impeded free population movement and would almost certainly, in time, have led to friction between the communities and greater division and communalism than what had been enshrined in the discredited 1960 Constitution. The Greek Cypriot side, it must be made quite clear, did not reject the need to establish adequate local Government; and, in fact, Mr. Clerides did put forward suggestions concerning the recognition and establishment of local administration. No agreement, however, was reached on this issue. It can, indeed, be said that the Intercommunal talks would long ago have succeeded had the Turkish side not wanted to secure through Local Government a device for splitting up the island's Administration at the all important regional level with a view to establishing a separate Turkish Governmental structure defeating and, eventually, destroying the unity of the State.

Such Intercommunal talks have, of course, been frustrated by the Turkish invasion. It must not be forgotten, however, that substantial progress was achieved at such talks and that broad agreement was reached after protracted negotiations on a number of important topics. It is thought that to allow such results to be completely ignored by Turkey simply because there has been a change of circumstances as a result of an illegal military operation would not only sanction the use of force; even more important, it would throw doubt upon, and make a real mockery of, the very concept of negotiations freely entered into for the purpose of resolving a complex international and constitutional problem.

Another important development in the 1960-1974 period was the increasing involvement in the Cyprus question of the Big Powers.[40] America, for instance, did not really manifest an interest in the Cyprus problem before Cyprus became independent. There was no power vacuum to be filled and British control of Cyprus seemed capable of safeguarding American strategic interests in the area. Since independence, however, NATO military concerns in the Eastern Mediterranean and the growing importance of the Middle East have intensified concern over Cyprus. And "additional anxiety"[41] seems to have been caused to US policy makers by the Cyprus Government's alleged flirtations with the Soviet Union whose powerful fleet has in recent years decisively infiltrated the area and posed a challenge both to American hegemony in the area and the vital Southern flank of NATO.

More fully, the main reasons for American concern over Cyprus seem to be the following. First, as a result of ethnic ties and a complicated Treaty structure, this "local quarrel" has always threatened to produce an armed conflict between Greece and Turkey. Such a conflict, the American Government has always believed, should be averted at all costs. Adhesion to NATO, "in its very essence", means that NATO countries should not wage war on each other; and a generalised conflict between Greece and Turkey, the American Government has always feared, could easily lead to direct involvement by the Soviet Union. Secondly, as a result of the UN Security Council undertaking to keep peace on the island, the Cyprus problem was, throughout this period, an active item in the international diplomacy practised in New York. The US could not but take a keen interest in such an item. Thirdly, the American Government has always been suspicious of Archbishop Makarios' policies. It was not only that Archbishop Makarios had early on embarked upon an adventurous (and wholly justified) non-aligned course in the area of foreign policy, and that such course, particularly in the context of Middle Eastern developments, acutely worried the global policy makers of the State Department; Archbishop Makarios was always thought by the US Government to be dangerously flirtatious with Moscow. This apprehension, coupled with concern regarding the strength of the local Cyprus Communist Party, raised, in American eyes, the spectre of a serious and, perhaps, permanent intrusion of the Soviet Union into the strategic Eastern Mediterranean.

Three phases in American involvement in the problem of Cyprus seem to be capable of delineation. First, America's decisive action in preventing Turkish invasion in 1964. Secondly, American efforts at mediation, and the straining of the relations between Cyprus and the US upon the rejection of such mediation by the Cyprus Government; and, thirdly, the American Government's diplomatic handling of the 1974 Turkish invasion and the situation created in consequence thereof.

(a) As is well known, in the first week of January, 1964, Turkey was seriously contemplating an invasion of Cyprus for the purpose of occupying a portion thereof. President Johnson, in a letter sent to Prime Minister Inonu, dated 5th January, 1964, expressed grave concern regarding Turkish plans to invade Cyprus.[42] The proposed intervention by Turkey, President Johnson pointed out, would clearly be intended for the purpose of supporting an attempt by the Turkish Cypriot leadership to partition the island, "a solution which specifically is excluded by the Treaty of Guarantee". Further, that Treaty required consultation among the Guarantors and it was the view of the US that the possibilities of such consultation had by no means been exhausted. Moreover, by virtue of the bilateral agreement between the US and Turkey in the field of military assistance, Turkey was required to obtain US consent for the use of military assistance for purposes other than those for which such assistance was furnished and, the President stated, "in all candor", the US could not agree to the use of any US-supplied military equipment for a Turkish intervention in Cyprus. The Johnson letter was effective in averting a Turkish invasion, but was taken, in Turkey, as "a serious intervention in Turkey's sovereign affairs and caused a critical worsening of relations between the two countries". This may be one of the factors explaining America's failure to take any similar action in 1974, despite the fact that the arguments against the legality of a 1964 Turkish invasion put forward by President

Johnson seem directly applicable to Turkey's action in 1974. Also, throughout this period, America was obviously apprehensive about the possibility of a rapprochement between Turkey and the Soviet Union, and such apprehension, both then and now, accounts for many developments of, and turns in, American foreign policy. Indeed, during the following years, Turkey did embark upon sustained efforts to develop better relations with the Soviet Union, and this form of indirect pressure seems, as recent events indicate, to have been effective in convincing the Americans that their strategic interests in the area, particularly with a subservient military dictatorship in Athens, would be better served by greater favour to Turkey and by a tactical shift in their policies in the area in the direction of Turkish interests.

(b) Immediately after the 1964 crisis, American initiatives were launched for the purpose of resolving the problem. In January 1964, President Johnson met, separately, with Prime Minister Inonu and Prime Minister Papandreou but, despite intense American pressure, the Greek Prime Minister declined to abandon the UN framework. US efforts, however, resulted in talks being held at Geneva between Greek and Turkish Representatives under the aegis of the UN Mediator, with the participation of Dean Acheson, the former American Secretary of State. The Cyprus Government was not invited to participate in these talks. This was the origin and circumstances of the Acheson plan. This plan called for Union of Cyprus with Greece, subject to the following conditions: That Turkey receive the Greek Island of Kastellorizon, that two Turkish cantons be established in Cyprus, and that a military base be ceded to Turkey. In Acheson's own words, the plan was to bring Union of Cyprus with Greece, but also provide for Turkey " . . . a military presence unhampered by the need for tripartite consent at every turn. A sequestered base for ground, air and sea forces not only could be a defence for Cyprus but (could also) prevent its being used hostilely against Turkey, could defend the sea approaches to the south Turkish seaports, and be a constant reminder on the island of Turkish presence and interest". This, clearly, was a totally unacceptable plan, and was rightly denounced by Archbishop Makarios. Whatever the name of the plan, it was, in effect, a form of double enosis or partition. Also, it must not be forgotten, such a plan was engineered in the absence of any representative of the Cyprus Government. It is clear that the American Government, already predisposed against Archbishop Makarios' Government, was further annoyed by the rejection of Acheson's initiative. "The losers plainly are the NATO nations whose alliance has been gravely weakened, and especially, Greece and Turkey whose confidence both in one another and in the US and Great Britain has been strained. The gainers are the Archbishop . . . the Russians who have weakened NATO and, perhaps, gained another toehold in the Eastern Mediterranean, and Col. Nasser . . .". Such attitudes were reinforced by the failure of other American initiatives, such as the efforts of Cyrus Vance in 1967; by Makarios' insistence that the only acceptable framework for a solution of the Cyprus problem was that provided by the UN Charter; and by the Archbishop's further pursuit of a non-aligned policy. It must also be pointed out that in the UN General Assembly, the US voted against the Resolution emphasising respect for the sovereignty of Cyprus (see above), and, clearly, such vote could only have been taken as a sign that America, in the case of a further attempt to invade Cyprus, would either abstain completely from any involvement or else would adopt a much less stern attitude towards future Turkish aggression.

To summarise, the aims of US foreign policy towards Cyprus, throughout the 1960's, can be said to have been the following:

(1) To contain the conflict between the two Communities in Cyprus itself, ensuring that the intercommunal friction would not cause a large Graeco- Turkish war.

(2) To adopt a more or less ambivalent attitude towards the communal conflict, and

(3) to make every effort at excluding or minimising Soviet intrusion in the area.

(c) It remained to be seen, however, how the Americans would handle a situation such as the one in 1964, and how the development of detente between the super powers would affect, or influence, the Big Powers' responses to e.g. Turkish aggression. But it must be admitted, on the basis of recent developments in US-Cypriot relations, and in view of the State Department's increasing readiness to subject everything to strategic and political considerations, one could not realistically expect a balanced approach to such issues — and the situation from the point of view of the Government of the Republic and the Greek Cypriot majority was not improved either by the volatility of the Middle East, which made it imperative that Cyprus should not come under communist influence — real or suspected —, or by the seriously weakened position, both diplomatically and militarily, that Greece found itself in after seven years' oppressive dictatorship. Nor could one derive comfort either from the fact that America, despite its protestations to the contrary, clearly seemed to incline towards the "two communities" concept which, pushed to its logical extreme, might justify the physical separation of the two communities and the consequent partitioning of the island, or from the rather erratic performance of State Department diplomacy and American crisis management in previous episodes relating to the gradual unfolding of the Cyprus problem. But, despite such considerations which, as it has been suggested above, could not make Greek Cypriots confident that their interests as the overwhelming majority of Cyprus would be dealt with justly or accorded their proper weight by the American Government if it ever came to a serious crisis, not even the most pessimistic observer could anticipate American reactions in the tragic events that took place in the summer of 1974 — that the American Government would adopt such a pro-Turkish stance or that American foreign policy could consist of so many ambiguities, vacillations and miscalculations. More is said on this subject below. But when all is said and done, and irrespective of what may turn out to have been America's precise role in the crisis, on the basis of existing evidence one cannot but speak of America's complicity, at least through criminal inactivity, in the human and political tragedy of Cyprus.

Much more can be said with regard to the intensification of external involvements in the Cyprus problem, but this would not be the appropriate place for such an undertaking. One or two points will suffice. It has already been mentioned that a prime motive for the US's assumption of an active role in the Cyprus question was the desire to curb possible Soviet intrusion in the Eastern Mediterranean. What was Moscow's policy during this same period?

Two goals of such policy[43] can be detected beneath the ambiguities of Soviet public statements and the twists of the Soviet Union's tactical positions. Such goals, which have remained steady objectives of Soviet policy throughout, are the weakening of the southern flank of NATO and the demilitarisation of the island. Pursuit of the first goal means that aggravation of Graeco-Turkish relations and loss of faith and confidence in the US by either Greece or Turkey or both should be encouraged, and attempts to bring about the demilitarisation of the island, namely the removal of the British Sovereign Bases and the elimination of any possibility of Cyprus becoming a part of NATO, necessitate (since both Greece and Turkey belong to NATO and, as a result, either enosis or partition would suffice to bring Cyprus within the orbit of that Organisation) switching tactics and sides as the occasion demands.

As with all other major Powers, Moscow, particularly in view of the complexity of the issues and the diversity of the interests involved, acted, throughout the period we have been examining, in an opportunistic way, frequently changing the emphasis of its public pronouncements, retaining flexibility of action and continuously attempting to reinforce its influence over indigenous Communist elements in Cyprus. For instance, after the Johnson letter, Turkey adopted an anti-Western attitude, became amenable to Soviet approaches and attempted to effect a rapprochement with the Soviet Union. To such overtures Moscow was only too happy to respond. Russian leaders (e.g. see statement of President Podgorny in January 1965) began speaking of the "two communities" of Cyprus as both having sovereignty, and mentioned federation as a possible solution. Yet, on other occasions (and, as a matter of fact, immediately prior to the adoption of such pro-Turkish stance), the Soviet Union strongly castigated Turkish aggression. Premier Krushchev in August, 1964, charged that the Turkish air raids on Cyprus were part of an "imperialist plot", warned Turkey that it could not "drop bombs . . . with impunity", and expressed full support for Cyprus' independence and territorial integrity.

Similar ambiguity in tactical manoeuvring can be detected in Soviet attitudes over the recent crisis. Ambivalence and equivocation had (and have) to remain essential characteristics of Soviet policy since only in this way can the constant Soviet strategic objectives be served. As soon as the balance of power shifts or appears to shift dangerously in favour of either Greece or Turkey, the danger of Cyprus coming under direct NATO influence revives and new diplomatic overtures to redress the balance are called for. After the coup, it seemed as if the strategic balance had tilted towards Greece; adoption of an anti-Greek, anti-Western attitude became essential and inevitable. After it became clear, however, that Turkey, in invading Cyprus, intended not to restore constitutional legitimacy but rather to bring about drastic changes in the political structure of the island which might well endanger its non-aligned status, the contrary was the case in terms of the balance of Powers, the danger of partition became a very real one and anti-Turkish (but, of course, still anti-Western) statements started to emanate from the Kremlin. To sum up, the various shifts in Soviet allegiances are intended to do no more than reflect the various tactical phases and strategic developments of the Cyprus problem against a background of more or less constant and long-term policy objectives. Russia, as was made clear at the Geneva conference, is not really interested in the internal constitutional settlement to be agreed upon provided that Cyprus is not turned into "a bridgehead . . .an 'unsinkable air craft carrier' of NATO anchored in the Eastern Mediterranean".[44]

During this same period Britain ceased playing a decisive role in the political life of Cyprus. Its main interests appeared to be limited to the security of its sovereign military bases — bases which have so far not been threatened by the upheavals which have taken place around them. British policy always favoured the return to constitutional order in Cyprus by means of the intercommunal talks between the spokesmen of the two communities. The extensive commercial and business relations between Britain and its former colony; the human, cultural and scientific contacts between the two countries which rapidly developed in the post-independence era; the fact that Cyprus remains a member of the Commonwealth — all these developments led to a perceptible improvement in Anglo-Greek Cypriot relations and to British support for the continued independence of Cyprus. In spite, however, of the fact that Britain had been showing a more mature understanding of the political problems of Cyprus, during the July 1974 crisis it refrained from taking the necessary action to protect a state whose independence and integrity it had guaranteed. For that failure Britain bears an indirect responsibility for the brutal invasion and the occupation of almost half of Cyprus by the Turkish army. But more is said on this later.

Such then were the themes of the 1963-1974 period — intensification of Turkish aggression, external involvement in the affairs of Cyprus, increased but, ultimately, ineffective UN activity. Internally, there were both hopeful signs and indications at the same time, that, unless a constitutional settlement was speedily arrived at, a major tragedy might erupt, engulfing both Communities and, possibly Greece and Turkey as well, in armed conflict. The Intercommunal talks held out the hope of a constitutional settlement; increased financial prosperity among the Greek Cypriot Community could not but make it clear to the

Turkish Community that only through integration and unity could its financial situation be improved; and, on many occasions, the Cyprus Government offered substantial inducements to the Turkish Community to get out of its self-imposed segregation and once again participate in public life. At the same time, however, the Turkish Cypriot leadership, with strong Turkish support — financial and other — feverishly worked against any move towards integration and obstinately refused to respond to the Government's offers of co-operation. And, within the Greek Cypriot camp, there were increasing signs of fragmentation and division of loyalties which raised clearly the spectre of civil war and fratricidal strife. Moreover, the financial prosperity I have already mentioned seems to have lulled the Greek Cypriot Community into a false sense of security. As a result, our priorities were misplaced and both pursuit of material prosperity and continued exacerbation of partisan passions within the Greek Cypriot Community distorted the political vision and made the Intercommunal constitutional and political problem appear a secondary matter.

A more general point must be made. The formation of Turkish Cypriot enclaves, it should have been realised, was a very serious development. Such enclaves were not financially self sufficient, and, as a result, had to rely almost exclusively on assistance from Turkey mainland.[45] Such economic insufficiency seems to have been misinterpreted by the Greek Cypriot Community as a sign that time was on the Greek side and that the longer the Intercommunal negotiations dragged on, the better our position would become as compared to the Turkish one. It was not so. Time was not on our side. Reliance on Turkey meant not only a continuously increasing Turkish influence both in the actual administration of the areas controlled by the Turkish Cypriots and in the formulation of policies to be pursued regarding the intercommunal problem, but also involved on the Turkish Cypriot side (since Cyprus is, in Turkey, a "national" matter and a question of prestige) a stepped up determination to persist in self-segregation and further consolidate their hold on Cyprus territory. This territorial control (small at all times prior to the invasion, but control over part of Cyprus territory none the less) not only gave the world the impression (which, indeed, was not far from the truth) that there was a separate Turkish Cypriot administration functioning in the island but also provided the nucleus for the Turkish territorial expansion in Cyprus represented by the recent invasion and subsequent events.

Throughout the 1963-74 period there seemed to have been a feeling on the Greek Cypriot side that it was for the Greek side to dictate terms and that eventually the Turkish Cypriot Community would be forced by its own self-segregation and the economic deprivation that entailed to come to the negotiating table. This was a monumental mistake of basic policy. Not only did we fail to grasp the emotional and psychological aspects of the Cyprus problem for Turkey (a Turkey, moreover, facing such serious domestic problems at home that a Cyprus military operation could but seem a welcome diversion as well as a "national duty"), but we also identified "majority" with "power". In truth, the two terms were not synonymous. Unfortunately, it took an invasion for the Greek Cypriot side to recognise this. In fact, sound political judgment could only indicate that (a) Greece, in a war with Turkey, both by virtue of the geographical vulnerability of its eastern flank and on account of its seriously weakened condition as a result of disastrous dictatorial Government, could not defend Cyprus adequately, and that (b) the divisions among the Greek Cypriot Community, short of some miracle, would only become more accentuated with time and that this would not only lead to a weakening of our bargaining strength but also lead to a further hardening of the Turkish position. As a result of such perception (which, unfortunately, was not forthcoming) the only realistic and feasible policy was surely (and should have been) the pursuit of a settlement that would (a) preserve the unity of the state, (b) establish a balanced Central Government divested of the old divisive elements and (c) break up the enclaves by allowing free movement and settlement in all parts of the Republic, any regional arrangements to be adopted to be free of that geographic cohesion that would, in time, bring about new enclaves and the creation, within secure and established boundaries, of exclusively Greek and Turkish concentrations of inhabitants. Success on these three fronts (and this was very nearly achieved at the intercommunal discussions) would have paved the way for the creation of those conditions that would eventually make for an integrated society.

Alas, rhetoric, emotionalism and insufficient analysis of basic strategic considerations — coupled with an absence both of orderly political life and effective institutions for formulating and appraising policy — were dearer to the Greek Cypriot Community than either facing hard realities or developing coherent policies based not on narrow mindedness or an inflated view of one's own potential but on realism, common sense and sound judgment.

Throughout the same period, it is now clear, Turkish strategists were following a policy of wait and see. The Intercommunal discussions would continue and all efforts would be made to secure at such negotiations some kind of geographical settlement. It was a favourable settlement that was sought by Turkey and not a normalisation of conditions — hence, the Turkish refusal either to reciprocate Makarios' good will gestures or contemplate a stage by stage implementation of the results arrived at at the intercommunal discussions as such results were periodically agreed upon. And, it is clear that contingency plans existed relating to a possible invasion of Cyprus given the slightest pretext, with military preparations at an advanced stage.

Such internal developments then as the perpetuation of self-segregation by the Turkish Community and the apparent inability on the part of the Greek Cypriot Community as a whole to comprehend the dangers involved and appreciate the need for an early resolution of the constitutional and political problem, coupled, at the international level, with increased Turkish intransigence and a corrupt military Junta ruling Greece (which was doing so badly at home that it might well be tempted to resort to reckless adventures in Cyprus which, one could easily see, could but trigger off a Turkish response) should have alerted all that serious events might well be in the offing. The tragedy of Cyprus was, indeed, on its way.

III

THE TURKISH INVASION OF CYPRUS

INTRODUCTION

O N the 15th July, 1974, an attempt was made to over-throw the legitimate Government of Archbishop Makarios. The coup was engineered and staged against the Government by the military junta, then ruling Greece. It is not exactly clear what the intentions were either of the coup leaders or those people who found themselves in positions of authority after the coup, or even what the exact relationship was between the military who brought about the coup and those civilian, anti-Makarios elements who assumed authority on Monday, 15th July, 1974.[1] What is clear is that units of the Cyprus National Guard, led by officers from Greece serving with the National Guard, attacked on the 15th of July and destroyed with heavy weapons the Presidential Palace, seeking Archbishop Makarios' death. It does not seem unlikely that Makarios was the only target of the coup and that there was no intention either to interfere with the constitutional arrangements setting up the Cyprus Republic and securing the independence and non-aligned status of Cyprus or take any measures that would endanger the security of the Turkish Community. It was immediately announced that the institutional structure of the state would remain unaltered, that the Intercommunal discussions being held between the President of the House of Representatives, Mr. Clerides, and the Turkish Vice President, Mr. Denktash, for the purpose of amending the 1960 Constitution would continue, and that no change of foreign policy was envisaged.

The coup d' etat staged against Archbishop Makarios, a criminal and deplorable undertaking, was the prelude to the present tragedy in Cyprus. Turkey, using the coup as the pretext and purportedly acting under the Treaty of Guarantee, intervened militarily in Cyprus, in contravention of the Treaty itself, by invading the island on the 20th of July. This Treaty, it is argued below, did not and could not give such rights of military intervention as alleged by Turkey. Furthermore, it will be conclusively shown, the very conduct of Turkey's military operation in Cyprus has been throughout (and, particularly, in its later stages, by which time every deceptive appearance of justification is shamelessly thrown away and criminal reality openly acknowledged) in direct violation of the declared purposes of the Treaty. For, instead of protecting as a guarantor power the independence and territorial integrity of Cyprus, Turkey has destroyed both.[2]

Soon after the Turkish invasion of Cyprus, the Greek Junta fell and the Presidency of Cyprus was assumed by Mr. Clerides, the President of the House of Representatives. Mr. Clerides, who, according to the 1960 Constitution, is Archbishop Makarios' constitutional successor in the case of the latter's temporary absence or temporary incapacity to perform the duties of the Presidency, made it clear that he was assuming the duties of the President under the Constitution and in accordance with its provisions. As a result of such developments, it was clear and, in fact, widely believed that whatever the origins or intentions of the coup of the 15th of July, or Turkey's original justification or rationale, Turkey had lost any claim to legality for her continued presence on the island. The only objective of action under the Treaty of Guarantee, the Treaty itself unequivocally declares, is the re-establishment of the legitimate Constitutional order and the state of affairs brought into existence by the Treaty itself. Both these had been re-established. So, why were the Turkish troops remaining on the island, intensifying their aggression and extending their occupation?

Meanwhile, and as a direct result of Turkish aggression, the danger of a major war between Greece and Turkey was so acute that diplomats everywhere exerted frantic efforts to avert further intensification of conflict or the breaking out of a general Graeco-Turkish war. The Security Council had already adopted on the 20th of July Resolution 353 which called for an immediate ceasefire and demanded an immediate end to foreign military intervention. Turkey, needless to say, refused to obey. At the same time, NATO, since both Greece and Turkey were members, ineffectually attempted to mediate. Britain too, which together with Greece and Turkey is a Guarantor of Cyprus' sovereignty, also attempted to intercede with the Turks, equally ineffectually. Since then, encouraged by the Big Powers' inactivity and the UN's ineffectiveness, Turkey has defied repeatedly-proclaimed ceasefires, shown absolute contempt for Security Council Resolutions and ruthlessly extended the territory of Cyprus under her control.

Two Geneva Conferences have since been called for the purpose of dealing with the Cyprus problem. Both are analysed below. Suffice it to say that at such negotiations the Turkish Delegation, to quote Mr. Callaghan, the British Foreign Secretary, who presided at such talks, behaved "arbitrarily and unreasonably". Finally, on the 14th of August, and only minutes after the second round of the Geneva Conference had broken down as a result of Turkish intransigence and bad faith, the Turkish army once more began operations in Cyprus by land, sea and air, and, in fact, partitioned the island in two.

Such — as events have clearly proved — was the intention of Turkey from the beginning. Far from the Turkish invasion being directed towards a re-establishment of the Constitutional order, already, on the 24th of July, the Turks, at that time in control of a comparatively small strip of land in Northern Cyprus, spoke of the Kyrenia corridor forever remaining in Turkish hands; and Mr. Denktash, on that same day, revealed that Turkish Cypriots had begun to move into Greek houses and properties in Kyrenia evacuated by the Greek Cypriots. "This was a natural thing", Mr. Denktash claimed, even though such properties were in Greek Cypriot ownership. "The Kyrenia corridor was an essential door and window for the Turkish Cypriots and had to be kept". As a result, he concluded, "Kyrenia . . . would be transformed into a completely Turkish area". So, even at that time, the Turkish leadership was quite frank about its intentions — not the restoration of Constitutional legitimacy which had been disturbed but the transformation of part of Cyprus "into a completely Turkish area", something that is nowhere sanctioned or even envisaged by the 1960 Constitution which the Turks, allegedly, were seeking to re-establish. And that area, on account of the criminal negligence of the Big Powers and the unwillingness of the United Nations to take effective action, has been gradually extended, to the point where there is real fear of the whole of Cyprus being taken over.

Cyprus is now living through the greatest tragedy of its history, with 200,000 refugees (i.e. 40% of its total Greek population), three of its six towns (Kyrenia, Famagusta and Morphou) and a hundred of its Greek villages occupied and destroyed by air attacks, shooting and shelling, and thousands of dead among the population, both combatant and non combatant.

Before, however, we proceed to an analysis of Turkey's

invocation of the Treaty of Guarantee as providing justification for her actions, we must consider the main features and the immediate results of the Turkish Invasion.

CHARACTERISTICS OF THE INVASION.[3]

The ruthlessness and brutality of the Turkish forces during the military operations in Cyprus have been amply documented and extensively commented upon in the World Press. There can, indeed, be no doubt that the invading Turkish army has thoughout shown complete disregard for the 1949 Geneva Conventions and the various International Law Rules concerning the conduct of hostilities. Besides the indiscriminate bombing, shelling and shooting of unarmed civilians and of such internationally protected institutions as infirmaries, hospitals, schools and even the Red Cross Centre of Cyprus, the Turkish army has also inflicted unprecedented harrassment on the civilian population of the area they have occupied in Northern Cyprus. The Turkish armed forces, after their above-mentioned occupation, systematically looted and plundered the properties of the inhabitants, very frequently arrested all the men of villages they were capturing, taking many of them to detention camps in Turkey, brutally molested women, children and elderly people, and indulged in repeated rapes, arsons, coldblooded murders of civilians and forced expulsion of the inhabitants from their homes.

These two aspects of the invasion — namely, the unprecedented ferocity and inhumanity of the Turkish forces on the one hand, and, on the other, the complete disregard of the human rights of the civilian population of the occupied areas after the successful conclusion of the military operations — must be carefully considered.

(A) The basic rule concerning the waging of war is that the right of belligerents to adopt means of injuring the enemy is not unlimited; or, to adopt a somewhat different formulation, the sole legitimate object which States should endeavour to accomplish during war is to weaken the military forces of the enemy[4]. From such principles, the following more specific rules have been derived which, it can be readily seen, Turkey has repeatedly and massively violated.

(a) Belligerents should refrain from deliberately attacking non combatants. This immunity to which the civilian population is entitled during hostilities has not been clearly defined by International Law, but, in spite of many examples of blatant disregard of it, still forms one of the main pillars of the law of war. An even more specific norm deriving from such general immunity is that bombardments directed against the civilian population as such, especially for the purpose of terrorising it, are prohibited. This rule is widely accepted in academic writings, attempts at codification and judicial decisions; and, despite many violations, has never been, in principle, contested. The XXth International Conference of the Red Cross, moreover, did not omit to restate it. It is obvious that Turkey, in its military operations in Cyprus, has never observed such prohibition. In fact, many cities came under heavy attacks from the Turkish Air Force and, in both phases of Turkish aggression, there were many civilian casualties as a result of such indiscriminate bombing. A distinction was never made between persons taking part in the hostilities and members of the civilian population not participating in such hostilities. As a result, precautions were never taken for the purpose of reducing to a minimum the damage inflicted on non combatants during attacks against military objectives. The precautions to which allusion is made could have included, for instance, the careful choice and identification of military objectives, precision in attack, abstention from Air Force bombing if such bombing could involve damage or injury to the civilian population, respect for and abstention from attack on civil defence organisations and other internationally protected Institutions etc. Such precautions were never taken by the attacking side, i.e. the Turkish Army and, in particular, the Turkish Air Force. As a result, the Air Force attacks upon Nicosia, Famagusta and Paphos were nothing short of calamitous in terms of casualties and murderous in terms of methods.

(b) An ancillary rule, also considered basic in the Law of War, is that target limitations must be recognised in principle and observed in practice. This is nothing but the accepted distinction between the fighting area and the zones behind the lines. It is, moreover, generally admitted that an objective is military only if its complete or partial destruction confers a clear military advantage. It is also held, as a corollary to the above, that any attacking force, before bombing an objective, must identify it and ascertain that it is military. Such target limitations were completely ignored by the Turkish military forces. Hospitals, both ordinary and psychiatric, hotels, schools and other educational institutions were repeatedly raided by Turkish planes. To give one or two examples, the Education Ministry's Central Store in Nicosia containing all the books, stationery and teaching aids ready for distribution to schools of all levels for use during the coming year was bombed and literally reduced to ashes on August 15th. The value of the contents of the store exceeds £500,000. This destruction has rendered almost impossible the operation of schools, especially primary ones, and urgent appeals have already been made for the immediate supply of basically needed materials. The Psychiatric Hospital of Athalassa was also bombed despite the clearly visible emblems and flags of the Red Cross and such bombing resulted in the death of many helpless inmates. The famous antiquities of Cyprus were themselves not spared. It is not only that a large number of important ancient monuments, museums, archaeological sites, movable antiquities and other items of cultural property are now in areas controlled by the Turkish army of invasion and are, therefore, inaccessible for inspection and protection by the legal authorities of the Republic of Cyprus, but also many monuments of archaeological significance have been barbarously destroyed by the Turks — among such antiquities, for instance, are the world famous mosaics of the House of Dionysus in the district of Paphos, which have suffered very serious damage as a result of Turkish bombing.

All the above were buildings or sites which could not, under any circumstances, have been considered as military objectives; they should clearly have been given the benefit of special immunity under the Geneva Conventions (I, Art. 19; IV, Art. 18), the Hague Regulations of 1907 (Art. 27), and the 1954 Hague Convention relating to the protection of cultural property (Art. 4), namely that belligerents should in particular spare charitable, religious, scientific, cultural and artistic establishments as well as historic monuments. None was spared. But, as said above, this was not all or even the main feature of the Turkish attacks. Mention has already been made of the vicious air raids on virtually undefended and densely inhabited towns and villages. Even when such localities could offer no resistance, the Turkish army did not abstain from attack and useless destruction.

(c) Other limitations which must be observed in the conduct of hostilities are those that relate to weapons and their use. In this respect, the basic rule is Article 23 (e) of the Regulations annexed to the IVth Hague Convention of 1907, namely: "It is forbidden to employ arms, projectiles or material calculated to cause unnecessary suffering"; yet, as is well known, napalm was extensively used by the Turkish forces in Cyprus. This caused enormous suffering and has been strongly condemned.

It can be clearly seen that Turkey not only waged war on Cyprus. It did so in a peculiarly vicious way, ignoring all limitations (i.e. limitations for benefit of non combatants, limitations relating to targets that can legitimately be attacked and limitations on use of weapons causing unnecessary suffering) which have normally been considered as regulating warfare and which must be observed if essential human values are to be safeguarded. To find other examples of invasion characterised by similar acts of brutality and destruction one has to go back to Attila's time, whose name, indeed, was aptly given to this particular invasion by the aggressor himself.

(B) Turkey, through her invading forces, has acted in utter disregard of customary and conventional International law. The following points must be particularly stressed.

1. Many citizens of the Republic from the occupied territories were seized and taken to Turkey, in breach especially of Art. 49 of Geneva Convention IV of the 12th August, 1949, which strictly prohibits individual or mass forcible transfers, as well as deportation of protected persons, from occupied territory to the territory of the Occupying Power or to that of any other country, occupied or not.

2. It is common knowledge that Turkey has been making efforts to bring from Turkey Turkish citizens to the occupied territory in breach of the last paragraph of the aforesaid Article, according to which the Occupying Power should not deport or transfer parts of its own civilian population into the territory it occupies.

3. Turkey also had a duty under customary and conventional International Law to administer the territory under its temporary control according to the existing laws and the existing rules of administration, ensuring public order and safety and respecting family honour and rights, individual lives, private property, religious convictions and liberty (Article 43 of the Hague Regulations). Such obligations have been clearly violated. In addition, Turkey, in flagrant violation of the principles of International Law, does not allow inhabitants of the occupied territory who were either expelled or were bound to flee, to return to their homes.[5]

4. It is also well known that Turkey, also in clear violation of International Law, has seized property, both movable and

immovable, in the occupied territory and engaged in an unprecedented orgy of plundering and looting. In addition, the occupied territories have been ruthlessly, and, apparently, quite incompetently, exploited.

The Turkish forces have not limited themselves to the systematic plunder and destruction of Cyprus. The population of the occupied territories, as already pointed out, has been very seriously maltreated. Murders, rapes, assaults, harrassment, intimidation, all have taken place on a quite horrifying scale. It must also be pointed out that such acts as indiscriminate killing, mass and individual deportation and detention, rape, torture, general degrading treatment, plunder and destruction of properties fall under several of the provisions of the European Convention on Human Rights and its Protocols (i.e. Articles 2 (right to life), 3 (prohibition of torture, inhuman or degrading treatment and punishment), 4 (prohibition of slavery or servitude and forced Labour), 5 (right to liberty and security of person), 8 (right to family life and respect for home), 14 (prohibition of discrimination), Art. 1 of the First Protocol (right to peaceful enjoyment of possessions)).

THE CONSEQUENCES OF THE INVASION.

When we now direct our attention to the consequences of the invasion, special attention must clearly focus on the refugee problem created.[6] The whole of Cyprus has been turned into a vast refugee camp. More than 200,000 people, representing about 40% of the Greek population of the island, have been forced to leave their homes and live in refugee camps, under lamentable conditions, underfed and facing a serious problem of survival. If this is coupled with the fact that the displaced persons abandoned their homes without being able to take anything with them, and that 70% of the general stocks of food, agricultural and industrial products have remained in the cut-off areas and are, therefore, inaccessible, one can easily assess the magnitude of the enormous problem of sheltering and maintaining these unfortunate people that faces the Government. Particularly is this so if one realises that of 200,000 refugees only 27,400 can be regarded as being able to maintain themselves. The remaining 170,000 are in need of constant care and attention. Their subsistence alone requires an expenditure which, at the most conservative estimate, amounts to 500 mils (50p) per day for each refugee. "These refugees are everywhere present. To drive along the roads of the southern portion of the island is to drive through an endless refugee camp. Refugees (are) encamped under trees, along the roadside, under small huts, awaiting more permanent shelter. Every available public building and accommodation (is) filled with refugees — schools, churches, monasteries and civic buildings. District towns have been flooded with refugees, with . . . men swelling the unemployment rolls. Small towns along the way have doubled in size". The Government, of course, is doing everything in its power to alleviate the pain and misery of the refugees, but the dimensions of the problem are such that it is beyond its financial capabilities. Massive international aid is now required to keep these people alive.

It has already been mentioned that the displaced persons left their homes in such a hurry as a result of heavy bombing by enemy forces that virtually all their property has been abandoned to the mercy of the invading army. An indeterminate as yet number of the estimated over 50,000 households belonging to Greek Cypriots in this area have been destroyed, while most of them have been completely looted; the asset value of such properties is estimated to be not less than £250m, while movable property, at the most conservative valuation, ranges from between £50m to £100m. In addition, goods left in warehouses, fields, factories and shops in the occupied areas are worth many millions of pounds; their exact value cannot as yet be estimated. Suffice it to mention that goods worth £10m were stored in the Famagusta port warehouses. Furthermore, 100,000 tons of cereals valued at £6m and considerable stocks of potatoes and olive oil, also of very great value, are in the hands of the occupying army.

One wishes that the above alone were the economic consequences of the invasion. But this is not so. As has already been mentioned above, 40% of the territory of the Republic are now under Turkish occupation. The area involved comprises almost all the fertile Messaoria plain, the Kyrenia District, and the Karpasia Peninsula. This area is the almost exclusive cereal, carob, and olive producing, and the main citrus, vegetable, meat, milk and egg producing area of Cyprus. It contains ⅔rds of tourist activities, 55-60% of industrial activity, 65% of cultivated land, 60% of underground water resources, 60% of mining and quarrying activities, the main deep port of Cyprus at Famagusta — at which 83% of general cargo was prior to the invasion being handled — and the specialised port at Karavostassi, through which 85% of minerals were handled. It is also well known that the Kyrenia District, the most beautiful of the island, was also the most developed from the tourist point of view. In other words, the economic significance of this area is much more important than size. It is estimated that about 70% of total gross production from all sources emanates from this area, not to mention the immense wealth of physical assets, resources and structures situated there in the form of hotel and hotel apartments, houses, factories, orchards etc. The Turkish forces have, therefore, occupied the most productive part of the island, leaving the rest to the Greek Cypriots.

It is, of course, very difficult at this time to quantify accurately either the wider consequences of the invasion or the repercussions of such invasion on the economy and future of Cyprus. The intensity of the adverse consequences will, of course, inevitably depend on the final solution to be given to the Cyprus problem and the rapidity or otherwise of such a settlement and its implementation. It can be easily seen, however, even as things are at present, that an impossible economic situation has been created,[7] not only for the Greeks of the island, but for the people of Cyprus as a whole. Here, special mention will only be made of some areas of the economy which have been particularly affected, and of such other functions or services whose non operation or disruption as a result of the invasion has produced special suffering or inconvenience for the Cyprus people.

(1) The blow suffered by agriculture is considerable. Agriculture has been aptly characterised as the backbone of the economy. It normally provides employment to 96,000 people, contributes on average 20% of the G.N.P., is the major foreign exchange earner of the economy and supplies for further processing valuable materials to industry. Not only has considerable production been lost but also vast agricultural investment has been seized by force and has either been destroyed or is in serious danger of destruction. More than 45 sq. miles of citrus plantations, representing 80% and more of the total area planted with citrus trees, are facing the immediate danger of irreparable damage on account of non attendance and insufficient irrigation. Cyprus' lost animal stock is worth more than £11m and its annual production in terms of meat, milk, eggs, wool etc. was normally £12m.

(2) Industry in Cyprus has been severely affected. Cyprus' industrial potential was considerable, and, recently, industry was

investing heavily in all sectors. Now, many manufacturing industries have ceased production either because of physical destruction of factories by enemy action, or because many factories are situated in areas controlled by the Turkish army. Such factories employed 32% of manufacturing labour and produced 26% of output, that is about £12m annually. These industries have now come to a standstill and their fixed assets, valued at more than £30m, will be destroyed in time because of lack of maintenance. Many other industries have been, or will be, seriously affected. Some of them border on the dangerous zone and, as a result of continuous harrassment by the Turkish army, have not been able to resume commercial operations. Other industries which are relying on local raw materials now under the control of the Turkish army are already facing severe raw materials shortages. The mining industry must be specially referred to. Such industry, before the invasion a sizeable foreign exchange earner, was a dynamic sector of the economy, but its activities have been severely disrupted by the invasion.

(3) Tourism has been hardest hit of all. Before the invasion, tourism was booming and could have been described as the main pillar upon which the Government was basing its efforts to diversify the economy. In 1973, for example, tourism brought in £29m of foreign exchange earnings and provided employment for about 10,000 people. According to the estimates of the Tourist Board, the target for 1977 was £42m of foreign exchange earnings. Such plans, of course, must be abandoned. Not only have many tourist resorts been destroyed or irreparably damaged as a result of enemy action, but, as has already been mentioned, the area under Turkish occupation is the richest in the island both in terms of structures situated there and in terms of potential tourist development. Tourism, as a result of the losses sketched out above, has been completely paralysed, and is very unlikely in the near future (even if a settlement is before long arrived at) to be a considerable foreign-exchange-earning sector.

It must not be forgotten that many services have been adversely affected as a result of the Turkish invasion and that the disruption of such services, whilst such disruption continues, means that the Government of the Republic will not be able to reactivate the economy.

Important ports are now under the control of the Turkish army. Not only have the assets represented by such ports been lost for the Government but also sea communications have been seriously affected, the Limassol port being, in effect, the only one which can be used for navigation, and even for such port the insurance required has become exorbitant. Equally, if not more important, the Nicosia International Airport, a service of inestimable economic significance for Cyprus, was heavily bombed and is not operating at present. The closure of the airport (which handled 787,000 passengers in 1973) has caused a very serious loss of revenue to the Government, has brought about the cutting off of the only air communication with the world and has resulted in the complete dislocation of exports. All this was pointed out by Mr. Callaghan, the British Foreign Secretary, in Geneva. He said that the opening of the Airport was essential if Cyprus was ever to recover economically and he offered the services of the Air Force personnel of the Sovereign Bases for the purposes of reconstruction and reactivation of the Airport. He realised, of course, that the control of the Airport facilities had become a sensitive political issue, and he therefore suggested that the Airport be run, provisionally, by the British. Such offer was immediately accepted by both the Greek and Greek Cypriot Delegations but was, predictably, turned down by the Turkish side who have insisted throughout that all such issues must be resolved in the context of a general political settlement and that no gradual or phased progress towards normalization can be contemplated otherwise than as part of an overall "package deal". In the context of transport and communications, it must further be pointed out that in consequence of the destruction of the road network, the free movement of persons and goods has become impossible.

The Social Services are also encountering very great difficulties in their operation. Particularly is this so with the Educational system. Not less than 31% of the island's Greek Cypriot elementary schools and 38% of the secondary schools are in the area occupied by the Turks. Of course, it is not only that many school buildings are out of use either because they are actually in the Turkish occupied areas or in close proximity to such areas, or even because many school buildings now have to be used as places for housing refugees; the school population and its teachers have, in a very large number of cases, been dispersed and are now living as refugees in camps or in the overcrowded homes of friends and relatives. And one need hardly say that, quite apart from the purely practical problems involved in the need to reorganise schools and curricula in such a way as to be able to cope with the unprecedented situation created, the psychological atmosphere of the refugee camp or crowded home is not conducive to study and learning.

In the health sector nightmarish difficulties confront the Government. The Public Health Services are seriously pressed in consequence of hospitals having been destroyed or abandoned. In addition, pharmaceutical material is in short supply, and serious public health hazards have been created by the refugee problem. With 200,000 Greek Cypriots having been reduced overnight to the abject status of refugees, the public health situation understandably causes acute worry, and the possibility of outbreaks of serious epidemic diseases is a constant threat that might add further disaster to an already biblical catastrophe.

The political consequences of the Turkish invasion are well known. Almost half of Cyprus' territory has been taken over by the invaders. The foundations have been laid for a future partitioning of the island and annexation of the two parts thereof to Greece and Turkey respectively. And, whatever the precise settlement to be arrived at, the constitutional framework of the Republic (i.e. the 1960 Constitution) will need to be drastically revised. In this sense, the invasion has destroyed both the constitutional structure of the Republic and its political framework. But it is denied — and this point is amplified later — that the invasion succeeded in depriving the formal constitutional arrangements of the Republic of legal validity. Cyprus is still an independent and sovereign State, internationally recognised and a member State of the United Nations, and it is believed that the 1960 Constitution still represents the institutional structure of the Republic. But, "there can be no turning back the clock". Everybody recognises that a new Governmental and political structure will have to be fashioned. What should such structure be? Possible settlements range from partition to the establishment of a unitary state. The Turkish side insist upon a rigid territorial separation of the two communities of the island within secure boundaries, a proposed solution that the Greek Cypriot side has unequivocally rejected in the past and cannot possibly accept now, particularly if such solution is accompanied by a compulsory population movement and the virtual destruction of Central Authority. The Greek Cypriot side, in its turn, is prepared to accept some kind of geographically defined settlement but only on condition that such settlement does not endanger the basic unity of the state and does not necessitate a dislocation of the population patterns of Cyprus.

The very fact, however, that a rigid geographical federation on the basis of the Attila or some such line can be seriously put forward as a solution to the Cyprus problem irrespective of the vast population movement that would be necessitated thereby (at least 147,000 Greek Cypriots — or some 29.3% of the total Greek Cypriot population — would be moved out of the northern area for the purpose of implementing any such plan) shows how serious the political consequences of the invasion have been and how drastic the alterations effected in the balance of power, both internal and international.

It is not difficult to summarize the results of the Turkish invasion and occupation of Cyprus. The Turkish invasion has turned a prosperous island "into shambles". In political terms, it has violated the integrity and sovereignty of an independent State. In economic terms, it has shattered the island's flourishing development. And in human terms, it has brought personal tragedy to thousands of families and a nightmare of death and horror and grief.[8]

Perhaps, obvious conclusions can be drawn as to the purpose of the Turkish invasion simply from setting out the results of such invasion and adverting to many publicly made statements by Turkish leaders both before and after the 20th July. But, 'the legal aridities' of the situation, as Mr. Callaghan said at Geneva, cannot be ignored. It is now proposed (a) to inquire into the alleged justification by Turkey of its invasion of Cyprus, (b) briefly look at the Declaration of Geneva, the second round of talks there and the reasons behind the failure of such talks, (c) consider (1) International responsibility for the Turkish invasion and occupation of Cyprus and (2) the broader International implications of Turkey's actions, and (d) suggest ways in which the problem should be approached from the point of view of procedure.

THE TURKISH INVASION AND THE TREATY OF GUARANTEE

Turkey allegedly invaded Cyprus as a Guarantor Power, and in pursuance of Article 4 of the Treaty of Guarantee[9] which provides that in the event of a breach of the provisions of the Treaty, under which the Republic of Cyprus undertakes to ensure "the maintenance of its Independence, territorial integrity and security, as well as respect for its Constitution", Greece, Turkey and the U.K. should consult together "with respect to the representations or measures necessary to ensure observance" of the above provisions. Article 4 concludes as follows: "In so far as common or concerted action may not prove possible, each of the three Guaranteeing Powers reserves the right to take action with the sole aim of re-establishing the state of affairs created by the present Treaty."

The Treaty of Guarantee expressly envisages, by Art. 4, joint consultations between Greece, Turkey and the U.K., before any action in pursuance of such Treaty is taken. When Turkey perceived a threat to the independence, the territorial integrity and security of Cyprus as a result of the coup of the 15th July, the machinery of joint consultations should have been initiated and only on the completion or real failure of such consultations should unilateral action have been contemplated, let alone undertaken. It is abundantly clear that such machinery was not put into operation. Mr. Ecevit, the Turkish Prime Minister, it is true, went to London after the Cyprus coup for the purpose of holding talks with the British Government, but, as Mr. Callaghan, the British Foreign Secretary, himself said at Geneva, before Greece, as a guarantor, could be brought into the picture (as was the British intention), Turkey undertook unilateral action in Cyprus. It is further believed that alleged exchanges of view between the Greek and Turkish Governments, which exchanges took place through the American Under-Secretary of State, Mr. Sisco, cannot, on any construction of Art. 4, however strained, be said to amount to the formal consultations envisaged by the said Article and which, as is apparent on a cursory examination of Art. 4 as a whole, form a condition precedent to any action to be undertaken by any of the guarantors acting unilaterally.

Further, the suggestion that Turkey was entitled, by reason of Article IV of the Treaty, to use force (and the *kind* of force) in the exercise of her right to preserve the Cyprus settlement is refuted by many arguments, used both cumulatively and in the alternative.

(a) The exercise of the right of the guarantors to act, whether collectively or individually, is dependent upon a breach of the Treaty (see Article IV: 'In the event of a breach of the provisions of the present Treaty' ...). It can be asserted and plausibly maintained that no such breach occurred. There is not the slightest evidence to suggest that, as a result of the coup of the 15th July, either the independence or the territorial integrity of Cyprus was endangered. Indeed, those people who found themselves in governmental positions immediately after the Coup clearly stated that they did not contemplate any change in the status of Cyprus as an independent state; that they did not anticipate any change in the foreign policy of the Republic; and that their only purpose was to remove from power Archbishop Makarios. Nor, during the short period when the coup leaders were in positions of authority, was there any indication that there would be either a revision or an alteration in the status of Cyprus as an independent, non-aligned state.

Was there, however, a relevant failure as regards "Respect for the Constitution," another of the obligations resting on the Republic of Cyprus as a result of Art. 2 of the Treaty of Guarantee? Prima facie, the above mentioned obligation means that the Republic is bound to observe the terms of its Constitution and to change it only in accordance with the procedures therein contained. However, a strong case can be made that (a) "Respect for the Constitution" (in the same way that, in the past, it was not read as requiring the Republic to adhere to the letter of an instrument which experience had shown to be unworkable but, instead, allowed the qualified revision of such Constitution by the operation of the principle of necessity) should not be taken as having been departed from whenever there is a change or alteration in the governmental structure unprovided for or going contrary to the requirements or express provisions of the Constitution; and that (b) what took place in Cyprus on the 15th July was not a Revolution in the Kelsenian sense which alone must be taken as completely abrogating the juridical order and as totally overthrowing the existing system but a coup which was animated by a limited objective, namely the removal of the President of the Republic. The Constitution, as observed above, was declared by the Coup Leaders to have remained unaffected by what had happened and many of their actions lend support to the view that this indeed was their intention. The spirit of the requirement of respect for the Constitution can, therefore, be said not to have been violated.

It must be acknowledged, however, that a strong case can be made that there was a relevant interference with the Constitutional arrangements setting up the Republic, that there had been intervention in the affairs of Cyprus by the Greek Government disturbing Cyprus' sovereignty and that, as a result, rights regarding the restoration of the legitimate Constitutional order were acquired by the Guarantor Powers. What is clear is that both the facts of the coup of the 15th July and the provisions of the Treaty lend themselves to different interpretations regarding what can amount to, or what is sufficient for, a breach of the Treaty, and that, by virtue of such Treaty and the facility whereby divergent arguments of some plausibility can be made in relation thereto, the three Guarantors were in effect given the power of intervening in Cyprus whenever something had happened which might be interpreted as a breach of the Treaty. This consideration, as argued elsewhere, militates against the validity of such Treaty.

(b) In any event, even assuming hypothetically that a state of affairs had developed which might be regarded, in some quarters, as constituting a breach of the Treaty, there is still nothing in the Treaty which warrants a forcible intervention by Turkey. It is true that the second paragraph of Art. IV of the Treaty refers to 'the right to take action' but any such right (even assuming that it encompasses the right to use force which, it must be noted, is nowhere specifically mentioned in Article 4) must be read subject to the provisions of Articles 2 (4) and 103 of the Charter of the United Nations. The latter provides that in the event of a conflict between the obligations of Members of the UN under the Charter and their obligations under any other International Agreement, their obligations under the Charter shall prevail. The former prohibits the use or threat of force against the territorial integrity or political independence of a member. If Art. IV of the Treaty implies the use of force, clearly it cannot stand with Art 2 (4) of the Charter; and, by reason of Art. 103 of the Charter, the latter must prevail.

Another argument militating against the unilateral use of force by Turkey lies in Article 53 of the Charter. This provides that '. . . no enforcement action shall be taken under regional arrangements or by regional agencies without the authorisation of the Security Council . . .'. It would not now be paradoxical to classify the Treaty of Guarantee as a Regional Arrangement; and there is evidence to suggest that the U.K. has so regarded this Treaty.

(c) Another consideration excluding the use of force by Turkey is that a guarantor power, under the Treaty, is only permitted to take that action which can result in the re-establishment of the state of affairs created by the present Treaty. As regards this, two points can be made:

(1) that the unilateral use of force by Turkey (or, indeed, any other power) cannot itself re-establish the state of affairs created by

the present Treaty; and that since this is so, and since the only aim of intervention under the Treaty is the re-establishment of the previously existing Constitutional Order, permissible intervention under the Treaty does not include resort to dynamic or military action, but only other measures; (2) whether dynamic action is contemplated by Art. 4 or not, the re-establishment of the state of affairs created by the Treaty was not (and certainly is not) the aim of Turkey. As is clear from what was set out above regarding the results of the invasion, and as is made clearer in other parts of the present study, the true aim of Turkey is the destruction of Cyprus' territorial integrity, the partitioning of the island into two separate, geographical zones — one to be administered by Turkish Cypriots and the other by Greek Cypriots — and the bringing about by forcible means both of a vast movement of population and the establishment of an unworkable system of geographical federalism. Even if there was some initial justification for some kind of action by Turkey, such justification had disappeared on Mr. Clerides' accession to power in Cyprus, Mr. Clerides representing legality and the Constitutional Order that had been disturbed. Even if this is not accepted (and there is no reason why it should not be accepted, particularly when one takes into account Mr. Karamanlis' contemporaneous advent to power in Greece), once the Geneva Conference of the Guarantors had convened and diplomatic initiatives were set in motion within the framework of the Treaty of Guarantee itself for the re-establishment of Constitutional Order and the orderly resolution of the problem, surely the time had come when the Turkish army would cease its aggression? And, at the very latest, at the second round of the Geneva talks, when even the British expressed satisfaction with the assurances and views of the Greek Cypriot Delegation concerning the orderly resolution of the Cyprus problem, the time obviously had come when the coup had been purged, constitutionalism re-established, and when the Turkish troops, given adequate assurances regarding the security of the Turkish Community, should have begun to withdraw.

Not much will be said here regarding the validity, continued or otherwise, of the said Treaty of Guarantee. Suffice it to say that its validity, original or continued, can be questioned, and that a plausible case can be made that such Treaty not only constitutes a fetter upon the Independence of Cyprus — demanding in effect the consent of three other States before its Constitution can be modified and, as a result, thwarting the will of the overwhelming majority of the population — but that it is also quite inconsistent with the international position of Cyprus as a fully Independent State.[10]

Furthermore, even if the Treaty of Guarantee was originally a valid Treaty, a strong case can be made that it is no longer of any force (and was of no force during the Turkish invasion, or at other relevant stages in Turkish operations, in which case Turkey's action was aggression pure and simple). In this connection, one must remember that a material breach of a multilateral Treaty by one of the parties entitles any other party to invoke the breach as a ground for suspending the operation of the Treaty in whole or in part in the relations between itself and the defaulting State and/or simply treat such Treaty as of no further legal validity. It can now be strongly maintained that such a material breach took place either by reason of Turkey's general belligerency regarding Cyprus since 1963 or by virtue of Turkey's initial military thrust in Cyprus or, at the latest, by Turkey's refusal to withdraw her troops from Cyprus once constitutional legitimacy (in the person of Mr Clerides) had returned.

Be that as it may, and assuming for present purposes the full legal effect of the Treaty of Guarantee, it can be immediately observed that Turkey has massively violated such Treaty, by invasion, aggression, and occupation of the territory of the Republic. It is abundantly clear that the invasion by Turkey on the 20th July, and as such invasion has unfolded and developed, was not at all made for the sake of the re-establishment of the 1960 Constitution, but was a naked act of aggression intended to secure a strong bargaining position for Turkey with a view to imposing on Cyprus a federal geographical system of government amounting in effect to partition.

The conclusion drawn from all the above is that Turkey's invocation of the Treaty of Guarantee as affording a right of Intervention is baseless and without foundation in either fact or law. Such alleged justification is, in fact, nothing short of preposterous.

Another point to be discussed because it touches upon Turkey's invocation of the Treaty, and on a host of other points as well, relates to the continued legal validity of the 1960 Constitution (of which, it will be remembered, the Treaty of Guarantee forms an integral part). At Geneva and elsewhere, both the Turkish and Turkish-Cypriot Delegations put forward the view that the 1960 Constitution was inoperative, that events has somehow robbed it of efficacy. But Mr Günes, the then Turkish Foreign Secretary, did not pause to investigate the inter-relationship between the Treaty of Guarantee and the Constitution. As is made clear above, the only possible justification for Turkey's invasion was the restoration of the 1960 Constitution. Yet, at the same time as he was putting forward his Treaty of Guarantee argument, Mr Günes insisted that Cyprus had no Constitution and was in need of one. The reconciliation of these two lines of argument would be a major feat of juristic imagination and was not attempted by the Turkish Foreign Minister. Here, it must be strongly emphasised that the 1960 Constitution is valid and legally effective.[11] It is true that, as a result of the 1963 incidents, and because of the departure of Turkish officials from the machinery of government, the Constitution has been somewhat departed from, but such deviations from the letter of the Constitutional Instrument must be (and have been) predicated upon the Doctrine of Necessity. In Attorney-General of the Republic v Mustafa Ibrahim[12], the Supreme Court of Cyprus, "in its all-important function of transforming legal theory into living law, applied to the facts of daily life for the preservation of social order"[13], was faced with the question whether the legal doctrine of necessity should or should not be read into the provisions of the written Constitution of Cyprus. The unanimous view of the Court was in the affirmative. Necessity, for the Court, created law — it superseded rules. Salus Populi suprema lex. Indeed, any other answer would have been paradoxical. Organs of government set up under a Constitution are vested expressly with the competence granted to them by such Constitution, "but they have always an implied duty to govern too".[14] It would be absurd to accept that if, for one reason or another, an emergency arises, which cannot be met within the express letter of the Constitution, then such organs need not take the measures absolutely necessary in the matter, and that they would be entitled to abdicate their responsibilities and watch helplessly the disintegration of the country or an essential function of the State, such as the Administration of Justice. "The Government and the Legislature", the Court stressed, "are empowered and bound to see that legislative measures are taken . . . .".[15] This doctrine of necessity has been applied in many other countries of the Commonwealth, and its existence is not questioned by academic writers. There is need, of course, for such doctrine of necessity to be carefully circumscribed, but at times when, due to supervening events, substantive Constitutional provisions cannot operate, "it is not logical or proper to hold that measures designed to ensure continuance of essential functions of the State, and being otherwise valid in substance, are invalid or not in force because of lack of formalities arising out of the situation which the measures taken were designed to meet".[16]

But such interpretation of the Constitution (which interpretation, it must be once more emphasised, goes no further than to include the doctrine of necessity in exceptional circumstances in the Constitution as an implied exception to particular provisions of the Constitution — and this in order to ensure the very existence of the State) does not derogate from the essential validity of the Constitution or endanger its legal status. There can be no doubt that the 1960 Constitution is valid but that its full implementation and operation have not been possible.[17] This, indeed, was also the view, as expressed at Geneva, of the British Foreign Secretary, who, more than once, said that the 1960 Constitution was "the only Constitution there was" and that discussions among the Guarantors could continue only in so far as the prohibition against the imposition of a Constitution on the people of Cyprus was not infringed.[18]

THE GENEVA CONFERENCE

On the invasion of Cyprus, the Security Council, by its various Resolutions, and, particularly, by Resolution No. 353, "deeply deploring the outbreak of violence and continued bloodshed, gravely concerned about the situation which led to a serious threat to International peace" and "equally concerned about the necessity to restore the Constitutional structure of the Republic of Cyprus, established and guaranteed by International Agreements", *called upon* all states to respect the Sovereignty, Independence and territorial Integrity of Cyprus; called upon all parties to cease all firing; demanded an immediate end to foreign military intervention; requested the withdrawal without delay from the Republic of Cyprus of foreign military personnel, present otherwise than under the authority of International Agreements; and called on Greece, Turkey and the U.K. "to enter into negotiations without delay for the restoration of peace in the area and Constitutional Government in Cyprus".

In a purported compliance with the last request of the Security Council, and "having regard to the International Agreements signed at Nicosia on the 16th August, 1960", the Foreign

Ministers of Greece, Turkey and the U.K. held discussions in
Geneva from the 25-30 July, 1974. The three Foreign Ministers
declared that, in order to stabilise the situation, the areas in the
Republic of Cyprus controlled by opposing armed forces should
not be extended; they called on all forces to desist from all
offensive or hostile activities; and concluded that a number of
immediate measures should be put into immediate effect (s.3) (i.e.
A security zone should be established; all the Turkish enclaves
occupied by Greek and Greek Cypriot forces should be
immediately evacuated; military personnel and civilians detained
as a result of the hostilities should be exchanged or released
within the shortest time possible). In s.4, the three Foreign
Ministers, reaffirming that Resolution 353 of the Security
Council should be implemented in the shortest possible time,
agreed that "within the framework of a just and lasting solution
acceptable to all the parties concerned and as peace, security and
mutual confidence are established in the island", measures
should be elaborated that would lead to the "timely and phased
reduction of the number of armed forces" in the Republic of
Cyprus. Finally, in s.5, the three Foreign Ministers, "deeply
conscious of their responsibilities as regards the maintenance of
the independence, territorial Integrity and Security of the
Republic of Cyprus", agreed that negotiations, as provided for in
Resolution 353 of the Security Council, should be carried on with
the least possible delay to secure "(a) the restoration of peace in the
area and (b) the re-establishment of Constitutional Government in
Cyprus". They also agreed that representatives of the Greek
Cypriot and Turkish-Cypriot Communities should "participate in
the talks relating to the Constitution."

"Among the Constitutional questions to be discussed", it was
concluded, "should be that of an immediate return to
constitutional legitimacy, the Vice President assuming the
functions provided for under the 1960 Constitution." As a final
observation, the Ministers noted the existence in practice in the
Republic of Cyprus of two autonomous administrations, that of
the Greek Cypriot Community and that of the Turkish Cypriot
Community.

Some observations are called for with regard to the Declaration
of Geneva.[19] The three Foreign Ministers met together as a result
of Resolution 353 of the Security Council and in pursuance of
their rights and obligations as provided under the Treaty of
Guarantee. Hence, nothing in the Declaration should run counter

either to the above Resolution or to the obligations of the three powers as guarantors. It is regretfully concluded that this is not so. Resolution 353, as pointed out by Mr Tornaritis, the Attorney-General of the Republic, demanded an immediate end to foreign military intervention and the withdrawal, without delay, from the Republic of Cyprus of foreign military personnel. The Declaration of Geneva, in s.4, only mentioned measures which should be elaborated and which would, in time, — and within the framework of a just and lasting solution, and as peace and security are established — "lead to the timely and phased reduction of the number of armed forces." As now regards the Treaty of Guarantee and its relationship to the Declaration of Geneva, the contradiction is even more apparent. The three Foreign Ministers who signed the Declaration — it cannot be emphasised strongly enough — were acting in a purported exercise of the powers of their States as Guarantors of the Constitutional Order established by the 1960 Constitution, and had no other competence, either to dictate a particular solution to the Cyprus problem or insist on any particular settlement. Such problems must be left to the people of Cyprus as a whole. The guarantors, having guaranteed the Independence, territorial Integrity and Security of Cyprus, could only (a) take some immediate measures for the normalization of the situation and (b) order and ensure an immediate return to the legality of the Constitutional order which they had pledged themselves to protect. It would, therefore, have been more proper had the Geneva Declaration, after the setting in train, as a matter of urgency, of some measures for the adjustment and regularization of the situation in Cyprus, ordered an immediate return to the 1960 Constitution and the removal of any threat to the Independence and territorial Integrity of the Republic. Instead, the Declaration (1) appeared to contemplate only a phased reduction of Turkish troops, (2) seemed to extend some recognition to the illegal Turkish administration, (3) had no reference to the State of Cyprus as such, but merely called upon the representatives of the two Communities to "participate in the talks relating to the Constitution". Also, it is not clear exactly what subsequent discussion the three Ministers had in mind. At one point, it seems that the restoration of peace and the re-establishment of the Constitution would be the only topics for discussions at such other meetings. A little later, however, the Declaration is worded in a rather ambiguous way as if other matters would also be discussed — the return to the 1960

Constitution being only one of them — and as if the guarantors as well as the State of Cyprus would participate in the talks relating to the Constitution, whereas the correct legal position is that such Constitutional talks, i.e. talks relating to the restructuring of the Constitutional Order of Cyprus, can only be participated in by the people of Cyprus, the other powers to act, at most, in an advisory capacity.

Yet, these points, admittedly not very serious ones, are counter-balanced by other considerations. For a start, there was only a de facto recognition of the fact that a Turkish Cypriot administration was functioning in the island, the juridical existence of the Republic of Cyprus is throughout taken for granted and there is no suggestion that, as a result of the invasion or other event, the State of Cyprus ceased to exist. Finally, para. 5 contemplates a return to Constitutional legitimacy and the re-establishment of Constitutional Government in Cyprus, and provides — this being the likeliest interpretation — that any subsequent negotiations should be carried on with the express purpose of securing these two objectives. Similarly, the 1960 Constitution, together with the International Agreements signed at Nicosia on the 16th August, 1960, are also explicitly mentioned in the Declaration. Needless to say, this Declaration, with all that it provided, was completely ignored by Turkey which, to this moment, continues to 'administer' and exploit the territory under its occupation, violates ceasefires and Security Council Resolutions alike, and defies all internationally accepted canons of behaviour.

The second Geneva Conference convened on the 9th August, 1974. At this Conference, Acting President Clerides, the leader of the Greek Cypriot Delegation, maintained the following: (a) the Geneva Conference had no jurisdiction regarding the imposition of a Constitution on the people of the Republic of Cyprus, and, consequently, the insistence of the Turkish Delegation on agreed principles regarding the Constitutional future of Cyprus was untenable. Indeed, the re-establishment of the 1960 Constitution was the only course consistent both with the Declaration of Geneva and with the status and obligations of the three powers as Guarantors. (b) The Acting President expressed his readiness to return immediately to the 1960 Constitution and set up a government with the Turkish Cypriot Community, the Turkish Vice-President assuming his functions and powers thereunder. This, indeed, the Greek-Cypriot Delegation maintained, was

Turkey's only justification for the invasion of Cyprus; for, if the invasion was, as was alleged, perpetrated under the Treaty of Guarantee, the restoration of the 1960 Constitution was the only legitimate course. If Turkey did not accept this analysis, but insisted on providing another solution to the constitutional problem, an effort was being made to impose a constitution on the people of Cyprus. This was nothing but aggression, and well beyond the powers of the Guarantors. Clearly, the Cypriot Acting President said, the 1960 Constitution needed far reaching amendment but such departures from the 1960 Constitutional arrangements could only be decided upon, and introduced, by the people of Cyprus. The intercommunal discussions for amending the Constitution should therefore continue once the 1960 Constitution was restored.

Such a course, which, indeed, seems unanswerable, was strongly resisted by the Turkish Foreign Minister. Mr. Günes used terms suggesting that Cyprus was in need of a Constitution; and that it was for the Conference to give Cyprus the Constitution needed. Moreover, he demanded an immediate acceptance of the Turkish plans for the geographical division of Cyprus; and was throughout the Conference threatening to use force to implement what came to be known as the Attila plan if the Turkish proposals were not adopted by the Conference.

More specifically and in greater detail, three plans were put forward during the Geneva Conference. On Monday, 12th August, the Denktash proposals were communicated to the other Delegations. Their substance was unacceptable (since they envisaged a rigid, bizonal geographical federation) and, procedurally, it had already been made abundantly clear that the Greek Cypriot Delegation could not recognise any competence in the Conference to impose a new Constitutional settlement on the people of Cyprus. Late that same Monday, the second set of Turkish proposals was leaked to the press. Such proposals came to be known as the Günes plan. Such plan (which envisaged the creation of six Turkish areas or zones in Cyprus) was also rejected. There still exists some misconception regarding the Günes plan, and it is still widely believed that this plan reflected a change in Turkish attitudes in the direction of moderation and that it possibly afforded a basis for meaningful negotiations. Nothing could be further from the truth. Confusion has been caused by the designation of such plan as "cantonal", a peculiarly imprecise expression, particularly when not carefully analysed. Not only did the Günes proposals amount to the imposition of a geographically defined solution. But, also, according to such plan, the Turkish Regional Administration was to have entire control of its own area within settled geographical boundaries, regulating every type of service within the relevant regions and being entrusted with sole control of all essential Governmental functions. So, even if the Günes plan was geographically more acceptable (something that cannot be accepted without qualification), by way of powers and functions — which, as I argue below, is the most crucial point — such plan was as objectionable, if not more so, than the Denktash one.

The proposals of the Greek Cypriot Delegation were predicated upon the need to maintain an "integral republic", yet made ample allowance for elements which were considered important by the British Delegation (elements such as the bicommunal character of the State, communal autonomy, the establishment of areas of local administration etc.) and which, it is believed, afforded the basis for further discussion and negotiation. Such proposals were not even considered by the Turkish side.

It must also not be forgotten that the Turkish demands were put forward as non negotiable and were coupled with a time limit within which they had to be accepted.

Indeed, such was the intimidation employed by the Turkish side, and so undisguised the blackmail policies they pursued throughout the duration of the Conference, that the London Times in a leading article on the 14th August, 1974, felt impelled to ask "What is Turkey up to?". As correctly observed by such editorial, it looked as though the Turks, through the quite deliberate creation and maintenance of artificial tension, were setting the stage for a further outbreak of fighting in Cyprus in which they could take over a larger area of Cyprus by force. By this time most observers had come to acknowledge that Turkey had become (whatever may have been the original merits of the case) the chief violator of the Treaty and it was widely stated that the other signatories, Greece and Great Britain, had both the right and the duty to take action against Turkey were such action to be warranted by developments. When, at the end of the Conference, both Acting President Clerides and Mr. Mavros, the Greek Foreign Secretary, asked for an adjournment of 36 hours to consider the Turkish proposals, and such a request was favourably regarded by Mr. Callaghan, Mr. Günes again refused to consider such adjournment. The Turkish proposals, he said, were well known to everybody (even though they had been communicated to the Greek Cypriot Delegation at 10 o'clock the night before). There was need for an immediate answer. And that answer had to be acceptance of the Turkish proposals. In the last hour of the session it had become clear to all those present that Mr. Günes was merely playing out time, and that the Turkish Government had decided to take by force what they had so far failed to obtain by argument. The Conference broke up at approximately 3.00 a.m., but not before Mr. Callaghan used stern language castigating Turkish intransigence and bad faith. Immediately afterwards, heavy bombing of Nicosia began and the Turkish Armed forces began to march once again for full implementation of the Attila plan.

In this way, the question that The Times had asked was all too quickly and brutally answered. Indeed, the whole Geneva Conference, or at least Turkey's part in it, was exposed as nothing but a smokescreen for their military preparations, as nothing but cynical deception. But this was not all. Insult and affront to common sense were added to injury. Even the military thrust which followed the failure of the Geneva Conference, and as a result of which Cyprus was, in effect, partitioned in two, was presented as simply an extension and consolidation of the original invasion launched on the 20th July, when the world at large had naively accepted that Turkey was acting within her rights as a guarantor of Cypriot independence under the 1960 Treaty. The transparency of such justification was, at long last, obvious even to the uninitiated. Even the Turks themselves cannot have been surprised to find that the attitude of the world at large to their new action was very different from what it had been towards their first venture. On the 20th July, it could be plausibly asserted, Cyprus was under the effective control of Brigadier Joannides and under the nominal authority of Mr. Sampson. Since then, however, and before the beginning of the second round of talks, everything had changed. The Greek military Junta had been replaced by Mr. Karamanlis' civilian Government and Mr. Sampson by Mr. Clerides. Both changes had been welcomed at the time by the Turkish Government. Mr. Clerides and Mr. Denktash knew each other well and had been negotiating with each other for a long time in the context of the Intercommunal talks at which, clearly, quite considerable progress had been achieved. As a result of such factors, there had seemed, at the opening of the second round of the Geneva Conference, a reasonably good chance that after much hard bargaining a constitutional settlement could emerge acceptable to both sides. Such a settlement, of course, was only visible, if at all, in the barest outlines. But there did seem common ground between the two sides on the basis of which an eventual agreement could be reached. All parties, for instance, before attending the Geneva Conference had indicated agreement with the proposition that Cyprus had to remain one whole sovereign and independent country; that it should not be partitioned; that it should not be united with either Greece or Turkey, or be wholly aligned with one or the other or with any major power. In addition, everybody seemed to agree that the 1960 Constitution had serious shortcomings that needed to be remedied so that it would both provide sufficient assurance of security to the Turkish Community, and, at the same time, ensure the effective functioning of the State. Such security could best be achieved by, among other things, the introduction of some kind of regional element, and Governmental viability could best be ensured by the maintenance of State unity and the recognition of strong Central Authority. Also, an investigation of the positions of Greece and Turkey respectively at the opening of the second phase of the Geneva talks did seem to afford to the independent observer some reason for optimism. Both the Greek and Turkish Governments were (and, perhaps, still are) under severe pressure at home, with powerful armies breathing down their necks and public opinion in a volatile state. Both needed to bring home something that could be made to look like victory, yet neither — logically or given the interdependence of Greek and Turkish interests — could afford the consequences of humiliating the other. So, there did seem, both at the internal level and by reference to the likely international implications likely to be triggered off by moderation and extremism respectively, some community of interest between Greece, Turkey and the Greeks and Turks of Cyprus, in favour of strenuous and well intentioned efforts towards the working out of a fair and workable settlement. But, self evidently, such a settlement needed time, and Turkey, as described above, absolutely refused either to provide such time or exhibit minimum good faith, surely necessary prerequisites for the successful conclusion of any negotiations.

THE TURKISH INVASION: INTERNATIONAL RESPONSIBILITY AND INTERNATIONAL IMPLICATIONS

At this time, after the ruthless implementation of the Attila plan, and before any definite settlement is in sight, two questions have to be asked. First, could anything have been done in time for the purpose of averting the Cyprus disaster, and if so what? And secondly, what measures should be adopted by the world community at present regarding the Turkish occupation of a great part of the territory of Cyprus? It is thought that both questions are of great importance and should not be dismissed either as useless historical excursions (in the first case) or as abstract speculation (in the second).

As regards the first part of our enquiry it is a matter of very great regret that the Great Powers did not take effective action against Turkey either before the 20th July or after their initial military thrust. It should surely have been apparent, whatever the precise legal situation regarding the coup, that Turkey was preparing to launch an attack upon Cyprus, which, whatever its outcome, could not possibly result in the re-establishment of the 1960 Constitution. At this point, measures should have been taken and procedures initiated which would be aimed at restoring constitutional order in Cyprus, re-establishing political normality and dissuading Turkey from invading. And after the first stage of the Turkish invasion, particularly when the Turkish forces were clearly proved to have massively violated the early ceasefires while trying to improve their positions — something that should have belied all the Turkish statements regarding the strictly limited objectives of their invasion and its legal justifiability — surely the time had come when the Great Powers involved in the situation should have taken effective action. By the "Powers involved" in this context one means essentially the US, which is the main arms supplier and economic patron of Turkey; and by "effective action" one, at this — then early — stage, does not necessarily mean American military intervention — other sanctions, it is strongly believed, could have worked. For instance, a threat to cut off military aid to Turkey, economic sanctions or even making it clear to the Turkish Government, in stern terms, that, Constitutional legitimacy having been restored to Cyprus, the Turkish troops should be immediately withdrawn and negotiations held for the purpose of determining the future of the island, could, at the right time, have borne fruit. If one, indeed, compares the attitude of a previous American Government towards another Turkish attempt at invading Cyprus to the behaviour of the present Administration, the conclusion that has already been drawn by many observers, namely that the US was criminally inactive in its handling of the Turkish invasion, seems to follow naturally.[20] Particularly is this so if one considers the events of the second round of the Geneva Conference when the US, despite having been repeatedly warned of Turkish expansionist policies, made it clear that it had not the slightest intention of embarking upon any substantial steps for averting further Turkish aggression. Much has already been said regarding America's involvement and role in recent events. A more systematic treatment of this subject is, therefore, called for.[21]

American policy over the recent Cyprus tragedy has been, at best, one of hasty improvisation, its diplomatic efforts being throughout incredibly naive, insensitive and ineffective; at worst, such policy has been a coldly calculating one, desperately aiming at a minimisation of disturbances within NATO and totally oblivious to the true dimensions, both political and human, of the present crisis.[22] It is, of course, easy to make accusations and try to shift the blame onto someone else's shoulders but this is not the intention of the present chapter. It is here accepted that: (a) sufficient evidence is lacking for a final allocation of responsibility and for any definite evaluation of American policy over Cyprus; (b) it may be a mistake, or rather an oversimplification, even to try and attribute a coherent policy to the US, in the sense that there are many agencies entrusted with the formulation and carrying out of American foreign policy (CIA, the State Department, the Pentagon, the Presidency), and such agencies should not be presumed to be always in agreement or even to be acting in concert; and (c), personally, I have never attempted to hide the fact that overall lack of planning and short-sighted policies on the part of the Greek Cypriot side over the 14 years of Independence have, to a considerable extent, contributed to bringing about the present disaster. But when all this is said and all allowances are made, the US must assume a heavy responsibility for the Cyprus tragedy. Such prime responsibility cannot be evaded, not only because of the US's own position in the area, exercised both through NATO commands and the Sixth Fleet or because of the US's exceptionally close and influential ties with both Greece and Turkey ever since the launching of the Truman Doctrine programmes of military and economic assistance in 1947. The main reason why Washington bears a heavy share of the blame for the Cyprus tragedy is to be found in its own diplomatic performance throughout the crisis.

To begin with, there are substantial grounds for believing that the US had an opportunity to prevent the fatal coup against President Makarios, but let it pass because of a long held dislike and distrust of the Archbishop and an unwillingness to offend the then military rulers of Greece, whom the US, it must not be forgotten, had helped and assisted throughout their repressive rule of Greece. Trying to establish what happened at this period is complicated by the fact that the US apparently was in the habit of communicating with the Junta via the CIA station-chief, while the regular Embassy channels in Athens were rarely used. In any case, much more forthright and forceful measures should and could have been employed at this early, critical stage, for the half hearted, complacent tactics of the US failed to deter the Junta. After the coup, Washington might have persuaded Turkey to hold back on military intervention if the Secretary of State, Dr. Kissinger, had given prompt, vigorous support to Britain's refusal to recognise the Cyprus regime, an offshoot of the Greek Junta, and also to London's demand that Athens should immediately recall the Greek officers who had directed the operation. If Washington had, at this early time, embarked upon initiatives directed towards a swift return of constitutional legitimacy, the invasion might well have been averted. Once again, however, the US dragged its feet and carefully refrained from committing itself. The State Department spokesman called for moderation, and, at the UN, Ambassador Scali said that "it would be a serious error to rush to judgment on an issue of this gravity". It may well be that these early American pro-Junta leanings were interpreted by Ankara as tacit US acceptance of the new state of affairs in Cyprus. Ankara, it is clear, immediately prepared for a military operation against Cyprus, and such activities were, obviously, within the knowledge of the State Department. Instead of decisive action to avert the impending catastrophe and contemporaneously launch serious diplomatic initiatives for an early return to constitutional legitimacy, Under Secretary Sisco was dispatched to shuttle ineffectively between Athens and Ankara, in a futile effort to effect a compromise. He does not seem to have seriously warned the Turks that they should not seek a military solution, even though one should have seen that a Turkish military operation would not only lead to a serious danger of war between Greece and Turkey but almost certainly result in at least a de facto partitioning of Cyprus.

After the Turks invaded Cyprus and massively violated the early ceasefires that had been negotiated, the pressing need was to dissuade Ankara from embarking on a reckless military adventure aimed at achieving by force the partition of the island and the forced separation of the two Communities. Here, again, Washington's reaction was too mild and too late. What was required was the kind of tough, clear message that President Johnson sent to Premier Inonu and which prevented a Turkish invasion in 1964. Decisive American action was particularly called for at the later stages of the Geneva Conference. Throughout this Conference, as described above, Turkey's arbitrary and unreasonable attitude was observed by all and quite generally adversely commented upon. The US, as already indicated above, refused to join in this universal condemnation; refused, at any stage, even to threaten a halt in American military aid to Turkey; and obstinately refused even to consider either a UN or a British sponsored initiative for the purpose of putting an end to Turkish aggression. Finally, in an incredible move of bad timing and opportunistic policy, the State Department, at the most crucial juncture of the talks, instead of exerting strong pressure on Turkey to remain at the negotiating table, issued a statement which stressed the equity of the Turkish position. This statement "recognised (that) the position of the Turkish community in Cyprus requires considerable improvement and protection", and went on to support "a greater degree of autonomy for them".[23] It clearly appeared both from the timing of the statement and the stress put on the Turkish grievances that Washington was supporting Ankara's position in Geneva. The results are well known, and have been described above. On the 14th of August, the Turkish army, by then heavily reinforced and wielding the advantage of complete air superiority, slashed across Cyprus. 40% of Cyprus came under Turkish military occupation. This vicious military advance had both a devastating effect on the population of the island and serious international repercussions. Greece withdrew militarily from NATO, great bitterness was felt against the US and the causes of international peace and non-alignment suffered a serious setback. American foreign policy was exposed as bankrupt, opportunistic and totally unprincipled. Not since the American involvement in South East Asia was there such an explosion of feeling about American foreign policy. Even today, despite all the above, the US has never really acknowledged that the territorial integrity and sovereignty of Cyprus have been violated through the invasion and occupation of a substantial part of the island by foreign troops; and in recent statements, American spokesmen seem to have given tacit recognition to Turkey's fait accompli in Cyprus and to have clearly associated themselves with a biregional settlement on the Island.[24]

There can be no question that there was bias towards Turkey.[25] Was such bias the product of miscalculation or design? It is thought that both were instrumental in the shaping of American policy regarding Cyprus. At first, it seemed as if the State Department did not really comprehend the issues at stake and the dangers on the horizon. Later, when partly as a result of such incompetence and incomprehension the Turks landed a substantial force in Cyprus and gained the initiative, American policy tilted decisevely and consciously in favour of Turkey as it was thought that such policy orientation was required if the losses within NATO were to be minimised or American strategic interests safeguarded. This policy failed in the end. Not only did it achieve the opposite result in the sense that the price the American Government has paid for coming down so obviously on the side of Turkey in the Cyprus conflict has already been high, and will almost certainly become higher; what is more important, this policy has totally failed the defenceless people of Cyprus and has seriously endangered international peace.[26]

NATO's role, too, has been extensively discussed. Many have said that NATO was justified in virtually abstaining from the tragic events of Cyprus and maintaining a position of declared neutrality. Such arguments are predicated upon the assumption that NATO was set up for the purpose of resisting aggression by the Warsaw Pact, and that it could therefore play no part in resisting aggression by one of its own signatory powers against another. In fact, as was correctly observed by Mr. Philip Noel Baker,[27] the NATO Treaty says: "The Parties reaffirm their faith in the purposes and principles of the Charter of the UN" (which Charter, of course, basically outlaws the use of national armed force); also, the parties to the North Atlantic Treaty declare themselves resolved to unite their efforts for collective defence and for the preservation of peace and security. In winding up the debate by which the House of Commons ratified the Treaty, Mr. Philip Noel Baker said this on behalf of the Government: "This is not an old power-politics alliance against Russia ... it is a pact against aggression and armed attack". Not only did the Warsaw pact not exist at the time of the setting up of NATO, but it has since been repeatedly declared by representatives of the Atlantic Alliance that the provision of support against aggression is the central objective of the Treaty. In addition, Art. 6 specifically includes "islands", of which Cyprus is one, in the area of Europe in which peace was guaranteed and, again to quote Mr. Philip Noel Baker, "to exclude Cyprus now because it is an Independent Democratic Republic, and no longer British, would be a sophistry indeed". The conclusion is difficult to resist that Turkey committed aggression in flagrant violation of the NATO pact; and her guilt is undiminished by the fact that she now, having achieved all her military objectives, seems more or less to adhere to the last ceasefire proclaimed. A NATO peaceful blockade, to be used for purposes of cutting off sea and air communications between Turkey and Cyprus, could easily have been taken by NATO and there is little doubt that such blockade, if taken on time, would not only have prevented the Cyprus tragedy, or at least its present magnitude, but would also have immeasurably increased the prestige of the North Atlantic Organisation itself.

Great Britain must also bear a considerable part of the responsibility for what happened. Great Britain, as one of the three guarantor powers, is bound by Art. 2 of the Treaty of Guarantee to recognise and guarantee the independence, territorial integrity and security of the Republic. If the guarantee means anything, it must surely mean that the UK is bound, should the island be attacked, to come to the defence of the Republic for the purpose of preserving its independence and territorial integrity. The UK did not do this even though it had powerful forces stationed on the island. This is to be regretted. Indeed, at Geneva, there seemed to be both full recognition and explicit acknowledgement of Britain's legal and moral duty in the circumstances — which, indeed, seems clear — but it was more than once suggested to the Greek Cypriot Delegation that Britain, as a result of her weakened military position and other such strategic considerations, could not unilaterally take dynamic action for the purpose of preventing Turkey's anticipated military expansion. Mr. Callaghan, however, at the last Plenary Conference, made it clear that he would be fully prepared to place British troops in Cyprus under UN Command were a concerted UN operation to be mounted for the purpose of stemming the Turkish advance; moreover, with

American assistance and co-operation, which, as Dr. Kissinger had already made clear to him, would not be forthcoming, he would once again have been prepared to commit himself to some kind of dynamic action against the Turkish aggressor. Furthermore, throughout the Geneva Conference, Mr. Callaghan valiantly attempted to dissuade the Turks from abandoning the negotiating table; toiled hard to narrow the gap between Greeks and Turks and eventually strongly criticised Turkish unreasonableness and bad faith. Despite all this, without American support British diplomatic efforts could not but be frustrated. American policy makers must have known this. To say that Dr. Kissinger showed, at best, considerable indifference to the desperation and agony of the people of Cyprus or that he exhibited, throughout the crisis, very questionable political judgment is to put it rather mildly. Mr. Callaghan, as observed above, showed, both at Geneva and elsewhere, a much better understanding of events and has exerted all diplomatic efforts for the purpose of finding an acceptable solution to the Cyprus problem. Regrettably, he has not been strong enough to influence the course of events, particularly after the Turks had landed substantial troops in Cyprus. Had Britain exhibited some of her older decisiveness, and either interfered or threatened to interfere immediately, events might have developed differently. To say, as some have said, that British policy so far in this affair has differed little, if at all, from that policy of appeasement practised so assiduously by certain pre-War British Governments is, perhaps, to put it rather too strongly.[28] But what has to be clearly recognised is that Britain had a legal obligation to come to the assistance of Cyprus once Cyprus' independence was threatened. Such obligation was never fulfilled.[29]

The chief lesson of recent events in Cyprus is that when a country thinks its army can pull off a quick smash and grab, it is liable to leave the diplomats and their fine adjustments, and, more important, international morality standing on the sidelines. It is the same lesson as the Russian occupation of Czechoslovakia, Nazi adventurism etc. The advantage that modern technology gives to an army with great local superiority of power — with the bigger tank force, with the air cover and the necessary manpower — means that such army can finish its business before the lumbering machinery of international discussion or dissuasion even starts to go into action. Nuclear weapons may have made big wars unlikely, but, as is obvious from the Cyprus crisis, there is plenty of scope in today's world for the quick, small war. Today does, indeed, seem to be the era of the smash and grab raid, and it may be that the ultimate lesson to be derived from the Cyprus tragedy is that people who do not want to be grabbed or enslaved must take their precautions. If this is so, armaments will have to be increased, World Organisations will tend to be distrusted and non-alignment will suffer irreparable damage.[30]

For there should be no mistaking that the Cyprus crisis is a major world problem and a great challenge to the International Community. Cyprus' treatment by the International Community, one way or the other, will almost certainly be a decisive landmark in the development of International Organisations and the continuation of efforts for the establishment of world peace. For, the question before the International Community and International Organisations is simple. Should the fate and the very existence of small countries be decided by gunboat diplomacy, by the use of force, by destruction and intimidation without the UN being in a position to act? As Archbishop Makarios said in his address before the UN General Assembly, "This is the problem of Cyprus today. And it is only natural for the people who suffer to wonder why we have laid our hopes in the UN and in the rules of International law and precepts of International morality, which the United Nations represent?"[31] One, indeed, hesitates to foresee where the drama of Cyprus may lead if the International Community were finally to fail in putting an end to the Turkish aggression and occupation of Cyprus. Not only will the confidence of the world in the effectiveness of the UN be finally, and irrevocably, shaken. Small states would never be safe since, as the Cyprus story will have conclusively demonstrated, their independence is, in fact, at the mercy of their most powerful neighbours. Furthermore, as already stated, the cause of non-alignment which Cyprus represented will have received a serious setback. "If Cyprus were not a non-aligned country, we perhaps might have had allies to come to our defence. But, the fact that we did not should not render us a victim of a power, a member of NATO, which has used the arms supplied to her for her defence to attack Cyprus".[32] The case of Cyprus is, as a result, a test case of non-alignment and beyond that a test case for the UN. If the UN Organisation fails to make Turkey respect the Charter and its Resolutions, its continued utility will be seriously questioned. Cyprus might even mark the beginning of the end for the UN just as Abyssinia did for the League of Nations. This price, surely, would be too high to pay.

In case such dangers are thought to be rather hypothetical or somewhat speculative, it is not difficult to point out the immediate dangers attending Turkish aggression and intransigence. If a just settlement, acceptable to all parties, is not quickly reached, and there is nothing more than a succession of pious UN Resolutions which Turkey is allowed to ignore, it should not be surprising if the Greek Cypriots adopt Palestinian tactics which, in turn, would tempt the Turks to take an even more inflexible attitude. In this way, Cyprus would infect the Eastern Mediterranean with chronic instability and violence—and this, it is abundantly clear, will do great damage both to Western interests and to the cause of International Peace. Nor will the Turkish Cypriots, or Turkey itself, find true security if there is no just resolution of the Cyprus problem. Turkey will very likely have a hostile Greece to contend with and it is not thought that the Turkish Cypriots will be able to obtain the security they hope for, or deserve, under the permanent protection of Turkish bayonets. Turkey's only acceptable course, even in terms of Turkish and Turkish Cypriot interests, will surely be to obtain conditions under which Turkish Cypriots will be able to live in security after the troops have left. Such conditions, it is believed, can be established and proposals will later be put forward suggesting how security can be achieved. Meanwhile, it must be emphasised that a promising start has been made both by the return to the island of constitutional legitimacy and by the fact that the Greek Cypriot side has repeatedly indicated its willingness to participate in genuine negotiations regarding the constitutional future of the island.

Despite all the above, a great part of Cyprus is still under Turkish occupation, and the Turks have refused to take those measures which will make possible the resumption of negotiations. Acting President Clerides has defined the Greek position on this issue as follows: There can be no negotiations unless the refugees are allowed to return to their homes; there can be no negotiations if the only purpose of attendance at negotiations will be the legitimization of a fait accompli; and, thirdly, there can be no meaningful negotiations if the Turkish forces remain in occupation of the area now under their control. It is not thought that such conditions are unreasonable. Quite to the contrary, without them there could be no true negotiations, but only a further effort, under the cloak of respectability that an international diplomatic conference would provide, to dictate a settlement to the Greek Cypriots and force them into capitulation.

What is to be done now? Unquestionably, the need now, given Turkey's intransigence, is for concerted international pressure on Turkey to ensure that the Turkish troops are withdrawn, that the Greek and Turkish Cypriot refugees are allowed to return safely and swiftly to their homes, and that negotiations can continue in good faith for finding a final settlement. For such pressure to succeed strong American and Western European support will be needed. What form should this pressure take? For a start, Turkey should immediately be denied any supplies of arms or spare parts so long as her troops are (and remain) in Cyprus. This in itself may not be a very effective deterrent. More importantly, it must be made quite clear to the Turks that there is no question of their obtaining international recognition for any kind of de facto partition of Cyprus or any kind of solution not freely negotiated and accepted by all the parties concerned, and they must also be firmly told that international support for the rights of Greek Cypriots (including the right to the independence and unity of their country) will continue and cannot be changed by any Turkish military successes. Ultimately, the threat that should face Turkey is that of being denied international respectability and of becoming an international outcast. But even this may not be enough. Further action, of a dynamic nature, must be taken against Turkey. Turkey, it is believed, has become so contemptuous of international order as to make military action against her the only recourse; and such action must be taken in the name of the United Nations. "It is inconceivable that the United Nations, which represent the conscience of humanity, should tolerate an aggressor applying the rule of the jungle and creating by brutal force faits accomplis". What is, indeed, the alternative? Cyprus will become another, and not less troubled, Palestine. There would be constant danger to the British Sovereign Bases and, more important, the perpetual fear of a generalised conflict between Greece and Turkey. And another betrayal of the UN charter will have been perpetrated. It is therefore absolutely essential not only for Cyprus but also for the UN and for mankind as a whole for the UN Organisation to step in decisively and effectively so that the territorial integrity and unity of Cyprus as a sovereign and independent State, member of the UN, can be restored, ensured and safeguarded. Among possible courses of action, and in order to prevent the aggravation of the situation, the UN could once again call upon the parties concerned to comply with such provisional measures as it deems necessary or desirable, such provisional measures to include withdrawal of all foreign troops from Cyprus, the restoration and maintenance of law and order and the immediate return of all refugees to their homes. In case such instructions or measures are ignored or disregarded, more UN troops should be immediately despatched to the island for the purpose of implementing any applicable Resolutions relating to Cyprus.

FORUM AND PROCEDURE

At Geneva, the Turkish Foreign Secretary seemed to regard the whole problem as, primarily, a matter for the Guarantors or, more specifically, for Greece and Turkey. He did not really envisage a positive role in any of the negotiations for the Republic of Cyprus or even for the two Communities. And, if ever there were any doubts about this attitude of Turkey's, such doubts have been dispelled by various statements of Mr. Günes since then. Mr. Günes is even reported to have said, in response to a remark by Mr. Callaghan that the two Cypriot Communities could solve their own problems, if the Turkish army would only let them: "it is not the Cypriots who decide the fate of Cyprus, it's the Turks and the Greeks, and all the rest is blah-blah". This answer, which does not even envisage a role for the two Communities in the eventual Constitutional set up of the island, is instructive as an exact indication of Turkey's intransigent approach to the Cyprus problem and its complete disregard for legality. This statement of Mr. Günes either does not accept the existence of Cyprus as an independent State, or, else, it seeks to impose a solution or a constitutional arrangement on an independent and sovereign country by naked force. Either way, Turkey's stance is devoid of any legal or political justification.

It is thought that the problem of Cyprus can only be solved by the people of Cyprus. Any other course would be nothing but an attempt at the imposition of a settlement on a Sovereign and Independent State and would amount to neo-colonialism. Once it is realised that the 1960 Constitution is valid, and that the function of the guarantors extends only to the restoration of such Constitution — any other action undertaken by them, with the obvious exception of ordinary pacification and regularisation action, being ultra vires — the rest follows naturally. The 1960 Constitution must be immediately reactivated and fully implemented and then Intercommunal discussions should be held between the two Communities for any amendments thereto that are thought necessary. There can be no doubt, of course, that Greece and Turkey are intricately involved in the problem of Cyprus and that they have a legitimate interest in the maintenance of peace in the island and the establishment of a Constitutional system ensuring full security for both Communities. It was because of such considerations that the later stages of the Intercommunal talks were attended by two Constitutional experts made available by Greece and Turkey respectively, and who, it was made clear by the Secretary-General of the United Nations himself at the opening of the reactivated talks at Nicosia, were present in a strictly advisory capacity.

Such arrangement, given the ties of the two Cyprus Communities with Greece and Turkey respectively and the fact that whatever happens in Cyprus will almost inevitably affect the wider Graeco-Turkish relations, is only logical and should continue. Likewise with the competence of a Conference such as the Geneva one consisting of the three guarantors and the two Communities. The primary task of such a Conference can only be the re-establishment of the lawful Constitutional order. A Declaration, however, providing a very general framework within which the two Communities would then proceed to hold detailed intercommunal discussions regarding the necessary amendment of the Constitution, particularly if such declaration contains negative criteria rather than positive principles, does not, at first sight, appear to be outside the jurisdictional competence of such a Conference. It would, however, be advisable for such a Declaration to emanate from the two Communities rather than from the Conference as a whole, even though a Declaration so emanating could be presented as also having the approval of the three guarantors.

But, it must be endlessly repeated, the problem eventually must be solved and be seen to be solved by the people of Cyprus. Any other way would not only fail to provide a durable Constitutional structure; it would, like the Zürich settlement, become a new source of friction between the two Communities, and, as a result, not only further disturb Graeco-Turkish relations but also greatly endanger International Peace and Security.

IV

A GENERAL STATEMENT OF THE CYPRUS PROBLEM[1]

THERE is very real danger that with so many spectacular events of late and with accusations being ceaselessly hurled at each other by all those concerned in the Cyprus problem, the essence of such problem will be lost sight of; whereas it is the belief of the present writer that when all is said and done, a settlement will have to be arrived at. Without such settlement there can be no permanent peace in the area and if a settlement is arrived at that is clearly unfair to one side or the other, or does nothing to deal with the underlying problem, further violence, on an even wider scale, could at any time erupt.

The Turkish Community of Cyprus are a small minority, but only in the immediate area of Cyprus itself. In a wider context, since they can always call upon Turkey to come to their assistance, they are part of the majority. Likewise with the Greek Cypriot Community. In Cyprus itself, the Greek Cypriots are the overwhelming majority of the population but in the strategically relevant area they are a very small and helpless minority, at the complete mercy of Turkey, as has been made abundantly clear in the recent crisis. Cyprus has always been a victim of geography, and it is to be seriously regretted that shortsightedness on the part of the Greek Cypriot Community and incredible distortion of our political priorities obscured this fact. Turkey itself, in her own turn, cannot be said to be indifferent to whether Greece is hostile or amicably disposed towards her. For, although Turkish politicians may compete as to who is to make the most aggressive pronouncements, it is possible that the more sophisticated politicians do take account of certain factors which argue not only for a more conciliatory attitude towards Greece, but also for determined efforts to achieve durable peace between the two countries:

(i) Despite self-confident poses, it is recognized that the American Government is the main, and perhaps the only, reliable supplier of military aid and credit. The recent expression of Congressional displeasure suggests that Turkey cannot take for granted this aid, and the running out of military supplies may cause restlessness among the military establishment, who until recently held effective power. So American opinion cannot be provoked indefinitely for fear that the American Government might bow to Congressional and public pressures and discontinue both aid and unqualified support.

(ii) Turkey needs friends in Europe, and the return of Greece to the Council of Europe and the EEC could influence European countries away from Turkey.

(iii) Turkey has *some* interest to bring Greece back to NATO because (a) this is important for her own defence system and (b) Turkey realises that in the eyes of her allies she is held responsible for the loss of Greece.

(iv) Invasion and occupation is a costly business; and although, if necessary, Turkey will stay in Cyprus indefinitely, she would prefer very much to be able to withdraw the bulk of her army.

(v) The invasion and occupation of Cyprus has done nothing to alter the international image of Turkey as a non-European, semi-civilized country; this, naturally, is hardly good for Tourism and cultural/educational relations. A fair settlement could go a long way towards rectifying this situation.

(vi) Last, but not least, the danger of a new military takeover cannot be discounted, particularly if there is any prolongation of current governmental instability. Lately, with a succession of caretaker governments and many abortive efforts to stitch together workable coalitions, Turkey's civilian rule has begun to bear a strong resemblance to no rule at all. And with inflation running at 30 per cent a year, American military supplies in jeopardy and the explosive Cyprus issue still unresolved — and it was this issue that caused the breakdown of Mr. Ecevit's governing coalition in the first place — the Turkish military could be having second thoughts about its voluntary abdication of power. Resolution of the Cyprus problem could help the principle of civilian Government.

Such and other considerations surely indicate that the achievement of a lasting peace on the basis of a fair overall settlement is the only way ahead for all the parties involved — Turkey included. Particularly is this so for the people of Cyprus who have never really known true peace since Independence and who, it is believed, given a chance, can achieve considerable success living and working together. To do this, it must be repeated, one must not be distracted away from the fundamentals of the problem. Before the problem of Cyprus can be solved it must be understood, and before it can be understood it must be stated clearly, and, in so far as possible, in scientific and value-free terms. It is elucidation of the obvious, rather than manipulation of the obscure, that would be a real service to efforts to arrive at a peaceful and satisfactory settlement of the Cyprus problem. In this chapter an attempt will be made to take a fresh look at the Cyprus problem and roughly indicate some directions which it would be fruitful to follow. More concrete suggestions will be put forward later.

The Constitutional conflict in Cyprus is basically a conflict between the two Communities, and must be so presented. It is true, of course, that a delicate network of other national and international interests involving Greece, Turkey, NATO, the United States and the Soviet Union, Great Britain and the European Community cannot but be taken into account in any final settlement; yet, in the final analysis, the problem of Cyprus must be solved by the Greek and Turkish Cypriots themselves, without outside interference.

The two ethnic groups of Cyprus, Greeks and Turks, are of substantially different size and this difference in size of the conflicting communities is the most important feature of the crisis that has existed for so long. The problem, given the basic recognition of all concerned that an Independent State must be preserved with full security for both communities, is the structuring of such a constitutional pattern that the above objective can be attained without either the destruction of the state or the endangering of the vital interests of the two communities. The Greek Cypriot position is (and has always been) that since the Greek Cypriots constitute the great majority of the population essential political decisions should be theirs to take, and that such a state of affairs can only be possible in the context of institutional arrangements securing an independent and integral state. It is recognised, of course, that both the security and the ethnic rights of the Turkish Community should be protected and secured and the Greek Cypriot position has been that such security should be achieved in the framework of a unitary state. Greek Cypriot policy has so far been predicated upon a rejection of the 'partnership' principle. It could not be accepted that the Turkish Community which is only 18% of the population of Cyprus should have collectively the same rights as the Greek Community which constitutes 82% of the population.

The Turks, on their part, believe that being the smaller and weaker ethnic group insufficient protection would be extended to them if they were treated simply as a privileged minority. Consequently, according to them, the state should be recognised as having a bicommunal character and the principle of partnership between the two Communities should be constitutionally adopted. The Turkish philosophy until recently was that a permanent solution should be found on the basis of Independence; that the Constitution of Cyprus must be based on the principle of the partnership of the two Communities so that the State would be a Cypriot one and not Greek Cypriot; and that both communal matters and local affairs should be left to the respective Communities. The Turkish Cypriot position was often declared to be that what mattered was not the numerical strength of the two Communities but that two national Communities existed in Cyprus and that these two Communities "own" the Independence of Cyprus.

There has, of course, been a dramatic change in Turkish attitudes regarding the solution to the Cyprus problem. As a result of the Turkish invasion two separate plans have been put forward; the Denktash Proposal aims at the creation within the Republic of Cyprus of two federated states with full control and autonomy within their respective geographical boundaries — and it demands that the area of the Turkish Cypriot Federated State should be no less than 34% of the Republic's territory. The Günes Plan demands the creation of a Turkish Cypriot autonomous zone comprising 6 districts, a main Turkish Cypriot district in the northern part of the island and five Turkish autonomous cantons, the administration of the Turkish zone being in entire control of the area within its geographical boundaries. Lately, however, "cantonal" plans seem to have been abandoned by Turkey and a rigid bizonal federation is insisted upon as the only political and constitutional scheme whereby the security of the Turkish Community can be provided for. One wonders why this is so. It is thought that two reasons have been instrumental in this abandonment of the Günes Plan. On the one hand, and given Turkey's apparent willingness to negotiate on the extent of the area to be put under Turkish regional control, there is greater approximation between such cantonal schemes and the proposals of the Greek Cypriot side which are predicated upon the recognition of areas of Turkish Regional Administration, than between such proposals and rigid biregional settlements; on the other, once cantonal or semi-cantonal systems are, in principle, adopted, the crucial question that still remains is, of course, that of the distribution of powers within the state (i.e. which powers should be given to the regional administrations and which should be reserved to the central authority). Once the emphasis, however, is shifted to the question of powers and functions, it can be clearly seen that the Turkish claim that full control or that full and complete powers should be exercised within the Turkish zones by the regional authorities to be set up lacks not only any excuse in the context of the realities of Cyprus but also any justification by way of comparative federalism.

The Greek position as expressed by Mr. Clerides on the 11th June, 1974, was that any solution to the Cyprus problem must be based on the concept of an independent, sovereign and unitary state with adequate participation in the affairs of government by the two Communities, with complete autonomy on matters provided for by the 1960 Constitution (religion, education, culture, personal status etc.) and with a degree of local government compatible with the concept of a unitary state. Likewise in Geneva, the proposals of Mr. Clerides insisted that Cyprus remain a sovereign, independent and integral Republic but also mentioned that there should be an agreed allocation of powers and functions between the central government having competence over state affairs and the Autonomous Communal Administrations which would exercise their powers and functions in areas consisting of the purely Greek and Turkish villages and municipalities respectively. The Clerides proposals contemplated that, for purposes of communal administration, such villages and municipalities could be grouped together by the respective communal authorities, mixed villages for the same purpose coming under the communal authorities of the community to which the majority of their inhabitants belong. Such proposals, as is well known, were unequivocally turned down by the Turkish side.

At first sight, there appears to be a complete divergence of view between the Turkish and Greek positions — the Turks insisting on an autonomous geographical area of very considerable extent and with full powers therein, and the Greek Cypriot position being an unequivocal rejection of any such settlement, limited local autonomy being the most the Greek Cypriot side has been prepared to concede — the main units for the exercise of such autonomous local power being groupings of Turkish and Greek villages respectively. The Greek Cypriot position, moreover, has been put forward as an administrative concession, not as a geographical one, and ideas of territorial boundaries and geographical cohesion are completely absent from Greek Cypriot proposals.

Later an effort will be made to elaborate another approach to the Constitutional problem of Cyprus — such approach, i.e. one based on Local Government or Regionalism, has been already indicated by the distinguished Attorney-General of the Republic in his very valuable work on Cyprus and Federalism.[2] The present proposals are somewhat different, although, as is obvious from what follows, I respectfully share the Attorney-General's belief in the imperative necessity to maintain inviolate and integral the Republic of Cyprus.

We must now take a general juridical glance at the Constitutional problems of Cyprus.

If an attempt is made to state such problem in a neutral but principled constitutional manner, it will be recognised that the problem is the setting up of such a constitutional pattern so that both (a) the political oppression (by the majority) of the smaller group which may be alienated from the state if its legitimate interests are not effectively protected and (b) the constant frustration and resentment of the predominant group which will also be alienated if it cannot take those decisions which are necessary for the pursuance of its interests, can be avoided. An attempt was made to deal with this problem by the 1960 Constitution.

The Zürich Constitution, as has been already said, is an example of an unworkable Constitution.[3] It attempted to deal with the problem of the existence in Cyprus of two ethnic Communities in entirely the wrong manner — instead of attempting to institutionalise bicommunal cooperation by workable provisions and by a proper allocation of functions and powers between the two Communities, it clearly enshrined the concept of political communal segregation. Not only was the Constitution of Cyprus (which, as stated above, was "conceived, drafted and (which) came into force whilst circumstances were such as not to render it the unquestionable outcome of the free choice of the Cyprus people or of its leadership"[4]) never ratified by an unfettered expression of judgment on behalf of the people of Cyprus, after Cyprus had become independent; the said Constitution has been justly characterised as "a tragic and occasionally an almost ludicrous document".[5] Furthermore, as is amply proved above, the 1960 Constitution is "probably the most rigid in the world. It is certainly the most detailed and...possibly...the most complicated".[6]

It is not difficult to draw up a damning indictment of the 1960 Constitution. This has already been done. It seems, however, that after one has stated the problem in the way suggested above, namely as a problem of distribution of power in the context of (and so as not to render impossible) a viable and efficiently functioning state, the defects of Zürich are even more obvious now than when we engaged in, perhaps, too detailed and refined an analysis of the 1960 Constitution. Too many structures were set up by the Zürich Constitution, and such structures made up an unduly expensive state machinery which was not only disproportionate to the size of the population and the resources of the Island but also positively inimical to the development of that "living law" which is so necessary for the overall satisfactory performance of any Constitutional system. In addition, not only were many arrangements and structures set up by the Zürich Constitution which were devoid of functional capacity; many unnecessarily complicated and uncoordinated mechanisms were provided for, and such mechanisms had a paralysing effect upon the functional capacity of the state.[7] In short, the whole of the 1960 Constitution is permeated with the rather naive belief that communal suspicion can only disappear through the multiplication of structures and countless awkwardly interacting mechanisms. As a result, redundant structures were created simply for distribution between the two Communities. The 1960 Constitution, it has been authoritatively stated, "is weighed down by checks and balances, procedural and substantive safeguards, guarantees and prohibitions".[8] Constitutionalism had, indeed, ran riot "in harness with communalism".[9] In retrospect, it can be clearly seen that the Zürich Constitution was fundamentally defective. It gave the Turks excessive powers, did nothing to satisfy deeply-felt resentment on the part of the Greek Cypriot Community, and, in effect, brought about a situation in which, contrary to all democratic principles, the will of the majority was subordinated not so much to the security of the Turkish minority or to the worthy cause of International Peace as to the tortuous imagination of the constitution makers.

When we now direct our attention to new constitutional arrangements for the Republic of Cyprus, we must surely conclude the following. A sound constitutional policy should aim at (a) a proper distribution of structures and functions between the two Communities; (b) the political reintegration of the Greek and Turkish Communities which in its turn depends on the successful institutionalisation of their cooperation in running the Republic of Cyprus and (c) provision for both communal autonomy and local government through decentralisation of authority not amounting to, or inevitably resulting in, the fragmentation or disintegration of the State. Such destruction of the State will be avoided if local autonomy is fully integrated, through various correctly functioning coordination mechanisms, within the unity of the State. It is therefore urged that in restructuring the present constitutional pattern all efforts should be directed towards establishing the foundations of a durable, efficacious and smoothly functioning State, avoiding, if possible, unduly complicated institutions and taking all necessary measures to ensure that a universally condemned solution such as partition is not inevitably but imperceptibly reached.[11]

The key to the problem of Cyprus, it has always been realised, is the provision of security for both communities and the general treatment accorded to the Turkish minority.[12] Nobody, of course, denies the importance of protecting minorities. Minorities must be fully protected and their rights, both ethnic and political, guaranteed and rendered fully effective. "But majorities also have rights".[13] It is surely wrong to raise a small minority to substantially equal status with the overwhelming majority in so far as political power is concerned. But such precisely was the result of the Zürich Constitution. In spite of its numerical weakness, its proportion in land ownership and its very small contribution to public expenditure, the Turkish minority, against all precedent and contrary to every democratic principle, apart from having its minority rights fully safeguarded by the Constitution, was effectively put on the same level politically with the Greek majority.

The existence of minorities, in close proximity with their mother country, is not a phenomenon peculiar to Cyprus. One comes across similar situations in many other countries. The extraordinary proposition has never been put forward, however, that such minorities should be given a privileged position with regard to their participation in Governmental functions or that they should be under the protection of the foreign country from which they derive their ethnic origin. Generally, minorities should have their ethnic and communal rights fully protected and should be subjected to no discrimination in the matter of political rights. When, however, a minority is singled out and given, over and above such protection, separate and preferential treatment — to an extent, moreover, that the normal operation of the State becomes impossible — not only will artificial, unrealistic and unworkable means have to be devised for the implementation of such policies, which, it can be easily seen, will be strenuously objected to by both the majority and the other minorities; such a system will almost inevitably result in communal segregation, in the exacerbation of already existing passions and in conflict between the Communities involved.

It has been said that if the Turkish Community were, say 40-50% of the total population of Cyprus, the problem would, in a way, have been much simpler. In that case, there would be every reason for adopting a system of government based on the joint entitlement of both Communities to the powers and prerogatives of office. Indeed, if the two Communities were of approximately equal numerical strength, the designations of majority and minority would not really have been appropriate. Similarly with the situation in which a minority is a very small fraction of the population, for instance, less than 10%. In that case there could be no reason for treating the minority concerned otherwise than as a minority, i.e. according to such minority the internationally recognised rights, both ethnic and political, and allowing the normal processes of democracy to operate. In Cyprus, the Turkish minority is approximately 18% of the total population of the island and, as an abstract matter, it is not thought that separate arrangements, concerning such minority should have been necessitated, particularly when one considers the intermingling of the communal populations. The Cyprus problem, however, as can be easily seen, cannot be dealt with in an academic manner. The Turkish Community absolutely refuses to allow itself to be treated simply as a minority. They regard themselves as a separate and distinct Community and Cyprus as an island consisting of two separate Communities. It has been explained above that the Turkish Cypriots' communal perception of the constitutional problem must in part be attributed to British policy. Whatever may be the origin, however, of such developments, it seems to be undeniable that the eventual settlement must provide for joint and balanced participation by both Communities in the processes of government. Furthermore, regional arrangements providing added security to the Turkish community must be resorted to. Detailed proposals are later put forward concerning such matters.

But if the Turkish Community of Cyprus, still only 18%, desire not only to participate in the exercise of governmental power with the Greek Cypriot Community, but to share such power with them on the basis of "joint entitlement", then such claims can only be described as unrealistic, divisive and unacceptable. And the same applies to proposals which would have the same effect, i.e. which would result in the Turkish Cypriot minority of 18% controlling, in effect, the exercise of governmental functions.

Yet, despite the force of such arguments, and the pro-claimed readiness of the Cyprus Government to bind itself in this matter by International Guarantees, the Turkish side has persisted in its attempt to give new force to the equal partnership principle. The restructured Constitution of Cyprus, so the Turkish philosophy goes, must be based on the equal partnership of the two Communities (this over and above their claims for the geographical division of the island, such desired geographical division being, in ultimate analysis, the most extreme manifestation of the "joint entitlement" philosophy). Also, the Turkish side obviously continues to postulate the theory that the numerical strength of the Communities is not a fact to be taken into consideration, attempting thus to equalise the 18% of the Turkish population to the 82% of the Greek. To such claims, it can only be answered that, though it goes without saying that every citizen of the Republic, whether a Greek or a Turk, shall have the same political and other rights, and that the Turkish Community will be fully entitled to its ethnic communal rights, the Greek Cypriot side can never accept that the Turkish Community, which is only 18% of the population and which contributes even less than that to the economy of Cyprus, should be entitled, collectively, to the same rights as the Greek Majority.

What should the principles be on which the future Constitutional structure of the Island must be based? The question, of course, of "What a Constitution should contain"[14] is one of the most difficult ones. Here, it will suffice to make a few salient points.

A Constitution should not be a strait-jacket. It should be allowed to become a living organism. As such, it will be, and should clearly be recognised as being, capable of growth — "of expansion and of adaptation to new conditions". Growth implies changes — political, economic and social. And growth there is bound to be. If we arrest Constitutional growth in its infancy by refusing to countenance it and by providing that the constitution should never be capable of adaptation, reassessment and readjustment, we will either, at the same time, be attempting to arrest social growth, a futile undertaking, or we will be refusing to absorb and legitimise such growth by constitutional expansion. Such refusal to allow growth that is both significant and inevitable to manifest itself in intellectual and moral conceptions — and, after all, what should a Constitution be other than a complex of legal and moral values — can only be catastrophic.

The Constitution should also be a living one, both in the sense that it is based on the traditions and the realities of the Island and in the avoidance of that complexity and prolixity of detail which one normally associates with codes rather than Constitutional charters. Clearly, in the case of Cyprus, with its peculiar problems and idiomatic complications, it is not possible to insist, with Marshall C.J. in McCullogh v Maryland, that only the great outlines of the Constitution be marked out and only its important objects designated, all "minor ingredients" to be deduced from the totality of the Constitutional scheme. It will be necessary to adopt not only sui generis provisions but also very specific and, in many areas of Government, very detailed formulations. Indeed, nothing less than explicit and detailed structuring of the State and full provision for the exact participation of both Communities in the affairs of government would satisfy the Turkish Community. But, on the other hand, and this is the basic tenet of the present chapter, we must neither frame, nor think of, the Constitution as a catalogue of specific answers to specific problems. A Constitution should be much more — it should be nothing less than "a charter for the governance of generations to come". To be sure, a Constitution must be written, its purposes must be clearly articulated and its intentions must be spelt out with respectable specificity. If, however, the hands of the organs of government are "most inconveniently tied", the Constitution simply will not be able to work, and even if it endures it will do so as an empty formula, unable to command moral support or provide a unifying focus for all the people of Cyprus.

Another point to be repeatedly made is that whatever the formal arrangements adopted, a Constitution can only be a skeleton. It is the acts and behaviour of those who operate it that bestow upon it a certain character and impart to it a given effect, thus personalising it. The Constitution, any Constitution, can only be incomplete.

Around it cluster (and will cluster) practices and conventions, political compromises, settled ways of doing things, understandings. Such multifarious ideas and habits often achieve the solidification necessary before one can speak of them as rules of law; even if such is not their fate, however, such clusters of conventions and practices still perform a role of vital importance. Not only can they be "the raw materials . . . from which national policy is wrought"; they also ensure that change does not come in violent spasms, that essential continuity is maintained.

Nevertheless, a well constructed Constitution is a necessity. It can provide the context in which political and other differences can be resolved without a resort to force or acrimony, and can constitute the framework in which both communal accommodation and cooperation can be first successfully institutionalised and then fully achieved.

This last point, which is brilliantly made by Professor Bickel, is crucial and must be further elaborated. In order to last and be stable, a Constitution must make it possible for future battles to be fought out by men who, on both sides of contested issues, can in good faith profess allegiance for the organic law of the state and the system of government established thereby. The Constitutional provisions, in general, must be capable, by virtue of appropriate drafting, of containing many intercommunal differences and of "embracing either result of most trials of political strength".[15] Only in such a way can a Constitution acquire symbolic value, not only as the ultimate criterion of legitimacy but also as the ordered framework within which political controversy is not only acceptable but also positively desirable. If a Constitution purports to settle, in detail and for all time, all the issues that are likely to confront those who are entrusted with the operation of the system, as the 1960 Constitution did, such Constitution invites either abandonment or frequent amendment. "The familiarity of amendment will breed a species of contempt and incapacitate the document for symbolic service".[16] One could perhaps say that such statements are more appropriate for a politically advanced society which, moreover, is not plagued by the kind of communalism and blind nationalism that have become a real cancerous growth on the Island of Cyprus. It is the fervent belief of the writer, however, that the development of a mature political life and the elimination of the kind of communalism that has so much disfigured Cypriot public life are inextricably connected. The development of the concept of political duty and the emergence of civic consciousness are, in the ultimate analysis, the only factors capable of bringing about the erosion of the old pernicious influences and destructive communal prejudices.

Certain general principles on which, it is believed, the solution of the Cyprus problem must be based are the following:

1) Cyprus must remain an independent, unitary, integral and sovereign state.

2) All Communities and minorities should have complete autonomy in matters of religion, education, personal status.

3) The internationally recognised human rights as provided by the European Convention on Human Rights and all its Protocols, supplemented as necessary by rights included in the European Social Charter and by rights provided in the Universal Declaration of Human Rights, should be incorporated and entrenched in the Constitution, and fully protected by an appropriate remedial apparatus. Such remedial apparatus can be internationally reinforced.

4) Adequate and balanced participation by the Turkish Community in the affairs of government should be provided for, such participation, naturally, to be fixed by the Constitution.

5) Adequate local or regional Government should be recognised.

V

CYPRUS AND POLITICAL FEDERATION[1]

THE word Federation has figured extensively in Turkish claims with regard to the Constitutional structure of Cyprus. At times such claims have been spelt out with some particularity — on other occasions, they have remained vague, depending for their appeal on the respectable pedigree of concepts such as Federation, Autonomy, etc. In substance, however, the Turkish claims have not changed over the years. This is pointed out by Dr. Plaza in his Report on Cyprus (paragraph 16) who mentions, in this connection, the Turkish Government's *continued* belief "that only the geographical separation of the two communities could provide adequate protection for the Turkish Cypriot community". One can also refer for substantiation of such a thesis to a multitude of Turkish and Turkish Cypriot statements over the years supporting geographical federation or the outright partitioning of the island as the only possible solutions to the Cyprus problem. Thus, Mr. Kemal Satir, former Vice-President of Turkey, in a public statement in 1964, said that: "Cyprus will be divided into two sections, one of which will join Turkey". In June 1964, Mr. Erkin, then Foreign Minister of Turkey, clearly spelled out what his Government's intentions were when he said, in a newspaper interview in Athens, that: "the radical solution ... would be to cede one part of Cyprus to Greece and the other, closest to the Turkish Asiatic coast, to Turkey". Hardly three months later, on the 8th September, 1964, the former Prime Minister of Turkey, Ismet Inonou, addressing the Turkish National Assembly, with reference to the Geneva talks of that year, said: "officially, we promoted the federation concept, rather than the partition thesis, so as to remain within the provisions of the Treaty". This, of course, is another clear indication of the tactical nature of the use of federation as an official camouflage of partition. Even in the Security Council itself, the then Permanent Representative, Mr. Eralp, brought out that purpose when he declared that 'a federal regime' is the only solution. That the ulterior aim of partition is annexation transpires also from "Halkin Sesi", the then mouthpiece of Dr. Kütchuk, which, in its editorial of 9th August 1965, wrote: "Cyprus is another Alexandretta in the history of Turkey. The power of Turkey will ensure an honourable life for the Turkish Cypriots in the same way as it did in Alexandretta by annexing it and bringing it under Turkish domination. The road in this direction has been opened by the Turkish fighters at Kokkina who are now fighting in every corner of Cyprus". It can well be seen that in the case of Cyprus the concept of federation, implying partition, has always been directly opposed to the independence and territorial integrity of the country, and has always been calculated to defeat it. Finally, it must be noticed that, as recently as the 27th March 1974, and whilst the intercommunal discussions — which were predicated upon the need to maintain an independent and unitary Cyprus — were continuing, the Turkish Prime Minister, Mr. Ecevit, referring to the Cyprus problem, is reported to have supported the establishment of a "federal state". Such statement not only, at the time, undermined the local talks but is also an infallible indication of Turkey's real objectives for Cyprus.

There is also a great similarity between the Turkish position as put before the U.N. Mediator and the recent proposals of Mr. Denktash submitted at Geneva. The dividing line that Dr. Kutchuk, the then Vice-President, had suggested in 1964 as appropriate for the delimitation of the Turkish Zone ran from the village of Yalia on the north-western coast through the towns of Nicosia in the centre, and Famagusta in the east. The zone, lying north of this line, was said to have an area of about 1,084 sq. miles or 38% of the total area of the Republic. In the recent Denktash proposals, it was demanded of the Greek Cypriot delegation that ir recognise: (a) the binational character of the Republic of Cyprus; (b) that the Republic should be composed of two Federated States "with full control and autonomy within their respective geographical boundaries" and, (c) that the area of the Turkish Cypriot Federated State should cover 34% of the territory of the Republic "falling north of a general line starting from the Limnitis-Lefka area in the west and running towards the east, passing through the Turkish controlled part of Nicosia, including the Turkish part of Famagusta and ending at the port of Famagusta". It can be seen that the geographical lines envisaged by the various Turkish proposals and on the basis of which the territorial Federation of Cyprus has been sought have not changed much.

It has not been the same with the powers and functions that are sought for the desired Turkish autonomous administration. Par. 74 of the Plaza Report indicates that the Turks had asked that both the two separate communal areas "enjoy self-government in all matters falling outside federal affairs", and, in par. 75, it was stated that under the above proposal, the federal authority would be competent to deal with the subjects of foreign affairs, defence, the federal budget, customs, commerce, banking, currency, standards of measurement, nationality, passport matters, post and telecommunication services and criminal legislation and jurisdiction. In the more recent proposals the federal jurisdiction is even more attenuated. Thus, in 2 (b) of the Denktash proposal it is said that the two Federated States should have *full* control and autonomy within their respective geographical boundaries, and this demand is not made any more palatable by the declaration of 2 (c) that, in determining the competence to be left to the federal government, the binational nature of the state should be taken into account and the federal competence exercised accordingly. Even more revealing about Turkish intentions with regard to the powers and functions to be assigned to the proposed Federated States within the "United Republic of Cyprus" are the proposals contained in the Turkish pro-government newspaper "Milliyet". These reports have been attributed to "officials", and there is no doubting their emanation from governmental sources. The administrations of the proposed regions, according to "Milliyet", "will have full autonomy on political administration, economy, finance, education, domestic security and national defence". The two autonomous administrations, "Milliyet" further states, "will be able to act freely in finance, education, domestic security, justice and commerce". They will also "regulate every type of service within their own regions". What is obviously envisaged by these proposals is not so much "a federal system" but the bringing about of partition and the designation of it as "federation". Before we go further, and delve briefly into the subject of Federalism and the applicability or inapplicability thereof to the conditions and the people of Cyprus, it is imperative that we should have in mind the warning of Dr. Plaza against oversimplification; it is not enough to advocate a solution to the problem of Cyprus without investigating all the likely repercussions of such arrangement, nor is it enough to support a given constitutional structure without closely studying the likely effects that the imposition of such structure will bring about as regards the people of Cyprus as a whole.

Before we even advert to the problem of defining a federal system, one must notice something that, by and large, has gone unobserved; namely, that in most discussions of federalism the problem has been one of a number of independent states deciding to relinquish part of their sovereignty for the increased benefits that will result from political association — the problems of federal government, that is, have, generally, been the problems of states resolving to come together for some purposes but retaining, at the same time, a large measure of their original independence. In Cyprus, as must be obviously apparent, the issue is different. It is not the coming together of independent states that is sought, but the fragmentation of an existing State, the virtual abdication of its sovereignty and the destruction of central authority to the detriment of both communities.

Federal Government is the system of government embodying "predominantly a division of powers between general and regional authorities, each of which, in its own sphere, is coordinate with the others and independent of them".[2] It is clear that political federation pre-supposes some territorial basis, and must be distinguished from possible forms of functional federalism.[3] Here, a parenthesis must be inserted. Terminological confusion and linguistic ambiguity have, here as elsewhere, bedevilled both a formulation of the problem and its comprehension. Functional federalism is an imprecise expression, yet the Turkish side is on record as having repeatedly expressed the view that the Zürich settlement was the setting up of such a functional federative system. What they clearly mean is that the governmental system imported thereby was based on political and governmental functions being distributed between the two Communities. And Professor Friedrich in his 'Trends of Federalism in Theory and Practice' has written that 'the Federalism chosen for Cyprus was what might be called "corporate federalism" ', the basis of such federalism being not some territorial plan but the community or nationality to which a person belongs. Personally, together with both Lord Radcliffe[4] and Dr. Plaza, I prefer to think of federalism as predicated upon some geographical basis. Fixed communal participation in government (both the Zürich model and, to some extent, what I later propose myself) need not be called functional or corporate federal schemes. Neither simplicity of formulation nor clarity of conception — surely cardinal virtues in constitutional theory — are advanced by any such appellation. Whatever may be the case in abstract theory, however, it is abundantly clear from what was set out above that political federation based on the recognition of a distinct geographical zone within which almost absolute political authority would be exercisable is the governmental structure desired by the Turks. "The establishment of a federal regime requires a territorial basis, and this basis does not exist", says Dr. Plaza in par. 150 of his Report. The absence of this territorial basis which alone is fatal to Turkish claims will be further elaborated later on. The case against a geographical federation, however, need not stop with demonstrating that such a territorial basis does not exist. It should also be asserted that the general "prerequisites" of federal government are not apparent in the case of Cyprus, and that a return to the principles of an integral and unified state is, as a result, better calculated (than other solutions) for the safeguarding of the various interests involved in the problem of Cyprus.

Professor Wheare in his "Federal Government" considers "a desire to be under a single government" as of vital importance for the constitution of a Federation. Absent such a desire, the creation of a Federal State should not be suggested. (It is true that, as pointed out above, discussions of "prerequisites" for federalism take place in the context of a choice between the kind of association that "federalism" represents and complete independence. But it will be here suggested that the kind of factors that could elsewhere militate in favour of independence, in the case of Cyprus — and absent a geographical separation — point in the direction of an independent and unified state, the security of both communities being achieved otherwise.) Nobody can say that the intention of the Turks is coloured by a desire to be under a single government. Rather, their often-stated objective is the setting up of an independent regional government, the principle of "one state" being retained for purposes of appearance and international deception.

A factor that Professor Wheare gives considerable prominence to as almost invariably present in the setting up of modern federations is the "sense of military insecurity and of the consequent need for common defence". The federation, that is, binds the constituent parts thereof "always to fight on the same side", as John Stuart Mill observes in his "Representative Government"; and if they have such feelings towards one another "or such diversity of feelings towards their neighbours" that they would generally prefer to fight on opposite sides, the federal tie is not likely to be "of long duration", nor will it be well observed. Such, indeed, will be the case with Cyprus were a geographical federation to be established. The Greek and Turkish communities would never develop a sense of nationhood, but would naturally rely on Greece and Turkey respectively in matters of defence, etc. Federation in Cyprus would inevitably lead to partition and annexation of the constituent parts thereof to other states, a solution which is, today, universally condemned. This was also the view of the U.N. Mediator. He stated (par. 154) that the arguments for the geographical separation of the two communities had not convinced him that it would not inevitably lead to partition.

"A hope of economic advantage from union" seems to be another of the factors that have been operative in the structuring of many political federations. Again, nothing could be further from the minds of the Turkish leadership. It is not their intention to set up a viable government, but rather to appropriate to themselves the great area of productive Cyprus, deprive the government of authority as regards finance, trade and industry and leave the rest of the territory for the Greek community. Indeed, a federation does not seem capable of being set up (or, in our case, carved out of the integral state of Cyprus) without careful consideration of the relative resources of the contemplated units in the proposed federation. All the created units (including the federal government) must possess, or retain, sufficient resources for the purpose of financing themselves. It is very unlikely that this will be the case with Cyprus. Not only will financial stagnation be the result of geographical separation but it is inevitable that increased reliance on Greece and Turkey respectively in this, as in other matters, will lead to partition.

Another fact which is obvious, but not sufficiently taken into account, is that "size" is of considerable importance in determining whether to set up a federation or not. Size, of course, reflects on many aspects of the governmental structure envisaged. It should be clear, however, that federation is more appropriate to large units than to small ones. It is not only that in most of the federal systems of the world today geographical factors have been instrumental in the development of the desire to be separate and that such geographical factors cannot be said to be present in a small country like Cyprus (area 9,251 sq. Klm)[5] — one must not forget that federal geographical government is expensive and legalistic, and that in the case of a small country it is almost bound to be too expensive and too legalistic. One need not go as far as Harold Laski and declare that "the epoch of federalism is over"[6] — the federal solution clearly continues to appeal to constitution-makers, and where its prerequisites are present, federal government can indeed provide the governmental structure which can accommodate the frequently coexisting forces of unification and diversity.[7] What is claimed here is that federal government, particularly in its traditional form, with its compartmenting of functions, rigidity, and inherent conservatism, is not the appropriate form of government for Cyprus. Where it is not the desire to derive profit from economic union that leads to demands for separatist administrations but rather the desire to break up a unitary government, one can assume (as in the case of Cyprus one must assume) that the spirit for cooperation which lies at the root of most federations will be absent from any comparable ventures undertaken here (and that such lack of cooperation will be manifested by those who seek the break-up of the State in the first place).

The consequent problems that will almost certainly arise can be easily foreseen: fragmentation of authority, weak government (whereas what is needed in a country like Cyprus is strong, decisive government), double expenditure, general duplication of efforts and services, the development of friction between the centre and the circumference, etc. Size is important in another respect. If federal government is to work there must be available a supply of men with capacity to govern, "a supply sufficient not for one government only but for many". Federal Government makes a big demand on all of a community's resources, human as well as otherwise. Cyprus, with a population of only 650,000, and a limited availability of material resources, should neither be expected to supply readily so many trained and capable men, nor be subjected to the burdens of divided and inefficient Government and Separatist Administrations.

The above brief look at some of the general prerequisites of federation makes one very doubtful whether Cyprus (with its small size and population, and limited resources) can be considered appropriate ground for the experiment of political federalism on a geographical basis. Nor must we forget that it can be, and has been, claimed, with considerable justification, that "the essence of federalism lies not in the constitutional or institutional structure but in the society itself".[8] Federal government, indeed, can be described as a device whereby the federal qualities of a society are articulated, given expression to and protected. And Cyprus society lacks all and any federal qualities. Those forces — namely, economic, social, political, and cultural ones — that have made resort to the form of federation necessary in the case of other developing countries are demonstrably absent in the case of Cyprus. A more thorough look at the realities of the island fully confirms this view.

It is, first of all, important to understand that "the distinctive features of the two communities (i.e. traditions, customs, religion) do not imply that in normal times they have been separated from each other". (The Plaza Report, par. 18). Nor are the two communities substantially separated now, despite the continued attempts of the Turkish leadership to bring about de facto separation. Greek Cypriots and Turkish Cypriots have always been spread widely over the whole island — "not according to any fixed geographical pattern but rather as a result of the usual factors behind the movement and settlement of people over many generations".[9] All the main cities are mixed in population, even though the two communities tend to concentrate in different sectors of such cities. As to the villages, out of a total of 627, 123 are purely Turkish, 112 are mixed and the rest are purely Greek. The area, too, now claimed by the Turks (and which amounts to approximately 35% of the total territory of the Republic) is mainly inhabited by Greek Cypriots (80% Greeks and 20% Turks).

Yet, despite the great dimensions, both human and social, of what is surely a crucial problem, Turkish proposals have not been very consistent with regard to the movement of population that might be required were a geographical federation to be imposed on the people of Cyprus. Dr. Kutchuk, when seeking a geographical basis for the state of affairs created by the Zürich Agreement (see Plaza Report), advocated a compulsory exchange of populations in order to bring about a state of affairs in which each community would occupy a separate part of the island. In the more recent proposals, however, very little is said as to what is surely a problem of the first magnitude. In the 'Milliyet' article referred to above, it was said that Greeks and Turks would be allowed to live in each other's part of the island if they wished; "if not they will go to the region set out for their kinsmen"; the same was said by both Mr. Günes and Mr. Denktash at the Geneva Conference. A slightly different version has, however, appeared in a statement of Mr.

Ecevit. He said that he did not expect a forcible movement of population, but he thought that this would come about naturally; and all indications are that Turkish efforts will be aimed at moving all the Greek Cypriot population into the "Greek-Cypriot region" were a geographical solution to be adopted. This process, as is well known, has already begun (and, indeed, has been almost completed). And, legally, a federal geographical system makes little sense if the population or community for whom the separate arrangements have been enacted are not assembled together in the created region. As Lord Radcliffe said in his Report, "Federation of Communities which does not involve also federation of territories" seems "a very difficult constitutional form". There is another problem. If one supports the creation of a Turkish Cypriot region to be governed by a Turkish Cypriot administration, and one does not at the same time advocate some kind of population movement, one will be inevitably led to depriving the great majority of the proposed region of the right to vote, since as already indicated above 80% of the people north of the Attila line are Greek Cypriots. One is, consequently, inexorably led to the conclusion that territorial separation coupled with separation of the communities, is, and has always been, the true aim of Turkish policy.

It is obvious that removal and re-settlement of population on the scale required (and it is the Denktash proposals that we are primarily discussing) would create very great difficulties. New villages would have to be built, new roads, new water supplies, etc; also, one cannot assume that the remaining part of the island (considerably less productive than the territory above the Attila Line) will easily absorb the Greek Cypriot population uprooted from their homes and occupations. "Moreover, this would be a compulsory movement of a kind that would seem to impose severe hardships on the families involved as it would be impossible for all of them, or perhaps even the majority of them, to obtain an exchange of land or occupation suited to their needs or experience". (The Plaza Report, par. 153).

Geographical separation, in addition to the multifarious objections — moral, political, economic — to which it has been subjected, suffers from the defect that it fails to ensure that in the name of which it is put forward, namely the security of all Cyprus communities. The proposed Federated States would be separated by an artificial line "cutting through inter-dependent parts of homogeneous areas, including ... the cities of Nicosia, and

Famagusta". (par. 154); and even though Turkish proposals have not made clear whether they are envisaging a fortified line or a merely administrative one, it appears that the latter is intended, or, at least, that more or less free movement of people will be allowed through this line. It is almost certain that such a line of division will be the cause not only of many administrative difficulties but also of much friction between the two communities. In addition, as it was argued above, if the dependence of the two envisaged Federated States on Greece and Turkey respectively is likely to be such that, in truth, whatever the formal status of the states created is, a new frontier between Turkey and Greece has been created then a new source of danger to international peace and security will have been added — particularly, one must add, if such frontier is not formalised by the legal annexation of the two federated states to Greece and Turkey respectively. This was also the view of the UN Mediator. The cause of peace and International security, therefore, both for the two communities directly involved and for the other countries interested, cannot be promoted by the creation of an artificial line dividing Cyprus into two parts and by arrangements resulting in immense dislocation of peaceful life, "the uprooting of people ... immense hardship and human misery".[10]

If one now adverts to the economic facts only briefly sketched above, the restructuring of the Cypriot state on the basis of a geographical federation, particularly along the lines at present suggested, appears utterly impossible, inconceivable in practice and a sure recipe for future disaster. Such separation, resulting in the artificial creation of areas rich in certain resources on the one hand and areas characterised by a complete absence of economic resources on the other, could bring about the economic break-down of the whole island — particularly as Cyprus, due to the nature and special distribution of its resources, is — from the geographical point of view — an economic entity characterised by great inter-dependence of, and close inter-relationship among, its micro-regions and resources. Financial unification could lead to prosperity for all the people of Cyprus. Geographical separation will result in stagnation, economic depression and cannot but militate against the development of a peacefully united people. One, on the basis of such undisputed facts, cannot, in common with Dr. Plaza (par. 155), "help wondering whether the physical division of the minority from the majority should not be considered a desperate step in the wrong direction".

There is another angle from which Turkish claims ought to be examined — the aspect of what Lord Radcliffe called "liberal and democratic conceptions" concerning political power. In the 'Milliyet' article, not only is 34% of Cyprus demanded for the Turkish Community but it is also asked that equal representation be accorded to the two communities in the Federal Government. This is nothing less than "a claim by 18% of a population to share political power equally with 80%" (Lord Radcliffe), and cannot possibly be supported either on the basis of what we referred to above as liberal and democratic principles of modern government or because no other means can prove effective for the protection of the essential interests of the Turkish community. But it is not only equal representation for the two communities in the proposed Federal Government that can lead to a standstill in political life — with the frustration that invariably accompanies it — and result in the denial to the majority of the population over the whole field of self-government of the power to have its will reflected in effective action; the creation of a Turkish area for the Turkish community is also nothing less than a denial of self-government for the Greek Cypriot majority, and will bring about not only the paralysis of effective executive government but also the creation of a bad precedent for the world. It is not consistent either with justice or with sound principles of government that each minority should be entitled to its own geographical area. The security of minorities should be safe-guarded within the State and special guarantees, if need be, should be exacted in relation thereto.

The protection and security of the Turkish Cypriot community is, indeed, "one of the most important aspects of the Cyprus problem" (Plaza Report, par. 156), and everything possible must be done to ensure it, "including safeguards of an exceptional type" (par. 156). What is questioned is not that the Turkish Cypriot community is entitled to improved security, but whether geographical separation is the way whereby the needed security can be provided. For the arguments given above it is believed that not only will the physical division of the minority from the majority not achieve its stated objective, but that, on the contrary, the security of both communities will decrease and an important step towards the full partitioning of the island will have been taken — with all the consequent dangers, both Internal and International, that this could entail.

The imposition of federalism is not the answer to the problems of Cyprus.[11] Decentralisation of authority within a unitary state, rather than the forced separation of Greeks and Turks within distinct and fixed geographical areas, should be the solution resorted to. Federal government, in the case of Cyprus, will surely prove an obstacle to political and social integration and will no doubt hinder the formulation and administration of economic plans; furthermore, the control of the stability and the direction of the progress of the economy by use of active monetary and fiscal policies will inevitably suffer by the implementation of federal experiments; and, finally, both the effectiveness of social planning and the provision of social services will be seriously handicapped by any such solution.

But, as made clear above, such will not be the only, or even the principal, drawbacks of federation in the case of Cyprus. Is it not a cruel and insane policy in effect to divide a small and economically homogeneous island into two geographical zones with separate administrations and hardly any opportunity for association between the two main communities? If two peoples cannot live with each other, then surely they cannot live next to each other. And it is not only an essential thesis of the present work, but also an article of faith of the present writer, that the people of Cyprus, both Greek and Turk, can live with one another, together achieve the peace, and prosper in unity and co-existence. Both communities bear the visible scars of conflict and protracted intercommunal acrimony — both, at present, are stifling under the yoke of the Turkish army of occupation. Both, it is believed, are ready for a lasting and durable peace.

VI

THE CENTRAL GOVERNMENT

W E shall now propose a concrete plan for the restructuring of the Central Government.[1] In doing so, we must not forget that what we are aiming for is the establishment of viable and efficient Government. The constitutional arrangements to be arrived at for the purpose of constituting the three Powers of Government — the legislative, the executive and the judiciary — must, therefore, not be too costly, divisive or cumbersome, nor, again, should they be so detailed that no room for compromise is left. For, whatever the precise constitutional structure eventually adopted, intercommunal conflict and friction in Government there are bound to be and no machinery, Governmental or other, can be devised whereby such conflict or friction can be prevented from arising or totally suppressed. What must be aimed for is the devising of such constitutional machinery that intercommunal conflict can be reduced and peacefully resolved. Zürich had brought into operation too institutionalised a Governmental pattern. It was as if the framers of the 1960 Constitution believed that a Constitution, appropriately drafted and seemingly resolving all problems in advance, can save a people, whatever their actions and behaviour, from self destruction. The example of Cyprus has once more proved the fallacy of such thinking.

In a setting such as the Cypriot one, with generations of intercommunal conflict, tension and increased recent bitterness, the most that can be hoped for is that (a) conflict should not be accentuated by the Constitution and (b) that the Constitutional structure be so devised that conflicts can be resolved or worked out by the people themselves. It was because of the incredibly rigid institutionalisation of bicommunal participation in the Central Government that the development of genuine communal co-operation did not materialise. The essence of the 1960 Constitutional arrangements seemed to be an effort to impose an unworkable pattern of communal participation on the people of Cyprus. What should be aimed for now is the *achievement* of communal co-operation and co-existence in the context of

Governmental arrangements which will encourage such co-operation and co-existence by allowing them to develop. It should be repeated that tension there is bound to be whatever the precise Constitutional structure. A rigid and artificial pattern of Central Government will never cope with the stress of intercommunal tension and initial reluctance to co-operate. If the pattern is too rigid and attempts to provide, in a fixed way, for every conceivable eventuality, almost any constitutional question, as has been clearly seen above, will become controversial, such controversial issues will remain unresolved, unresolved issues will accumulate, conflict will intensify, positions will become increasingly entrenched and non-negotiable and the ship of State will before long capsize, having lost in the process all functional relevance. Such has been the sad cycle of communal and constitutional life in Cyprus in the recent past and such must not be allowed to happen again. To forestall, or rather help forestall, such developments in the future, the mistakes of the past should be avoided and a sounder constitutional policy pursued.

Ideally, as has been often stressed in this study, a completely unitary state, with adequate protection for minorities, should have been the preferable system of Government, but for the reasons emphasised elsewhere this does not seem possible. That two ethnic Communities exist in Cyprus will still have to be the starting point for any consideration of the setting up and organisation of the three Powers of Government, the legislature, the judiciary, and the executive. But we must not over-emphasise communal separation nor should communalism be allowed to run rampant in the structuring of Governmental mechanisms and institutions. Sui generis provisions are, of course, necessary until cohesion of interests and voluntary co-operation between the two Communities are brought about by wise leadership, mutual forbearance, generosity, restraint and good Government. But the point made here is that we must mould a regime in which Greeks and Turks *can* co-operate and where economic, social and other conditions will bring them closer together as time heals the wounds and compromise on the part of both Communities points the way towards a happier future.

The proposals regarding the organisation of the Central Government which will be put forward now are not intended to be exhaustive. Rather, it is the purpose of the following remarks to indicate what may be appropriate arrangements in the light of the general observations made above.

Legislature. We will first discuss the Legislature. Our discussion will be divided into: Composition; System of election; Competence and Restrictions upon Competence.

(a) *Composition.* The Elected Assembly which will be the main legislative organ of Cyprus should be called, as in the past, the House of Representatives. It should consist of Greek and Turkish Representatives in proportion to the Greek and Turkish populations of the island. For instance, if the House of Representatives consists of 75 members, there should be 60 Greeks and 15 Turks. The writer would rather see a smaller Elected Assembly as it is thought that a small legislative organ will be more efficient. This, however, is a matter of detail, in no way affecting the principle proposed.

The House of Representatives will elect from amongst its members its Speaker or President. Such Speaker or President will be elected by majority vote, all the Representatives participating in the election, no distinction, in this matter, being drawn between the Greek and Turkish members of the House. Candidates for election to the office of President of the House must be proposed by at least two members of the House and seconded by at least another three. Again, no distinction is drawn between Greek and Turkish Representatives. It is also thought that the House should elect a Vice President, again by general majority vote, such Vice President to be necessarily Turkish only when the President whose election, as a result, will have to take place first, proves to be a Greek Cypriot. Likewise, if the President of the House turns out to be a Turkish Cypriot, then the Vice President, whose main function will be to deputise for the President in the latter's absence or temporary incapacity, should be a Greek. The term of office of the House should be for a period of five years and general elections for the House of Representatives should duly take place as provided by the Electoral laws. Extension of the House of Representatives' term of office should only be possible in times of grave national emergency, and such an extension, before coming into operation, must be voted upon by a two thirds majority of the Members of the House of Representatives, no distinction again being drawn between Greek and Turkish Members.

(b) *System of election to the House.* How should the Members of the House of Representatives be elected? The assumption throughout has been that two electoral rolls are called for, one for Greek Cypriots and another for Turkish Cypriots, and such a system of minority representation has been advocated as self evident and as the only way of securing the rights of the Turkish minority. The idea, however, that minority Communities should be guaranteed special representation as such in the Legislature is not only seldom acceptable today but also suffers from serious drawbacks, and one should not be too hasty in recommending, even for Cyprus, such departures from liberal and progressive ideas without at least a thorough consideration of possible alternatives. Such a system of minority representation, which has been described as "a canker on the body politic, eating deeper and deeper into the vital energies of the people, breeding self interest, suspicion and animosity..."[2] and which was referred to by a distinguished commentator as a "malignant growth",[3] not only has a poor record, but also has incurred almost universal condemnation on account of its tendency "to magnify existing communal differences, in as much as the communities are stirred to fuller self consciousness".[4] Indeed, it needs little documentation to show that "Communalism stands for divided loyalties" and that it inhibits the development of a responsible body of citizens. It would, therefore, be most desirable if the system of two electoral rolls was abandoned and Elections to the House of Representatives were held on a common electoral roll. Thus, in any election for the House, that candidate would be returned who had secured a majority of the votes cast. Perhaps it would be necessary, even in the context of the abolition of the system of the two electoral rolls, to introduce some limiting or qualifying principle (at least as a transitional measure), namely that a Turkish Cypriot candidate would not be returned unless he had secured a given percentage of the Turkish votes cast. The problem, however, is: Can a satisfactory common roll system be found acceptable to both sides? The Turkish side has always insisted on two electoral rolls, because, it seems, of grave doubts about whether a common electoral roll system can be found which will (a) ensure adequate representation of the Turkish community and (b) safeguard the Turkish side from having imposed on it, by virtue of the Greek majority, Turkish Representatives who would not be acceptable to the Turkish community. (This second objective is, to an extent, provided for by the qualifying principle mentioned above). Such objectives could perhaps be attained by other means which do not, however, commend themselves either for their honesty or their political efficacy. In particular, it may be possible to appease minorities by so delimiting electoral constituencies as to ensure, or, at least, enhance the probability, that an adequate number of Representatives of the relevant communal Group will be returned. It can be argued, however, that such a method of "judicious boundary fixing" only accentuates the problem by e.g. making it imperative that electoral areas be agreed upon not so much on the basis of conventional electoral considerations as with the ulterior objective of securing 'fair' representation for the minority community. Likewise, the other methods which have on occasion been used for assuring minorities of legislative representation, such as manipulation of the franchise, artificial weighting of some votes etc., are open to similar objections, not only on account of their artificiality but also by reason of the departures they themselves entail from what Lord Radcliffe called "liberal or progressive ideas".

Lord Radcliffe himself, in his Constitutional proposals for Cyprus,[5] wondered whether it would be possible to propose some mitigation of the drawbacks of perpetuating communal separation (which would be enshrined by means of separate electoral rolls) by, perhaps, introducing a system whereby there would be a general roll (on which Turkish Cypriots would be able to register as well as the Greek Cypriots) in addition to a Turkish Communal roll whose main utility would be to absolutely guarantee the Turkish Community an adequate number of seats. Such an arrangement has much to commend it. By designating one of the rolls as general it would be made clear that the State, as a matter of principle, sets it face against segregationist policies, and, by introducing into Cyprus some scheme for a common roll, candidates, conscious of their dependence upon a mixed constituency of voters, would be encouraged not to pursue strictly communal policies but to direct their attention to the wider issues presented. I will not go into the details of such possible electoral arrangements apart from pointing out that such arrangements, however beneficial they may be in the long run, would be bound to be very complicated and involve considerable departure from the principle of simplicity, which is of considerable importance itself in constitutional drafting. In particular, it would have to be decided whether the Turkish Cypriots should be able to register on both rolls, i.e. have their own communal roll by reference to which they would be assured of, for instance, X number of Representatives and, in addition, also be able to register on the general roll. In that case, limitations would obviously have to be established in relation thereto lest a disproportionate number of Turkish candidates is elected to the House of Representatives.

Such electoral schemes, not only go counter to simplicity; they have not really been tried in practice and it is not clear how they would, or whether they could, be operated. Such thoughts led Lord Radcliffe[6] to propose that there should be two different communal rolls and that there should be no possibility of any Turkish Cypriots registering on the general roll. I agree with Lord Radcliffe that "theory is one thing and electoral management another". Much as I would like to see the system of special communal representation disappear, I do not find myself able to recommend any alternative common roll schemes which would be able to satisfy the Turkish Community. We therefore come to the conclusion that it is inevitable that, in as involved a situation as the Cypriot one, Communal representation on the basis of distinct ethnic rolls will have to be retained. A possibility, however, that must not be ignored is that the more cohesive a geographical settlement becomes the less scope there may be for such a system of representation.

(c) *Competence.* Decisions of the House should be taken, generally, by a majority vote, except for those cases where special considerations apply and where, as a result, it is thought that more demanding procedures should be gone through before a given result is achieved. Three different cases are here identified.

First, we have the cases of "the Electoral law and any amendment thereof" and of Regional Government (see below). Since special importance attaches to such arrangements from the Turkish point of view and since the Turkish Community has always considered the Electoral laws and any Regional arrangements to be made as of vital significance for its preservation and well being as a Community, both the electoral set up of Cyprus and its future Regional Institutions (if such are not embedded in the Constitution) should not be capable of amendment or modification by simple majority vote, but a two-thirds majority of Members of the House of Representatives should be required before any such amendment or modification can be effected. Ideally, no distinction in this matter should be drawn between Greek and Turkish Members of the House but it is very likely that the Turkish side will accept nothing short of an effective veto regarding such matters and, very probably, a special majority among the Turkish Members of the House will be absolutely insisted upon as a prerequisite to any change in that direction.

Secondly, all Constitutional clauses should not be capable of amendment otherwise than through some special majority formula. It could be provided, for instance, that the Constitution, being the Supreme law of the land, should be amended only by e.g. a two-thirds majority of the House or some such reinforced majority, or, alternatively, a distinction could be drawn in this area between those parts of the Constitution which refer to the Institutional structures or set up of the Republic and those clauses which embody and are intended to secure Human rights for all the people of Cyprus. It could be provided that Human rights clauses should only be capable of amendment by e.g. a three-quarters majority of the House of Representatives as opposed to e.g. a two-thirds majority demanded in the case of proposed alterations to the institutional structure of the State.

Thirdly, those parts of the Constitution which either expressly or by necessary implication and common knowledge are particularly intended to safeguard the Turkish minority should be in a category by themselves for purposes of amendment, abolition or modification. Such constitutional clauses, for example, would be the ones setting up the Turkish Communal Chambers or a Turkish Branch of the House of Representatives or any other body which would be entrusted with jurisdiction in the area of Turkish Communal rights, and those which confer specific rights on the Turkish community. For the amendment of such constitutional clauses, a special majority should be necessary not only among the Representatives in general but also among the Turkish Members of the House. It seems that only a provision which assures the Turkish Community of an effective veto in connection with such matters will satisfy the Turkish side and, indeed, it is not unreasonable that they be held entitled to such reinforced protection. As a result, a special majority of the House (e.g. a three-quarters majority) should be necessary before any of these constitutional clauses can be changed, and such majority must likewise include a two-thirds majority of the Turkish members.

The administration of justice. It is believed that the organisation of the judiciary is one of the most important issues in the restructuring of the Cyprus Constitution. This is believed to be so for two reasons. (a) I believe that in the context of the need to develop appropriate instruments for the effective protection of human rights in general and minority rights in particular, resort to an independent and impartial tribunal is ultimately the greatest safeguard of civil and other rights. I also consider that an independent and properly constituted tribunal can become the appropriate forum before which intercommunal disputes can be resolved and that if intercommunal disputes can be resolved (or appropriate machinery devised for dealing with such disputes), a large part of the political difficulties of self Government will disappear with them. It is indeed a fallacy to believe that the Court, any Court, can save a people intent on its own self-destruction — "a society so riven that the spirit of moderation is gone, no court can save". But in the context of Cyprus, our choice, so far as the protection of minority rights is concerned, seems to be the following. We either develop cumbrous and complicated structures and mechanisms for such protection, with an accompanying and inelegant panoply of checks and restrictions and special majorities, or we place our emphasis on a forum and our trust in an institution where the passion of partisanship and the influence of communalism have not as yet entered in as distorting a fashion as in the case of the other political and more representative Institutions. A system that depends for its survival on an independent judiciary seems to stand a better chance of success than one whose main pillar of support is distortion of the distribution of political power for the achievement of collateral ends. In the context of Cyprus, I view a fearless and impartial court (coupled with other devices to be dealt with later) as a more effective instrument of protection of minority rights and orderly intercommunal dispute settlement than a representative but, possibly, communalism-infected assembly. It is indeed a grave responsibility for a judicial tribunal to be invested with what are, in effect, political powers. But, after all, such functions have been discharged acceptably by the Courts of "many countries under many systems",[7] and it does not seem inapposite to allot similar responsibility to the judicial power in the proposed Constitutional settlement. (b) Secondly, I believe that there are many able lawyers both among the Greek and among the Turkish Communities and it is obvious that particularly friendly feelings still obtain among lawyers on both sides. Most of the Cypriot lawyers have shared a common legal education and it is believed that in no other profession in Cyprus does such cohesion of professional attitudes and interests exist. Such cohesiveness and such community of ideas must surely be utilised, and they will be utilised (as opposed to suppressed) if intercommunal co-operation is allowed further to develop by not imposing too many restrictions on the discharge of the judicial function. It is, moreover, believed that judges, much more than other public servants or persons, can achieve, by virtue of their position and the circumstances in which they normally exercise their calling, that detachment which is absolutely essential if communalism is to give way before the true unity of the whole people.

The 1960 Constitution separated the Administration of Justice on the basis of communal criteria by providing that in all cases, civil and criminal, a Greek should be tried by a Greek judge, a Turk by a Turkish judge and that cases, however trivial, involving both Greeks and Turks, should be tried by a mixed Court composed of Greek and Turkish judges. This division, as argued above, was not only, in terms of the efficient administration of Justice, completely unnecessary but was also seriously detrimental to the cause of Justice itself. Before the Constitution of 1960 came into force, the Court system had been operating extremely well for many years, Justice being administered in an even handed way and impartially by judges of both Communities on jurisdictional and not communal criteria. It is thought that it is of paramount importance to return to such a system of the administration of Justice. Justice must be one of those politically neutral zones which must not be allowed to be infected by communalism. Any separation in the area of the judiciary tends to develop a conception of the judges as being advocates in the causes of their respective Communities and what is even worse is that the judges themselves will eventually tend to regard themselves as being entrusted, no less than more representative elements, with the protection of the members of their respective Communities. As a result, it is earnestly hoped that the unification and independence of the judiciary will be established and positively secured in the new Constitution of Cyprus.[8]

Another two preliminary observations must be made before we proceed to discuss the organisation and composition of the judiciary. (a) The general point made above about the inadvisability of having too many formal Governmental structures established by the Constitution holds good in the area of the judiciary no less than elsewhere. Not only is the possibility raised of conflicting jurisdictions and consequent friction but another point, to be forever before those entrusted with constitution drafting, is that such structures and institutions depend for their support on the tax payer and it is not consistent either with good government or with progressive policies that the citizen be heavily taxed, particularly if such taxes are channelled into the maintenance of redundant institutional arrangements whereas they could be employed more efficaciously elsewhere. As a result there does not appear to be any justification for the existence of two superior tribunals, as was the case with the 1960 Constitution. (b) Until recently it seems to have been considered essential that the Supreme Judicial Tribunal be presided over by someone from outside Cyprus and that the number of Supreme Court justices from inside Cyprus be equally balanced between Greek and Turkish Cypriots. I think there is very little justification for either of these two positions. To choose someone who by his origin does not belong to either Community is not only in effect to perpetuate communal segregation in an important area of public life and declare one's loss of faith in the possibility of achieving detachment among those exercising the judicial function; it is also to refuse to educate Cypriots, both Greeks and Turks, in the responsibilities of high office and crucial decision making. The main defect of the old Supreme Constitutional Court was that, by virtue of its bizarre composition, such court had in effect become indistinguishable from any other political forum. It is therefore suggested that there should no longer be a foreigner appointed as President of the Court but that the composition of the Court be such that the Court appear to be the embodiment of political and communal neutrality. It is also thought that the Turkish Cypriots should be represented in the judiciary in proportion to their population.

I will now put forward more or less concrete proposals for the organisation, composition and competence of the Judiciary. The judicial organs of the State should be set up by direct constitutional provisions. The establishment of special courts under any name whatsoever should be expressly prohibited otherwise than through constitutional amendment, unless, of course, allowance is made in the Constitution itself for special or specialised Courts. The Judiciary should consist of the Supreme Court, Criminal District Courts, Civil District Courts, and such other subordinate Criminal and Civil Courts, whether of first instance or of appeal, as may be provided by law, such law not being in conflict with any constitutional provision. It has already been mentioned that the Turkish Cypriots should be represented on the judicial bodies of the State proportionately to their population, namely approximately 20%.

The Supreme Court. The Supreme Court should consist of between 6 to 9 judges, and again the Turkish Cypriots should be represented thereon in proportion to their numerical strength.

One of the judges of the Supreme Court should be the President of the Court and it is believed that the senior member of the Court, i.e. the member of the Court who has served thereon the longest, should be the President; likewise, on his retirement, the member of the Court next in line of seniority should become President of the Court.

When we come to the appointment of the judges of the Supreme Court, various modes of appointment come to mind. One can either entrust this function to the executive, or a special body, to be called the Council of Judicature, can be constituted, such body, consisting of public officials and others well placed and properly qualified for the performance of this duty, to be in sole charge of all judicial appointments. Various problems arise whichever procedure is adopted. If one chooses the former way, namely that judges, or at least those of the Supreme Court, should be appointed by the executive, the principal problem is whether all judges should be appointed by the President (who will be a Greek) or by the President and Vice President (who will be a Turk) acting jointly or, perhaps, whether some other combination of these two executive organs would be preferable in this connection — for instance, that Greek judges should be appointed by the President and Turkish judges by the Vice President. If one, however, prefers to remove the appointment of judges from the control of the executive and, as a result, the establishment of a Council of Judicature is contemplated, such Council to be invested with appropriate appointive powers, difficult problems arise as to the composition of such Council, its procedures and the ways whereby appointments will be made to the Council of Judicature itself. It seems to me that the combination of the two principal modes considered above would be most appropriate. Accordingly, it is thought that the appointment of the Supreme Court judges should be in the hands of the President, but that before any such appointment is made the President should consult with the Council of Judicature and only proceed to the appointment he has in mind if the Council of Judicature is of the view that the President's candidate is well qualified. The appointment, to repeat, would be that of the President but, in effect, the Council of Judicature would be able to veto any of the President's candidates on the ground of insufficient judicial qualifications or the presence of some positive disqualification. The President would have to submit to the Council either the name of someone he had decided to appoint to the Supreme Court or, perhaps, be allowed to suggest a panel of persons from amongst whom he would make the eventual appointment; and the Council would either approve of the qualifications of the particular individual proposed or e.g. express no reservations concerning the President's panel or, of course, express an unfavourable opinion. In the case of the Turkish judges of the Supreme Court, it is thought that they should also be appointed by the President of the Republic but that in their case the President should act on the recommendation of the Turkish Vice President. Subject to this qualification, the appointment procedures, i.e. prior consultation with Council of Judicature and requirement of no adverse comment on proposed judges by the Council, should also be applicable in the case of the Turkish members of the Supreme Court.

Other Courts — Council of Judicature. It is believed that all other judicial appointments (i.e. appointments to the District Criminal and Civil Courts and to any other judicial organs to be established under the Constitution) should be within the competence of the Council of Judicature. Not only judicial appointments but also termination of appointments, promotions, transfer of judges, disciplinary and all other such matters should be within such competence. What should the composition of such Council of Judicature be? Such body, it is believed, should consist of the President and two members of the Supreme Court (one of these three Judges being Turkish), the Attorney-General of the Republic, the Deputy Attorney-General of the Republic (these two officers not belonging to the same community), the Chairman of the Bar Council, two lawyers of at least 15 years' standing at the Bar, such lawyers to be chosen by the Supreme Court or, alternatively, proposed by the Bar Council and approved by the Supreme Court (one of these three lawyers to be a Turk), and three retired judges of the Supreme Court, one of whom, again, should be a Turk. Such people should be appointed by the President and the Vice President acting jointly.

Concerning the other courts to be established, no detailed scheme can be here proposed. Only a few general suggestions can be put forward. There should be two kinds of first instance courts, District Civil Courts and District Criminal Courts. Appeals from such courts will lie to the Supreme Court. Such first instance Civil and Criminal Courts will be local courts, and should, very roughly, be composed as follows. In the case of important civil matters or, where, for instance, the sum in issue is over a stated amount or where another such criterion is satisfied, there should be a court consisting of three members, such judges being district judges, appointed, as above, by the Council of Judicature. In those cases where either the amount in issue is below the sum stated in the court regulations to be enacted or where some other such criterion is not satisfied, such civil matters will be disposed of by a single district judge. Similarly with Criminal District Courts; in the case of minor criminal offences (i.e. breaches of bye-laws, traffic offences or other relatively minor offences which, for instance, do not involve imprisonment beyond a certain period) there will be a single judge, such judge being judge of both fact and law. In important criminal matters, however (such importance, clearly, to be measured by reference to the maximum sanctions to be incurred by the accused in case of conviction), there should be three judges, such judges being, again, district judges, appointed by the Council of Judicature. Appeals from both criminal and civil courts should lie to the Supreme Court in its appellate capacity. Appeals to the Supreme Court on civil and criminal matters should be heard by appellate panels of the Supreme Court, each panel consisting of three Supreme Court justices. Obviously, before an appeal can be heard, the various regulations of the Supreme Court (to be drafted by the Supreme Court itself) concerning appeals should be complied with. For this purpose, it may be helpful to introduce an Appeals Committee, consisting either of a number of Supreme Court justices sitting alone or of Supreme Court justices and a number of District Court judges sitting together. Such Appeals Committee will not only be in charge of any necessary drafting of regulations concerning appeals but would also be vested with the exercise of any discretion in this matter i.e. which cases were sufficiently complex or involved or important to justify an appeal even though the necessary formalities of the appeals procedure had not been complied with, etc. I am also attracted by the idea of the Appeals Committee recommending that in some cases which have come before them, the point raised was of such fundamental importance for the development of the law that the appeal should be heard by the whole Supreme Court sitting as a body.

Jurisdiction. It was suggested above (a) that the High Court and the Supreme Constitutional Court existing under the 1960 Constitution should be amalgamated and (b) that their jurisdictions should be vested in the Supreme Court. The Supreme Court will also have any other jurisdiction or powers as may be conferred upon it by the Constitution. It is particularly believed that the Supreme Court should be vested with administrative jurisdiction, primarily for the purpose of dealing with cases involving administrative matters and other such matters as may arise as a result of my proposals on regionalism in a later chapter. Briefly, it is there suggested that adequate local autonomy should be recognised and that measures should be enacted which will set up local administrative units. These proposals, which aim at the creation of a system of local Government not inconsistent with the maintenance of a unitary state, are far removed from any proposals which would aim at the creation of a state within a state, based on the full existence and autonomous functioning, within geographical areas, of all three powers of Government. Since, however, the local authorities which are suggested below will have delegated quasi-legislative powers to issue regulations, bye-laws, ordinances and other such orders relating to those matters which have been placed within their competence, judicial organs should exist for the purpose of adjudging such disputes and deciding cases arising in connection therewith. I believe it will be a major error to create special courts to deal with such cases and simultaneously provide that such courts will not be subject to the judicial machinery and procedures outlined above and/or that the power of appointment to such courts will be in the hands not of the Council of Judicature but in those of the respective local authorities. If we do create such courts to deal with Greek and Turkish local Government cases respectively and subordinate such judicial organs to the Regional or Local Authorities without integrating them with the State system of courts, a major step towards the separation of the two Communities at the crucial local governmental level will have been taken. I would suggest myself that cases involving alleged breaches of such local governmental regulations, bye laws, ordinances, etc, should be tried, in the first instance, by magistrates sitting either singly or, preferably, in small panels or groups of three or four, that such magistrates should be laymen of some education, good character, etc., and that such magistrates should be appointed not by the Local Authorities themselves but, like district judges, by the Council of Judicature. Moreover, appeals from such minor local governmental cases should lie to the Supreme Court sitting in an administrative capacity, the precise details concerning appeal procedures in this connection and the composition of both the local Magistrates' courts and the Supreme Court sitting in an administrative capacity to be dealt with by a specialist subcommittee to be appointed for this purpose. What should be made clear, however, is that such local courts, and all arrangements relating thereto, are an integral part of the State judiciary — not a separate system of courts organised along communal criteria and operating independently of State control.

It should also be made clear that the Supreme Court, in its administrative capacity, retains a general administrative jurisdiction, adjudicating finally in connection with complaints that acts or omissions of any organ, authority or person exercising any executive or administrative authority are contrary to the Constitution or any law regulating the exercise of executive power. Such complaints, of course, would have to be made by a person with appropriate locus standi, namely a legitimate and recognised interest, which, allegedly, has been adversely affected by the abuse or excess of power on the part of the State organ or authority involved.

The Supreme Court should also retain its power to pronounce on the constitutionality of legislation, whether such legislation emanates from the House of Representatives or the Communal Assemblies, whether such Assemblies are the old Communal Chambers or new bodies to be established by the Constitution. Again, such determination of constitutionality should be made either on a recourse by the President or Vice President of the Republic or by virtue of an appropriate reference made to the Supreme Court either by some other Governmental organ (including a lower Court before which the question of constitutionality was first raised) or by an individual with the required locus standi.

The Supreme Court, as already stated above, should, in addition to its constitutional and administrative powers, have the original, revisional and appellate jurisdiction vested in the High Court of Justice, and it should be further provided that any original, revisional or appellate jurisdiction of the Supreme Court should be exercised by such judge or judges as the Supreme Court itself shall determine, the various Rules of Court and other such special regulations being complied with. For instance, it could be provided that any appellate jurisdiction shall be exercised by at least three judges and that this number may be increased to five if the Appeals Committee of the Supreme Court is of the opinion that the case presents special difficulty and/or importance. It is believed that the jurisdiction of the Court on any constitutional matter should be exercised by the full Court. Should there be special provisions with regard to cases involving a Turkish element? The present writer would be inclined against such arrangements but some special provision safeguarding Turkish interests may be strongly insisted upon. It could, for instance, be provided that, at least for an experimental period of one year, in all constitutional cases involving a Turkish element where there has not been a unanimous decision, a further appeal can be had to the Privy Council. Or, alternatively, unanimity should be insisted upon in such cases, even though this may make for unseemly judical compromises and too restrictive a judicial attitude. The first course, i.e. appeal to the Privy Council, is to be preferred.

It is not thought that any provision such as article 159 should ever again find its way into the Constitutional Charter of a free people. Reasons have already been given why it is strongly believed that the introduction of any such provision could cause, in the long run, incalculable mischief both as regards the administration of Justice and as concerns efforts to bring the people of Cyprus together. It will be remembered that in effect the 1960 Constitution gave both Turkish and Greek Cypriots the constitutional right to have their case tried by a judge of their own Community, special provisions having to be made for mixed cases, i.e. cases with an intercommunal element. It is here suggested that the administration of Justice should be unified and that the judge who has jurisdiction should try the case or adjudicate on a claim, irrespective of the community to which the accused, litigant or litigants belong. This can be the only solution concerning the functioning of the Courts, and all other proposals which would result in disunity and separation at the judicial level should be stongly resisted; for instance, a compromise solution would be to make Art. 159 of the Constitution optional, in the sense that the judge who has jurisdiction should try the case unless objection is taken to his doing so by one or both of the litigants if such litigant or litigants belong to another Community and want their case adjudicated upon by a judge of the same communal origin. But such proposals would not, it is believed, solve the problem. Not only would such procedure be potentially embarrassing to the judge, counsel and litigants involved; what is more, the possibility cannot be discounted of litigants, at the early stages, being reluctant to be tried, or have their cases dealt with, by judges belonging to the other community, such reluctance being the result, not of justifiable doubt about the competence or impartiality of the members of the Cyprus Judiciary, but of misplaced suspicion and ill-conceived communal predjudice. Another compromise solution would be to retain Art. 159, or Art. 159 in its optional shape, for important cases, whereas for all other cases jurisdictional, and not communal, criteria would be determinative of who would try the case. This again is unsatisfactory. If we do want to build an integrated Cyprus, based on the principle of the harmonious and balanced partnership of the two Communities, we must not force upon the Cyprus people such provisions as Art. 159 which only engender communal acrimony. I would accept, however, that some (but not many) cases could present problems because of possible language difficulties. A Turk, for instance, is accused of a criminal act and he can only speak and understand Turkish. In such cases, the Supreme Court or a Committee of the Court should be vested with a discretion for the purpose of giving appropriate directions for the trial of such cases; or, alternatively, there would be a limit to the jurisdictional principle stated above, namely that the judge who has jurisdiction should try the case subject to limits intended to deal with any language problems and other practical difficulties which can occasionally arise. The ability of the accused to follow the proceedings should be the guiding criterion and in any cases of difficulty the Supreme Court should have power, on the application of any such party to civil or criminal proceedings, to give such directions as to the composition of the trial court and other such matters as justice may require.

The Executive. The Presidential regime should be retained. There should be a Greek Cypriot as President and a Turkish Cypriot as Vice President, the President and the Vice President to be elected by the two Communities respectively. It must be made clear that, ideally, it would have been preferable if such elections would not have to take place on the basis of separate electoral rolls — such ideal solution, however, is clearly unacceptable to the Turkish Community. As a result, the 1960 Constitutional set up in so far as it relates to the establishment of the Presidency and the Vice Presidency, such offices to "belong" to the Greek and Turkish Communities respectively, must be retained. But, as will soon become apparent, the substance of the 1960 Constitutional provisions relating to the Executive will have to be substantially modified. It should, of course, be provided that the President of the Republic will be the Head of State, and that the Vice President will be Vice Head of State, and it should no longer be the case that the Vice President does not deputise for the President in the event of the latter's absence or incapacity to act but that the President of the House does so instead. This provision produces a situation whereby, in the absence of the President, the Vice President is overlooked and the President of the House of Representatives steps above him and, inescapably, creates the impression that a person belonging to the Turkish Community and elected by it cannot deputise in a post the occupant of which bears responsibility to Cyprus as a whole. It is one of those separatist provisions which should be abolished.

The right of veto of the President and the Vice President of the Republic, it is strongly believed, must be abolished. The veto right must be distinguished from other provisions conferring the right to challenge laws before the Supreme Court and thus either delay their eventual promulgation and enactment or defeat them altogether. The Vice President, under the proposed Constitutional arrangements, should retain the right and duty to challenge before the Supreme Court any law or decision of the House of Representatives or the Budget on the ground that such law or decision etc., discriminates against the Turkish Community or encroaches upon the powers and area of competence entrusted to the Turkish Communal Chamber or other appropriate Turkish Communal or Administrative organs to be recognised under the Constitution. But rights of final veto — these rights being fundamentally different from other measures ensuring that laws and decisions on specific topics can be returned for reconsideration, such measures to be likewise retained in the proposed Constitution — are nothing but obstructive devices and can easily develop into vehicles of communal prejudice. It is not thought that they serve a useful purpose, either in terms of protecting the Turkish Community or in terms of bringing about some appropriate balance between the Executive and Legislative powers.

Further, the Turkish Vice President, in addition to his powers of referring laws and decisions of the House of Representatives to the Supreme Court and returning specific laws to the House for reconsideration, should be empowered (a) to promulgate all laws and decisions of the Turkish Communal Chamber or other appropriate Communal Legislative organ, (b) to nominate the Turkish Members of the Council of Ministers, the President being bound to act on such a recommendation and (c) to recommend Turkish Cypriots to the President for appointment to the Supreme Court and to other independent positions of authority — such positions having been allocated by the Constitution to the Turkish Community and the President, again, being bound to act upon such nomination. Of course, the Turkish Vice President should also be vested with all the appropriate ceremonial powers, such as having the right to attend all official functions, presentations of credentials, etc.

Executive power should, in the main, be exercised by the Council of Ministers, Turkish participation both in the Council and throughout the Executive being fixed at 20%, in proportion, that is, to their population. Decisions of the Council should be reached by majority and it may be that, at least for a transitional period, the Turkish Vice President should even be given direct power of suspending for a limited time the coming into operation of specific types of decisions. As indicated above, all Ministers, whose number should be designated by law, should be appointed by the President of the Republic who should also be the one to promulgate all laws of the House of Representatives and sign all instruments of important appointments. It may also be necessary to provide that one of the major ministries such as the Ministry of Finance or Foreign Affairs should always be vested in a member of the Turkish Community.

The Police. The organisation and composition of the Police present special problems. Not only are the Police the body primarily entrusted with the powers of law enforcement and keeping the peace but, ultimately, the protection of the Turkish Community, like that of all minorities, may depend on the appropriate structuring of the Police Forces, their effectiveness and their impartial enforcement of the laws. It is proposed that there should be a unitary Police force in which the Turkish Cypriots will be represented in proportion to their population. In particular, it is thought that the 1960 constitutional division of the Security Forces into Police and Gendarmerie should be abolished. The amalgamation of the two forces will cut down unecessary expenditure resulting from the duplication of separate commands with separate Headquarters etc., and will almost certainly improve the efficiency of the Security Forces.

The Commander and Deputy Commander of the Police should not belong to the same Community; further, such officers should be appointed by the President of the Republic, but in the case of the Turkish Cypriot to be appointed to one of these positions the recommendation of the Vice President should be acted upon. There should also be a Police Commission, consisting, inter alia, of the Commander and the Deputy Commander of the Police, two or three retired judges or persons with legal experience, and other persons considered appropriate for the discharge of the functions to be entrusted to such Police Commission which, among others, should include enlistment, promotions, transfers, dismissals etc.

It has been said above that the unification of the Police Force is essential. This, of course, is not inconsistent with the adoption of arrangements whereby police forces to be stationed in parts of the territory of the Republic inhabited in a proportion approaching one hundred per centum only by members of one Community will belong to that Community. Similarly, and as an extension of this, it can be provided that, generally, the police forces to be stationed in parts of the Republic inhabited by a mixed population of Greek and Turkish Cypriots will consist of Greek and Turkish members of the police force in proportion, wherever possible, to the population percentage of the relevant area.

It is suggested elsewhere that adequate local Government be recognised and established in Cyprus and tentative proposals are put forward in a later chapter regarding such local Governmental organisation, namely the demarcation of areas or localities within which local Governmental powers will be exercisable, the definition and setting up of local governmental units to be vested with such powers, and the establishment of methods of Central control and supervision of such local Governmental activities etc. Of course, the most important feature of such arrangements will be the fixing of local areas, in some of which the Turkish Community will enjoy the status of the majority community and it is almost inevitable that the Turkish side will demand that the local authorities should have the right and power to set up their own police organisations for keeping the peace and discharging those of the local governmental functions which can be characterised as police or security ones. Prima facie, such demands sound unreasonable on account of their manifest tendency to introduce disunity and complications in the organisation of the Police Forces of the Republic, and particularly is this so if quasi independent or wholly independent local police organisations are contemplated, such forces not to be integrated within the State security forces and to be subordinate not to the State but to the local authorities involved. Furthermore, if such demands result in the establishment of three separate police forces, the central one and two regional police authorities, such regional police authorities to be in absolute control of their respective Communities, not only will great fragmentation of authority result with consequent detrimental consequences upon the efficient discharge of police functions in general, but the stage may well have been set for future confrontation between such forces.

As a result of such patent disadvantages, such Turkish demands can only be accepted if the proposed local police forces perform indispensable services, either in the context of the provision of needed security for the Turkish minority or in terms of the discharge of essential functions not otherwise available. As regards the provision of security or, rather, the satisfaction of the Turkish Community's sense of security, it is not thought that special Communal police forces to be stationed locally are essential. The sense of security of the Turkish Community, it is thought, is amply satisfied, inter alia, by arrangements whereby in areas inhabited almost exclusively by Turkish Cypriots, the police will consist exclusively of Turkish Cypriots and in areas inhabited by a majority of Turkish Cypriots the majority of the police force to be stationed there will also be Turkish. Briefly, the applicable principle, namely that the composition of the police force should reflect population patterns, is precisely calculated to satisfy both Communities' sense of security. Hence, no separate police forces at the local level are called for by reference to security. What about the functions to be discharged by such proposed local organs and can such functions only be discharged or provided for in the context of the implementation of the Turkish demand? It may be that the local authorities should be able to have, among their employees, special inspectors, wardens etc, such officials to be entrusted with the enforcement of those bye-laws, regulations and ordinances made by the regional authorities within their areas of competence. It is thought that such officials should be civilian employees of the local authorities, distinct from the police. If, however, it is thought essential to entrust police or quasi-police functions to such local authorities, I can see no contradiction in assigning the performance of such functions to the police authorities of the State, the police, for such purposes, to receive instructions from the local authorities concerned. Alternatively, it may be apposite to provide, particularly if the employees now being considered are given true police functions, that such inspectors, wardens etc, will be part of the State police, forming, for example, a specialised Department.

The Public Service. Much has already been said with regard to this problem. Both Communities must participate in the Civil Service, but the proportion of Communal participation must be in accordance to the true ratio of the population of Greek and Turkish Cypriots. Great care should be taken so that all discrimination in appointments, promotions etc. can be eliminated, adequate remedies, of course, being provided by the Constitution. Equal protection of the laws must become a reality, and to achieve this the most vigorous safeguards against discrimination must be enacted. Perhaps a specialised agency entrusted with ensuring fair employment practices etc could be constituted and such agency, it is believed, would be greatly strengthened by UN participation, at least for a transitional period. The operation of the Public Service Commission must likewise be made more rational. Decisions at such Commission must be taken by simple majority.

The above proposals have been put forward very tentatively. They are basically predicated upon the maintenance of a unitary or at least united State. As I make clear later, however, the stronger the regional elements to be introduced (and the Turks insist on such arrangements) the less important the Central Government could become. But whatever the precise structuring of the State or the regional arrangements arrived at, a Central government there is bound to be since all the parties have expressed adherence to the principles of an Independent and Sovereign State; therefore, the composition and method of constitution of such Central Government are (and will always be) important issues.

Finally, two points, which, really, underlie all my proposals, should be made once more. Unification of authority should, wherever possible, be aimed for. And reasonable specificity and clarity in formulation should be combined with the necessary flexibility and room for compromise. All possible measures to ensure the protection of the Turkish minority should, of course, be taken and all institutional safeguards and devices should be employed for this purpose. But the constitution makers must never again disregard the equally imperative need to ensure the viability of the State or the proper functioning of Government. Nor should they forget Salmond's warning that a Constitution that will not bend will sooner or later break.

VII

REGIONALISM[1]

C YPRUS is small and unification of authority may be thought to afford the best chance of rapid economic growth and political and social integration. Under normal circumstances perhaps no special provision for local government or devolution of authority need have been contemplated, but Cyprus, as has been regretfully acknowledged above, both by virtue of the internationalisation of the problem and the serious tensions bearing on the total situation, is not any case. Special arrangements savouring of a geographical element are strongly insisted upon, and if there is to be any possibility of a settlement, one must recognise that the strongly expressed wishes of the Turkish minority in this regard cannot be ignored. But even to contemplate a biregional geographical federation, especially in the Turkish sense — I have made clear above — is to court disaster. Yet, some kind of geographically defined solution is inevitable. Such are the reasons that prompt the following suggestions.

The basic problem of Cyprus, it is respectfully suggested, must be seen and presented as a problem of Local Government, as a problem of Regionalism — not as a question of Federation. Federation, as I make clear in the Chapter on "Cyprus and Political Federation", normally refers to two or more Independent States coming together in a new form of Political Association, shedding in the process some of their powers whilst, at the same time, retaining others. Such a way of formulating the problem is particularly favoured by the Turks who have maintained that the Cypriot State no longer exists and that the Constitution of 1960 no longer retains any validity; such a thesis implies that there are already two effectively functioning states within the territory of Cyprus, and that such states should enter into a new form of political partnership. We must resolutely set our face against such a formulation. The State of Cyprus exists and nothing has happened which has deprived the 1960 Constitution of its validity. At the same time we must express our readiness to introduce the principles of Regionalism, or Local government, according, in this way, generous Local government to the areas or regions to be established.[2] Federalism, as it were, looks at the problem from above, Regionalism from below. Federalism demands that political power be divided between the Federal State and its component parts so that the general and regional governments are each, within their appropriate spheres, coordinate and independent. Regionalism, on the other hand, usually presupposes the Unity of the State but brings about administrative decentralization by giving adequate powers to territories, areas or regions within the state.[3] Where there exists administrative decentralization in the form of regionalism, however extensive such decentralization may be — provided, of course, that the Central authority retains ultimate control — then the unitary character of the State is not affected. It is obvious, of course, that, in substance, the line dividing regionalism and geographical federalism can be blurred and, often, evanescent; and that, often, extreme administrative decentralization, owing to the thin line dividing administrative from political power, can result in "localised federation", differing in name only from explicit recognition of the establishment of a federal geographical regime.[4] Such results must be avoided if we want to preserve an independent and unitary State — and, in this chapter, concrete proposals are put forward indicating how Regional or local government can be recognised without the unity of the state being thereby endangered. Zürich, it will be remembered, made the mistake of introducing, and embodying, many separatist and divisive elements at the top (i.e. the Central governmental structure). We must now be on the alert lest we introduce a separatist and segregationist policy in the realm of local government. If we fail in this regard, the resulting failure will be both more resounding and more catastrophic than Zürich.

Italy is referred to as a useful example of Regionalism, particularly as regards the methods and the philosophy of Central control. Art. 114 of the Italian Constitution establishes regions and guarantees their existence; the regions, however, are subject to the law of the State. Art. 117 allows the Regions to legislate with regard to a list of matters that follows but goes on to provide that such legislation must not conflict with the interests of the Nation or of the other Regions. It must also be pointed out that the "legislation" of the Regions amounts really to the issuing of regulations in the form of subsidiary legislation rather than being equivalent to the laws passed by the Legislature of the State. There also exists a Commissioner of Central Government (Art. 124) who exercises certain powers of supervision with regard to the Regions; and the Regions (by Art. 127) are subjected to the Constitutional Court. Specifically, the Government of the Republic is empowered by Art. 127, "when it considers that a law approved by the Regional Council exceeds the competence of the Region or conflicts with the interests of the Nation or with those of other Regions", to return such a law to the Regional Council. When, and if, the Regional Council approves it again by an absolute majority, the Government of the Republic may, within 15 days of communication of the fact, submit the question of its legitimacy to the Constitutional Court.[5]

The application of Regionalism or Local government in Cyprus should be seen as dividing itself into three distinct issues: (a) The status of the autonomous Turkish or other administration zones (or regions) together with a rough fixing of such areas, such rough fixing to be distinguished from an exact demarcation; (b) the functions, powers and set-up of such Units; and (c) Integration of such Units within the State.

But first, and before we examine what arrangements can be arrived at in this connexion without compromising our stand on a unitary and integral state, it is proposed to inquire briefly into the subject of Regionalism or Local Administration.

Such examination will be divided into three parts.
  (A) Basic Philosophy of Local Government and Decentralization of Authority.[6]
  (B) Normally accepted functions of Local Government.[7]
  (C) Methods of Control of Local Government.[8]

(A) Local Government may have a wide variety of meanings. It is, however, part of the "government" of a country, part of its governmental or constitutional structure. Since it is "local" it must, generally, relate to specific areas or regions of the country defined by locality. "The Institutions of local government are thus governmental organs having jurisdiction not over the whole of a country but over specific portions of it".[9] Local government must be primarily thought of as a system whereby local services are provided; but it must also be noted that local authorities are, generally, not merely executive or administrative agencies — in addition, "they exist not only to carry out duties but also to express opinions".[10] This representative function can take a variety of forms; local authorities, for instance, can urge other public bodies to carry out policies which will be of local advantage; another aspect of this representational activity is for one local authority to ask another, usually a larger one, to do something.

One of the assumptions on which systems of local government are based is that within the limits of the law, and in so far as the carrying on of their functions is concerned, local government authorities are independent. Such independence, which, moreover, is accompanied by a presumption that, within the powers which have been delegated to it, local services should be freely administered by the relevant local authority, is normally attested in various ways. Local authorities are, in general, independent of other local authorities. Secondly, local administrative councils are independent as to their composition. The Law, that is, usually lays down a code of procedure for election; it prescribes the qualifications and disqualifications for local office etc., but the councils themselves are freely elected. Thirdly, local or regional councils are normally independent as to their domestic procedures. The way, that is, in which local authorities go through their business is their own affair. Lastly, local authorities, particularly in England, are independent as units of administration.[11] They do not, as a rule, administer those services that have been given to them as the local agents of a central ministry; they administer them in their own right, as independent units of administration.

The other assumption on which systems of local government are usually based is that local government is predicated upon the distinction between political government and administration — that state affairs and political matters are reserved for the Central authorities of the State, whereas local problems and the dispensation of services are the legitimate preserve of local government. In defining local affairs, criteria such as the efficiency, the cost, the economy of operation, the uniformity of standards, the need for comprehensive planning, the local knowledge or interest, the tradition, the proper use of resources as well as the size and the inter-relationship of the problems to be tackled, should be taken into account. The problem of local government, it must be finally concluded, must not be made into a political one. Many mistakes could result from an artificial politicization of the problem — the various issues should be treated as technical and legal ones.

(B) The main services provided by local authorities can be roughly classified as follows: (a) Protection, (b) Welfare, (c) Public

Health, Roads, Housing, Planning, (d) Convenience, (e) Education etc. Generally, such services are concerned directly with the welfare of man or concern for his environment. A rough list of functions that could be delegated to regional authorities in a place like Cyprus can be said to include the following (a more detailed account is given later): (a) Public Health, sanitary services; (b) Animals; (c) Some limited powers over agriculture; (d) Streets and Public thoroughfares; (e) Markets, Fairs etc.; (f) Buildings, Land and Property; (g) Welfare services; (h) Administrative structure of such regional authorities.

(C) One of the most important aspects of local government is the way in which such government is integrated within the general Administration of the State. It is not only that modern day trends in political thought are favourable to broader avenues for state activity, or that some element of central supervision of local administration there must be if one wants to ensure that such administration will remain adequate and competent. It is inevitable that local government, in common with all systems of local administration, must be controlled by Central Authority "if equitable and just principles are to be maintained."[12] For, important as it is that adequate powers should be transferred if local government is to develop a life independent of duties which it performs as a virtual agency of the central government, "the process is surrounded by dangers":[13] on the financial side that the transferred services will languish for want of adequate resources, on the administrative side that standards will sag below tolerable levels, and on the political side that greater local powers will lead to political disintegration. It is, consequently, essential that state supervision should be retained so that both coordination of local and state activities and integration of Local Government within the State can be achieved. In England, for instance, control over local authorities is carried on by Parliament, Government and Administrative Departments, and the Courts. This fits the traditional tripartite division of political institutions into the Legislature, the Executive and the Judiciary, and even though this threefold distinction suffers from various analytical defects, it not only facilitates description but also serves to show how pervasive central control over local authorities normally is.

When we now turn to the problems presented by the establishment of local or regional government in Cyprus,[14] the following points must be borne in mind:

1. Such a legal basis for local government should be agreed

upon as not to deviate from the unity and territorial integrity of the State.

2. Such structures, or units, of local government should be set up as will take into account the realities of the island (e.g. the intermingling of Turks and Greeks throughout Cyprus, existence of many mixed villages etc.), the need to establish viable and efficient Regional government, and the imperative necessity of maintaining a unified State.

3. Such degree of State supervision should be exercised as will ensure the effective functioning of such local authorities without endangering the preservation of the State. Effective controls should exist.

These three points will be discussed in turn.

1. In discussing the possible philosophies of Local Government is Cyprus, Local Government, as above, must be emphatically predicated upon the distinction between political government and local administration — this distinction should be drawn advisedly in order to make it clear to the Turkish side that the government is not prepared to accept under the guise of local government or regional administration a rigid federal system. The main characteristics of such a federal system can be said to be the following: (a) a geographical area in which each state or district of the federation exercises its jurisdiction; (b) each state or district of the federation has its own government or authority undertaking or performing all three functions of government, i.e. executive, legislative and judicial; (c) each district or canton has its own police force and is responsible for policing its area.

Such a geographical system must not be accepted, as such acceptance (a) will result in a "state structure" which would compete with, and usually nullify, the Central State authority within the area of local autonomy and (b) will not ensure, due to the conditions of Cyprus, the economic viability of the areas to be created or their effective administration. Local government arrangements must be such as will conform to generally accepted rules and principles concerning such authorities and as will take into account the conditions of Cyprus. The Local Government authorities to be set up must be seen to possess delegated powers, such powers having been vested originally in the Central Government but having since been delegated to local administrative units for exercise in specified areas. "Local Government", that is, is and should be seen as an organizational arrangement concerning the application of a unified State authority, whereas a canton or wholly autonomous system of local administration, even if not exercising wholly original and uncontrolled powers, cannot but result in the destruction of the unity of the State.

2. This issue is seen to subdivide itself into (a) the appropriate units which will be recognised as local governmental units and the way they will correlate and (b) the localities, areas or regions wherein local administrative powers will be exercised.

(a) It seems inevitable that in Cyprus the first tier of local government should consist of the villages and municipalities. The second tier of local government should consist of the administrative regions, areas or localities. Each district (Cyprus being divided into six districts) could be divided into a number of administrative regions, the regions themselves to be demarcated in a number of possible ways (see below). The third tier of local goverment would be the Central Local Authorities (see below for more specific proposals) in combination with Central State organs, e.g. the District officer, a Commissioner of Local Government etc.

(b) Since the purpose of Local Government is the decentralisation of authority, efficiency and viable government cannot be lost sight of when considering what kind of locality to establish as the basic area or region of local administration. Some general considerations must be borne in mind. The demarcation of the relevant areas should not lose sight of topographical considerations and the similarity of the administrative, economic and social problems of the inhabitants of given regions. Moreover, the creation of the relevant administrative areas should not become a source of friction and conflict over jurisdiction and should not cause unnecessary and wasteful duplication of services. Finally, the establishment of local authority units should not result in hampering the free movement or settlement of the citizens of the Republic of Cyprus in any part of the Island. Basically, the envisaged scheme of local administration, while retaining each village as the basic unit of local administration, also accepts the principle that a number of villages, in geographical proximity to each other or for other reasons, can be grouped together for the purpose of forming cohesive areas of local administration. Below, three possible ways of such demarcation are put forward:

    (a) the grouping is effected on topographical and economic criteria;

(b) the grouping is based on communal criteria;

(c) areas, including both Greek and Turkish villages and their adjoining lands, are demarcated (this is a modified form of (a)).

3. Central control is, perhaps, the most important issue in connection with the proposed establishment of local government in Cyprus. More is said on this below. But, unless, central control is established (a) three separate governments in Cyprus would be created (i.e. the Central one, and the two Independent Local Administrations); (b) the system would prove unworkable, cumbersome and would inevitably lead to friction between the two Communities; (c) it would create three civil services and general triplication of all services, absorbing in effect the limited financial resources of the Republic; (d) effective planning for the whole of the Island would become impossible; and (e) partition would inevitably result.

It is agreed, of course, that e.g. the Turkish Local and Communal Authority should have, in the first instance, and within the limits of the law, power in the matter of Local Government. But such Local Authority should only be able to issue subsidiary legislation in the form of regulations, byelaws etc., and, of course, only in those matters that have been specifically assigned to it (see below) and should be subject to adequate supervision by the Government. (The controls should be executive e.g. through the District and other Commissioners; Legislative — here a special majority of the Turkish members of the House of Representatives should be required before the Local Government Law, which may well be embedded in the Constitution, can be changed; and Judicial, i.e. through the Supreme Court before which actions and regulations of the Local Authorities of debatable legality can be challenged).[15]

I now proceed to set out three distinct proposals for the organisation of Local and Regional Authorities in Cyprus:

A. The basic position of the Greek Cypriot side regarding the solution of the Cyprus problem is well known. It insists on the principles of a unitary and integral state and makes provision for limited communal autonomy and local government within institutional arrangements securing both the unity of the state and the security of the two Communities. Any geographical element is completely absent from the said position and there is only recognition that villages and municipalities, the basic units of local government, may be grouped together on topographical considerations and in the interest of increased effectiveness and enhanced viability. The relevant "local government" clause in any Declaration embodying the above mentioned position would go as follows: "the administrative region shall constitute the second tier of local government. Such regions shall consist of villages which, owing to topographical considerations and their general interests, may form an economically viable unit of local administration. Such regions will be under the supervision of the district officer and other central authorities".

B. In this, the first modification of the basic Greek Cypriot position, the concessions of the Greek Cypriot side would relate to the idea of grouping. We would recognise that Turkish villages and municipalities may be grouped together for the purpose of forming an administrative region or area, the Greek villages being excluded from such arrangement. Such communal grouping would be made by the Central Communal Authorities. An explicit formulation of this position would be the following: "for facilitating the smooth and economic running of local government, and with a view to making them into viable units able to carry on their constitutional functions and responsibilities, villages and municipalities may be grouped together. Greek and Turkish villages, however, shall not be grouped together unless such villages, by way of referendum, agree to be so grouped. There shall be two appropriate Central authorities in Cyprus in charge of local government, one for the Turkish villages and their areas and one for the Greek villages and their areas. The appropriate Central Communal Authorities shall perform the functions set out in Schedule X as incorporated in the Constitution. Adequate Central supervision will be exercised as follows . . .".

According to such formulation, there would be a number of local administration units scattered all over Cyprus. For instance, one such unit could consist of the Turkish municipality of Kyrenia, the Turkish municipality of Nicosia and the Turkish villages of Mandres, Geune Yli, Orta Keuy, Aghirda, Keumurju, Krini, Photta, Pileri, Kanli, the Turkish parts of Kazaphani and Lapithos and the Turkish part of Klepini. Other such units would be established in other parts of the Island, such grouping being entrusted to a Central Communal or Local Administration Authority (e.g. The Turkish members of the House of Representatives sitting separately). Such villages, or their village Boards, would be the first tier of Local Government, the Regional Council (in common with all other such Regional Councils) the second one and the Central Communal or Local Administration Authority the third one. Such bodies would function within a unitary and integral state. It could be said consistently with such analysis that the area sketched out above (i.e. the Kyrenia, Aghirda, Geun Yeli area) is "an administrative region", and, if so desired, a line may be drawn to indicate such administrative boundary, the Greek villages, falling within the line, being excluded from such arrangements.

An alternative formulation would be that the Turkish zone or region is a notional one, consisting of the various Turkish administrative areas or units around the island which, in their turn, include the purely Turkish villages.

As in Italy, care should be taken to ensure that any regulation-issuing activity is called subsidiary legislation or the issuing of regulations; and there should be explicit provision in the Constitution regarding conflicts between the Legislation of the State and the regulations or enactments of the Regions. The various devices for controlling Regional authorities will not be here analysed in any great detail, but they should, of course, be resorted to. And any executive power residing in the authorities of the said Regions should be recognised as power which has been delegated to such authorities by the Central government for the more effective administration of the Republic, not as an independent governmental or political power.

The financial resources of Local and Regional Government, according to such a Plan, could be provided by: (a) fees for the issuing of licences; (b) local forms of taxation such as local rates and the like; (c) possibly, Government grants; (d) fines, etc.

C. In the following, the system of local autonomy[16] is organised along different lines — whereas plan A refers to groupings of villages on geographical considerations and Plan B speaks of groupings of Turkish villages on ethnic or communal considerations, the present plan puts forwards the idea of the demarcation of administrative regions consisting of Greek and Turkish villages and the immediately adjoining area which the villages need for farming, grazing etc. If such an administrative region were demarcated, then, again, there would be a regional or local Government council consisting of both Greeks and Turks in proportion to their numerical strength in the relevant region or area. Each District, perhaps, would be subdivided into a number of such regions or areas of local administration, and there should, as indicated above, be appropriate arrangements for the supervision of the activities of the various Regional Boards so that both their increased effectiveness and the necessary coordination with Central and other Local authorities can be ensured.

Were any such plan to be eventually adopted and were our terminology and other points to be accepted, the total picture would be as follows:

1. The unity and integrity of the State would still be recognised.

2. A number of semi-autonomous administrative regions would be recognised. Such areas would be recognised as areas of local administration.

3. The first tier of local Government as regards these areas will be the villages and municipalities falling within them. The second tier will consist of the regional or area councils, there being one Council for each area or region. The third tier will be the appropriate Central Local and Communal Authorities or some combination of such Central Communal Authority and Central State Control. Another idea that could be tried in this connection and which seems to combine both the participation of the two Communities in the affairs of Local Government and the necessary Central supervision of the conduct of such affairs is the setting up of a special Ministry of Local Government, with separate Greek and Turkish Branches. What must be made clear is that, whatever the precise arrangements, the system of Local Government cannot and should not be made into "a state within the State", free from adequate Central supervision. Such supervision can be provided in a great variety of ways — both through the Courts and through coordinating bodies.

4. In so far as the other Turkish villages are concerned, various possible arrangements could be considered. (Here I am referring to Turkish villages which would not fall within the special regions or areas to be recognised). If these are grouped on ethnic criteria, then the first units of local Government would be the said villages and municipalities. The second tier would consist of the appropriate councils and the third tier again would be the Central Communal Authority, as above. Or, alternatively, such Turkish villages will not be grouped, or they will be grouped together with Greek Cypriot villages on topographical and economic considerations.

It must be stressed that all efforts should be made (a) to limit the powers and functions to be delegated and integrate them with those of the State and (b) ensure that the status of such areas is one of Local Administrative Regional Units, the recognition of such areas to be combined with immediately following provisions guaranteeing free movement of goods and people across the relevant administrative boundaries.

Two main points would arise were this to be the eventual solution — the status and extent of the areas of local adminstration and the powers and functions to be exercised within such areas. As regards the first point, much has already been said. The recognised boundaries should be expressly declared to be administrative ones. There would be full integration with the state and the structure of local government would be recognised as a part of the government of the Republic as a whole. And the extent and demarcation of such areas would, no doubt, demand much specialised work so that viable units of local administration are created.

The main problem would be in connection with the powers and functions to be accorded to the autonomous Administrations of such regions. The account that follows is applicable to all three plans sketched out above. Our efforts should be aimed at drawing a workable and proper line between State Matters, in which the central authority alone would have jurisdiction, and local ones which would be within the competence of the Regional Authorities or the Central Communal and Local Authorities (whether these last are distinct authorities set up for this purpose or bodies consisting e.g. of Greek and Turkish members of the House of Representatives or the old Communal Chambers or Separate branches of Ministry of Local Affairs to be specially created for the supervision of local government).

Turkish proposals that local administrations should have complete and full control within their respective boundaries are not only unworkable but also unprecedented. As becomes obvious from a study of the comparative constitutional position, (a) the Central State Authority in all the federative or regional systems is actively involved, and indeed, performing a predominant role, in connection with all the main headings under which modern State activity can subsumed, and (b) a division of powers along the lines suggested by the Turkish proposals (i.e. almost complete separation of functions) simply ignores both the close inter-relationship of so many social and economic factors in modern society and the specific realities, geographical and other, of Cyprus. As appears from a study of all Federal, Quasi Federal and Regional Constitutions, commerce, trade, industry, finance, economy, the management of money, the preservation of the environment, the utilisation of natural resources, agriculture, navigation, postal and other like services are to a great extent within the competence of the central authority.[17] If the regional authorities themselves are empowered to deal with such matters, and no adequate coordination machinery is set up for the achievemnt of cooperation between the two Communities and the subordination of such Regional Authorities to the Central State, economic depression and political frustration will be the inevitable result. It must be obvious that such functions cannot be discharged by Regional authorities. Political power and true governmental functions can only be exercised by the Central Government in which, of course, both Communities will be participating. Any other arrangement will almost inevitably lead to economic stagnation, increased reliance on Greece and Turkey respectively and the eventual partitioning of the island.

Instead, however, of considering the subject from the point of view of the main heads of modern state activity (something that would, perhaps, be appropriate were a true federation to be set up), one should consider it from the point of view of those functions which are generally recognised as pertaining to the welfare of the people (this being the main rationale of local government and decentralisation of authority). Such functions could include: public health and sanitary services (the sale of provisions; the inspection, regulation and control of shops and other such places; the inspection of food and other perishable articles; regulation, supervision and control of trades deemed to be offensive or dangerous; inspection, regulation and maintenance of drains, privies and other sanitary conveniences; the cleaning, removing and collection of any drainage, filth water, matter or things likely to be prejudicial to health; prevention or mitigation of contagious diseases; all other such purposes as are not specially provided for and which are necessary for the protection of the public health etc.); the control of animals; the regulation, control, repair, improvement and construction of streets and public thoroughfares; regulation of markets and fairs, both public and private; control over buildings and building operations; land and property; water and waterworks; hotels and lodging houses; creation of offices; the appointment of officers and servants, the provision of pensions and gratuities etc.

In addition, under such a scheme, Local Authorities would very probably be given (a) rights of subsidiary legislation or regulation on all matters relating to their own internal organisation and set up and (b) powers to provide by regulation or otherwise for the punishment of offenders against the rules, regulations, byelaws or laws of the authority; to appoint local peace officers and/or inspectors and men for the proper application of all the minor rules, regulations etc. passed by the authority; to improve land and other property for the general benefit of the inhabitants of the local authority; to issue licences, etc.

It must be once more emphasised that whatever the precise functions and powers to be given to such Regional or Local Authorities, it must be made clear that the purpose of local government (both generally and in the particular case of Cyprus) is to decentralise authority by giving it to the local areas concerned and not take powers and functions from the Government and the Central Legislature and give them on a centralised basis to the Communities.

Possible ways in which effective supervision of Regional Authorities by the Central Government can be achieved are:

1. A District Officer or a Government Commissioner (the Italian Constitution) exercising control over the activities of the Regional Administrations should be considered (see above).
2. Control through the Constitutional Court (see Italian Constitution. (Art. 127)).
3. Provisions in the Constitution for cases of conflict of regulations, gaps, residual powers, Inter-regional matters etc.[18]

I must finally summarise my proposals on Regionalism and Local Government. My essential point is that a geographical or locality element can be safely brought in without essential detriment to the unity of the State if (a) the problem is formulated as one of local government and (b) such local government is structured more or less as suggested above, namely on the basis of administrative areas or regions. The proposals I have put forward will result in the recognition of a number of Turkish areas of Local Administration. How such areas will be demarcated must obviously be left to precise and detailed study. Since my proposals do not envisage any compulsory population movement, such Turkish areas of Local Administration must obviously exist (or be recognised) in areas of the island where the Turkish Community already enjoys population superiority. The main area of Turkish Administration may be, if the Turkish Community so desires, the Turkish sector of Nicosia, the Turkish villages between Nicosia and Kyrenia and the Turkish sector of Kyrenia, plus the necessary adjoining land (or some such area similarly demarcated). Other local areas or units of administration will exist elsewhere. Local government structured along the lines suggested above both goes a long way towards satisfying Turkish demands for local autonomy and, since it is accompanied by proper safeguards and essential governmental controls — as well as a strong central authority —, does not deviate from the need to maintain an integral and unitary state.

It is believed that a bizonal system must be strongly resisted. What cannot be tolerated when we talk of federation should not be put up with when we discuss Regionalism. As I have already said, a bizonal system, whatever its correct designation, is not possible otherwise than in the context of a vast and compulsory population movement — and such would be catastrophic. It must be acknowledged, of course, that the phrase "Population movement" itself is not self-explanatory. Normally, such phrase refers to the antithetic and complementary movements of parts of both populations. It is common knowledge, however, that since the Turkish invasion Turkish Cypriots, often against their will, have been moved to the occupied Greek areas. To allow and legalise such practices in the shape in which they have been taking place would be nothing short of scandalous; for, as is again common knowledge, the above mentioned Turkish Cypriots have been settling in the houses, and taking over the properties, of Greek Cypriots — something not unlike robbery and open theft. The point made here is that if the Greek Cypriot refugees are allowed to return to their homes and resettle in their properties, it may be that some population movement on the part of the Turkish Community — new villages etc., to be built by the Turkish Administration — will be agreed to. This limited and one-sided population movement together with a truly voluntary movement and resettlement would take place in the context of demarcating zones of local administration and can be seen as devices whereby local majorities would be streamlined and made more cohesive.

Local or regional government, as outlined above, replaces possible or feared compulsion from above with ordered reciprocity, understanding and adjustment. One of the aspects of the above proposals is pluralistic, preserving possible local diversities and ensuring adequate local control. Also, my proposals help preserve such a measure of uniformity as will prevent clashes and facilitate cooperation — their fundamental tendency is harmonisation and their basic principle is solidarity.

Both international and internal pressures, however, are such that a further step may have to be taken in the direction of a geographically defined solution — a settlement falling in between a strictly defined bizonal geographical federation, on the one hand, and acceptable forms of local governmental and regional autonomy as sketched out above, on the other. Before such further step is described and its implications considered, a more general point must be made. The problem of Cyprus need not, and should not, depend on phraseology and semantics. Most phrases which have been used, and are still being used, in the battle of words over the question of Cyprus, phrases such as "geographical solutions", "population movements" etc., are, at best, ambiguous, and, at worst, positively misleading. They are imprecise symbols, encapsulating even more imprecise ideas. Particularly is this so with "geographical solutions". It could well be said that all local governmental proposals (including those here outlined) are nothing but geographic solutions, accompanied by the demarcation of areas and the delimitation of zones; yet, as has been clearly demonstrated, all are fully compatible both with the unity of the state and the preservation of true sovereignty. This is because the really vital point is not so much the importation of a geographic element in proposed solutions as the allocation of powers within the state. Not even 1% of Cyprus should be ceded if by "cede" we refer to the total abdication of sovereignty over such area, however small. Demarcation of zones, however, provided no compulsory population movement is forced upon the Cyprus people, need not lead to the evils I have associated in preceding chapters with geographical federation — if such demarcation is accompanied by proper allocation of powers, the Central government retaining all powers essential for the discharge of its functions. As a result of such considerations, the view of the writer is that both distribution of powers and population movement are much more important than fruitless logomachy over the desirability or otherwise of geographic solutions.

Coming now to the further step mentioned above — this further step being the last which can possibly be acceded to by the people of Cyprus — such settlement involves the recognition of a semi-cantonal system.[19] Geographically, this semi-cantonal system can be structured as follows: There would be a main area of Turkish Regional Administration in the north of the island; two or three or even more areas of Turkish local administration would be recognised elsewhere, for instance in the Lefka area, in the Polis area, in the Larnaca area, great care being taken in the delimitation of such areas so that both (a) the economic viability of such areas would be ensured and (b) a Turkish Cypriot majority would already exist within them. In so far as Turkish villages scattered around the island are concerned, these could be grouped on topographical considerations, as explained above, or in accordance with Plan B, namely communal criteria. In so far as questions of power distribution are concerned, it can obviously be seen that the more we strengthen Regionalism, both the more anaemic the central authority will become and the greater the alterations which we will have to bring about concerning the structuring of central government. The powers of such cantons, if cantons they are to be called, should still be primarily local governmental ones, and the rationale of the setting up of such cantons should still be the decentralisation of central authority for the more expeditious discharge of state business at the local level — not the establishment of independent, and fully constituted, by way of governmental prerogatives, authorities detracting from the unity and sovereignty of Cyprus. Finally, as regards population movement, what has been said above applies here as well. Population movement can only be agreed to if it takes the forms either of a voluntary population movement or of a one sided movement, the Turks moving, under an agreement, to predominantly Turkish areas for the purpose of rendering such areas more cohesive population-wise.[20]

But a bizonal federation as conceived by the Turks and accompanied by a compulsory population movement can only be disastrous for the reasons given above, and must be resolutely resisted. It should be realised, of course, that all the proposals here put forward are predicated upon the belief (which may well prove a naive one) that reason will be assigned some part in any eventual settlement — that military might and strategic considerations will not prove the decisive criterion at the table of negotiations as well as on the battlefield. And, as events have unfolded, to ensure that reason and common sense are not completely ignored but are allowed, at least to some extent, to determine the outlines of a constitutional and political settlement is, to a considerable degree, the responsibility of the great powers and the strong nations.

VIII

THE PROTECTION OF THE TURKISH
MINORITY[1]

THE security of the Turkish Cypriot minority — this has been repeatedly declared both by the Turkish and Turkish Cypriot sides to be the most important issue in the Cyprus situation[2] and, allegedly, the proposals for federating Cyprus have been put forward in the interests of providing that security.[3] It is the thesis of the present chapter that the Turkish Cypriot community can be safeguarded otherwise, and that the problem of minority protection and reassurance should be approached in this way and not through communal separation which, as proved in a preceding chapter, both in terms of its stated objective and in many other ways, would not only be totally inefficacious but, also, positively counter productive.

First of all, what kind of minority is the Turkish Cypriot Community? The question of the classification of minorities is a difficult one.[4] The possible criteria of classification of minorities are many and varied; quantitative factors, contiguity, the viewpoint of citizenship, origin and situation, the circumstances under which minorities were included within the State, desires and ambitions — such and many more have, on occasion, been put forward as providing both an authoritative guide to the definition and an accurate criterion to the classification of minorities. A purely theoretical approach to the problem of the Turkish minority, however, does not take us very far. Generally, the fundamental principle is that of non-discrimination — the rights of minorities, both political and economic, must be protected, and minorities must be allowed to preserve their distinctive ethnic and group charateristics and develop their own cultures.[5] But, on the other hand, minorities, on many occasions, have put forward claims to "special rights"[6] and "special prerogatives" and it has been authoritatively stated that such claims of minorities must be examined on their own merits "in the light of past and present circumstances as well as the light of the general principles of the Charter of the United Nations".[7]

The view has already been expressed that it would have been

much preferable if the Turkish minority were treated in the way indicated above, if it were, that is, effectively protected against discrimination and assured of the same rights as those accorded to all. Such course seems, unfortunately, impossible.[8] As a result of historical and geographic factors, as well as the divisive policies of the English Colonial Office before independence, the Turkish Cypriot Community of Cyprus, no longer characterised by a feeling of solidarity with the predominant group, is not satisfied either with preservation as a group or with development of its distinguishing characteristics. It also desires to participate in a fixed way in the affairs of State and attain some kind of administrative and local autonomy (in addition to its already recognised communal autonomy). Both desires, to a great extent, are satisfied by the proposals sketched out above. The organisation of the Central Government provides for fixed and balanced participation therein by the Turkish Cypriot Community, and the establishment of local or regional Government ensures, without disruption of State unity, considerable administrative autonomy.

Nevertheless, such structural accommodations are not enough. The following measures, to be explicitly adopted in the interests of minority protection, are thought to be absolutely essential.[9]

(1) An appropriate Bill of Rights should be enacted and appropriately entrenched in the Constitution. It is not thought that there would be any serious problem regarding the formulation of such a Bill of Rights. The Code of Fundamental Rights and Freedoms to be enacted should not be unlike the one already to be found in the 1960 Constitution; and on the 4th October, 1965, Archbishop Makarios, in a letter to the then Secretary General of the UN, informed him of his Government's readiness to indicate the rights and freedoms to be adopted in this connection. This list, which follows closely the Universal Declaration of Human Rights, met with general approval.

In addition to the rights and freedoms to be accorded to all, the Turkish minority — and all other minorities in Cyprus — should enjoy complete autonomy and freedom in matters relating to their respective religions, education, culture, personal status and all such related matters. More specifically, such rights should be the following:

(a) To enjoy their own culture;
(b) To use their own language;
(c) To establish their own schools;

(d) To profess and practise their own religion;
(e) To enjoy full autonomy in matters of personal status, such as marriage and divorce;
(f) To have their own educational, cultural and social organisations;
(g) To issue newspapers in their own language etc.

2. How will such rights be efficaciously enforced? Surely, this is the crux of the problem. For, security, according to their own declarations, is what the Turkish side wants. And what is security in this connection other than impartial enforcement of the laws and the existence and effective operation of adequate safeguards under law?

The safeguards and guarantees that should be insisted upon — and I would place my faith in — are the following: First, there should be effective safeguards and enforcement mechanisms under municipal law. Such, by virtue of my proposals sketched out above, would automatically exist and would be, it is believed, effectively operated (principally as a result of the totality of the Constitutional scheme I am proposing). Areas primarily inhabited by Turks, for instance, would be policed by Turkish policemen; in Turkish areas of local administration, the local Governmental organs would, generally, be Turkish; and, by virtue of the suggested structuring of the Courts and the proposed availability of municipal remedies, all citizens would be assured of the impartial administration of justice. But I would not stop here. Additional safeguards should exist under municipal law. It is felt that significant progress could be made by specifying positive and continuing responsibilities regarding the protection of the Turkish community and the more general enforcement of human rights, and "placing these responsibilities in resolute hands".[10] A body, for instance, along the lines of the Civil Rights Commission in the US could well perform valuable services in this field. Such a body, entrusted not only with the eradication of positive discrimination but also with the elimination of its root causes, should be composed of members of both Communities, the selection to be made by the President and Vice President jointly. Also, an Ombudsman on the Scandinavian pattern, whose specific duties would include the investigation of complaints of communal discrimination, should be given careful thought. And the explicit demarcation of politically and communally neutral zones[11] — such zones to include not only the judiciary but also the offices of Attorney-General, Director of Public Prosecutions (if such office be established) etc. — can go a long way in assuring both fairness of treatment and impartiality of administration. Finally, as observed in the Introduction, UN participation, perhaps temporarily or for a transitional period, in the law enforcement agencies of the state should be carefully considered.

3. In addition to effective safeguards under municipal law — both ordinary and extraordinary — international guarantees relating to the security of the Turkish Community, as well as to the integrity of the Republic of Cyprus, should be canvassed and carefully considered. Dr. Plaza has already put forward the intriguing possibility of the UN itself acting as the guarantor of any overall settlement arrived at, and such a course has much to commend it, provided, of course, that the UN has both the will and the resources effectively to oversee the prompt implementation and faithful observance of such settlement.[12] Furthermore, the Government of the Republic of Cyprus has indicated its willingness to accept the presence in Cyprus of a UN Commissioner with an adequate staff of observers and advisers who will observe, on such terms as the Secretary-General may direct, the Government's adherence to the rights and assurances referred to above.[13] Such UN Commissioner, permanently stationed, if need be, in Cyprus, should, in fact, be in overall superintendence of all efforts to assure effective implementation of human rights and guarantees against discrimination. It is not believed that many Governments have ever expressed readiness to subject their own internal machinery to international supervision in this way; yet, the Government of the Republic of Cyprus is on record as willing to go that far in its earnest desire to ensure justice for all.

To sum up, the security of the Turkish Community will be amply provided for by the ways indicated above. To strengthen law and set up appropriate law enforcement mechanisms and agencies — such, in the ultimate analysis, can be the only programme for communal peace. A word of caution, however, is called for. Minorities must be adequately protected and provided with all the facilities whereby they can preserve and develop their ethnic characteristics. They should not be idealised. Not only are some minorities "far from faultless"[14] but, also, excessive zeal in this direction can result in neglect for individual human rights and the setting up of a system of calculated obstructionism from which all will suffer. Gandhi indeed may have been right when he stated that civilisation should be judged by its treatment of minorities, but we must also not forget that the World Community will very likely be judged by its treatment of small and defenceless States viciously attacked and endangered. Security through law and an alert and enlightened public opinion for both majority and minority in an ordered framework of sovereign Independence — this, and not the exacerbation of further tension through artificial separation, should be the way ahead. As such it must also be the challenge of the future.

IX

DIVISION OR UNITY?[1]

D IVISION or unity? This is the basic issue confronting those in whose hands the future of Cyprus lies. The view of this author has already been made abundantly clear. As I see it, the one and only hopeful alternative to the disastrous policy of separatism pursued in the past and its poor relations such as geographical federation is a policy whose long term goal is a democracy in which all men, irrespective of ethnic origin or communal affiliation, can enjoy in peace and security the basic human freedoms and political rights in one integrated society. A strategy for integration — this is what we need in Cyprus. It is plain that there can be no real progress along the road to true peace and harmonious integration without a wholly fresh start — without the excision from the Constitutional, legal and social arrangements, and, indeed, in the course of time, from men's hearts, both of the gross distortion of ethnic prejudice and the pernicious influence of blind communalism.

Yet, to speak unqualifiedly of integration as such may be to court serious danger of misunderstanding. Have we not so far often spoken of a balanced partnership between the two Communities, of communal rights, of communal autonomy and of regional arrangements based partly on communal criteria, and is it not the case that such concepts and phraseology evoke the right to some kind of separate identity? How is the paradox to be resolved?[2]

If a sovereign political state incorporates more than one distinguishable cultural community — as is clearly the case with Cyprus — there are, broadly speaking, three types of possible long term development, even though in practice the combination of these types may produce many different variations.

First, we have the objective of "total integration". The guiding ideology is that the political state "ought" to be culturally homogeneous, or that there can be no other culture other than that of the political state. The fear is that the cohesive stability of society will be endangered by any variations that might be involved in different customs, values or behaviour and that the fabric of the state might be torn apart by the divisive influences of culturally distinguishable classes. Such theory does not only appear impossible to implement but is also inconsistent with modern theories of tolerance and pluralism. "For freedom in society means, above all, that we recognise the justice and the creativity of diversity, difference and conflict".[3] If, however, we speak not of total integration but simply of "integration within the state", which we then proceed to define as "equal opportunity accompanied by cultural diversity in an atmosphere of freedom",[4] many of the difficulties with this type of objective disappear.

Objective type two is that of balanced association, or, as I have referred to it before, balanced partnership. This formulation avoids terms such as majority and minority and proceeds to construct a system based on the preservation of a viable state which will accommodate distinctive group characteristics. In some cases, political federation may be the Governmental pattern best calculated to achieve this, but in those cases where the necessary federal prerequisites are not present and, as a result, federation is not a viable possibility, diversity must be protected and fostered otherwise, e.g. through regional arrangements, correct structuring of the Governmental and political processes, etc.

Finally, the third type of objective or long term development is that of "separate existence". This system is predicated upon cultural, political and economic self sufficiency for all the culturally distinguishable groups or classes (which self sufficiency, as demonstrated above, simply does not exist in the case of Cyprus), and proceeds to set up separatist structures and exclusively ethnic arrangements (which, owing to the conditions of Cyprus and the proximity to the island of Turkey and Greece, could only lead to partition, namely the total severance of any political link between Cyprus' two Communities and the annexation of the two zones or regions of the island to the two mother countries).

Either the first objective (as modified) or the second one would do for our present purpose which is none other than to indicate the outlines of what one can call the social philosophy of a new Cyprus. For, unfortunately, it is too late to declare and demand either that each person be viewed as himself and as himself alone and that our political and social perception not be distorted by group judgments which, in the first place, may have been generated or used as a result of the promptings of irrational emotions, or even that minority and group rights are a misleading formula, rights best thought of as inherent in each human being, irrespective of what kind of cultural or ethnic grouping he or she may belong to. This, indeed, may well be so in theory, and the above sentiments are noble ones, but to indulge in the naive belief that once we stop speaking of Greeks and Turks and substitute Cypriots for both all will be well, is but to indulge in fantasy and ignore the fundamentals of the problem. That two different ethnic groups exist in Cyprus must still be the starting point for any consideration of the social problem, in the same way that it provided the starting point for our constitutional treatment of this subject. Consequently, any recommendations to be advanced in this connection must be framed with this consideration in mind and our zeal for social reconstruction must be moderated by an awareness of the prevailing realities. But, of course, impossibility of total and instant integration does not mean that one should neglect areas of common interest where the two communities can co-operate, nor does it mean that statehood should not (or cannot) transcend diverse nationhoods. Mr. Clerides put it very well when he said:[5] "the only viable solution for Cyprus is to get Greeks and Turks working together and belonging to common institutions and developing common interests. This is quite compatible with a large measure of autonomy at the local level". The two Communities must be ready to absorb each other's values and join efforts in the building (and not simply the mechanical operation) of the State. It is this aspect of the Cyprus problem that I am now directing my attention to — how "to unite with ... differences intact ...".[6] For "when natural differences find their harmony, then it is true unity".[7] This is a point also made with great effect by Dr. Plaza who said that it was a matter for regret that "in the light of widespread modern conceptions of the need for the integration and assimilation of differing peoples in the interest of national unity"[8] so little was done in the past to breach the separateness of the Greek Cypriot and Turkish Cypriot Communities.

"To breach the separateness" and achieve feasible integration by means of active social engineering — this, then, should be our twin objectives. Such social integration and cultural interaction could not materialise in the past on account of the survival of narrow minded nationalism which pitted Greek against Turk and presented them both to the world and to each other not as partners and cohabitants jointly engaged in the new venture of

Independence, but as adversaries and antagonists. Indeed, so unfortunate were the circumstances of the achievement (or imposition) of Independence in 1960 and so artificial a concoction the Zürich settlement, that the survival of the nationalist movements on both the Greek and Turkish sides was inevitable. This, in its turn, prevented a firm line being drawn between pre-Independence revolutionary activity and the conduct of liberation campaigns, on the one hand, and, on the other, the Government and administration of a modern state with all its difficulties and complexities, which, surely, was the task facing Greeks and Turks alike after 1960. Different attitudes, habits, ideas, methods and style should have been brought to bear on the new post-Independence situation by both Communities, but this proved impossible. If we have derived any lesson from the past, it is surely that different attitudes towards both the State and each other on the part of both Communities are necessary if the Republic of Cyprus is to survive and prosper.

Above, I sketched proposals for constitutional reform, and I made it clear that I regard such constitutional reconstruction as essential. At the same time, and this has also been repeatedly indicated, it is of great importance not to be deluded into placing too much confidence in the value and efficacy of constitutions as such. As Lord Bryce pointed out, no constitution in the world can artificially create social unity and well being, if, in fact, the operative currents are flowing too strongly in an opposite direction. We cannot and should not rest all our hopes on parchment and on paper, but must strive to build the desire for peace and unity.

Again, a compromise must be aimed for. Just as inordinate legalism can give only a one-sided and distorted picture, it is as serious a mistake to underrate the role and psychological importance of constitutional and institutional forms in social and political behaviour. The relationship, in fact, between a society and its institutions is "a complex and dynamic one".[9] Institutions are normally the creation of the forces and currents within a society; but, also, institutions, when created, may themselves shape the pattern of society, both by determining new avenues of activity, political social and cultural, and by charting new channels within which social pressures can flow.

Here, it is intended to indicate a number of areas which until now and as a result of the separatism enshrined in our constitutional arrangements were areas of social stagnation and division. New institutional accomodations in such areas, it is strongly believed, can convert stagnation into fruitful social interaction. Education, the Arts, Sport — such are the areas I have in mind. This, of course, is too complex a subject to be dealt with in detail here. I will limit myself to essential clarification and a few suggestions. For, it does not need much evidence to prove that too nationalistic an attitude can lead to an outdated and artificially narrow conception of vital state services such as education, the most important of such concerns, or that the people of Cyprus have needs (security, peace, prosperity, freedom) that transend their ethnic origins and that such needs must find concrete satisfaction and fulfilment in institutional arrangements appropriate not only to the functions expected to be performed by the modern state but also to the imperative call for unity.

Communalism under the 1960 Constitution did not only permeate the legal arrangements set up but also narrowed the range of vision as regards the State and state services by presenting them not as essential for the development of a responsible citizenry but as mere appendages of diverse nationhoods. Education provides a striking example. Under the Zürich settlement, by which educational facilities were completely separate and in the charge of the two Communities, education was obviously conceived as the transmission of hereditary values integrally associated with, and arising from, the distinct heritages of the two Communities rather than as the imparting of essential knowledge or the assimilation of the neutral virtues of a common citizenship. The whole range of technical, scientific, vocational and advanced learning was neglected, not to say completely ignored. Education was allied to religion and both were made the absolute prerogative of the two Communities. Not only, in this way, was the State denied responsibility regarding education but also young Cypriots were deprived of the opportunity to associate together in the pursuit of learning free both of the parochialism of the past and the prejudices born of a divided allegiance. It is imperative, whatever the formal constitutional and governmental arrangements, that radical changes be brought about both in the conception of education and in the structures and institutions set up for the purpose of implementing such conception. It is obvious, of course, that both the Greek and the Turkish Cypriots will always feel part of the Hellenic and Turkish Worlds respectively and deeply cherish such links, and it would be quite wrong, as well as impossible, for any attempt to be made to sever such relations or completely submerge them under the neutralism of a state structure. Both Communities, particularly as matters stand at present, must retain some separate educational establishments and education, at some levels, must still be the prime responsibility of the two Communities. Yet, the demands of communalism, must, at some stage, bow before the needs of a common and united citizenship—this and no more is argued here.

Cyprus has already 15 intercommunal schools, the highest of which is the Higher Technological Institute, set up with the help of UNESCO funds to train technical secondary teachers, and high-grade technicians up to City and Guilds level. The Institute has functioned successfully with Greek and Turkish staff teaching in English. The success of the HTI argues that it is possible to bring Greeks and Turks under the same academic roof. Further, it is highly desirable to encourage and extend the scope of such intercommunal education as there is because (a) contact between young members of the two communities would undoubtedly serve the cause of mutual understanding and trust, and (b) subsequent co-operation between the Communities in the fields of industry and commerce will be enhanced. What then is realistic to propose given the fact that it is impossible, as argued above, totally to replace the community-based system of education by one integrated Cypriot system? The following suggestions are put forward with some diffidence.

1. While retaining the community-based system of education, the respective contents of the syllabuses must be modernised and made to conform to the need to develop the concept of Cypriot statehood. Absolutely imperative is the introduction of a "Citizenship" element in higher forms for the study of the fundamentals of the Constitution and the rights and duties of citizens.

2. The HTI must be enlarged so as to receive more students from both Communities, and its scope must be extended so as to give more technical and vocational courses, including some at ONC and HND levels. (In the UK alone there are some 3000 Cypriots doing sub-degree courses). Schools for the Tourist trade and other industries must also be established along the same lines, with a view to promoting the Cyprus economy.

3. It is not so desirable to establish an intercommunal University in Cyprus given the fact that many graduates are unemployed already. But already existing institutions for research e.g. Pedagogical Institute, Centre for Social Research, Centre for

Scientific Research could be reconstituted so that they could become centres for co-operation between Greek and Turkish scholars.

4. It might be useful to establish something like the Arts Council of G.B. to give grants in support of Greek-Turkish artistic, cultural, scientific and other activities, publications etc. Similarly, the Sports Council could be re-formed along intercommunal lines to promote contests between e.g. intercommunal clubs of different towns. Clearly such proposals can only be realised if public attitudes change to some extent at least, and the principle of intercommunal co-operation is accepted.

5. Broadcasting presents special difficulties. In all likelihood, special arrangements would have to be made concerning allocation of broadcasting and television time to the two Communities, but, of course, this should be combined with programmes of a supra-communal content. Likewise with many other activities which are, at present, conceived only in narrow communal terms. In general, it could be said that the establishment of separate facilities should, wherever possible, be discouraged and arrangements to share and use in common are much to be preferred.

I have above indicated some areas where fresh thought and a new approach seem to be required. There are, I am sure, many others.

The fundamental fact to which we must finally come back is that Greek and Turkish Cypriots have just one small island in which to live, and in this island they *must* live and work *together*. If this cohabitation and collaboration are to succed, and if Cyprus is to achieve peace and prosperity for all her people, it is necessary thet the two Communities should do more than grudgingly accept each other as permanent neighbours. They should come to develop a *positive sense* of common citizenship which transcends a mere recognition of geographical facts and legal arrangements, and which includes pride in, and loyalty to, a common Cypriot homeland. It is time to begin anew. Let both sides explore what problems unite us and what are the areas in which common bonds of friendship can be forged instead of forever belabouring those issues that divide us and those many, sore, painful points of the past. Is it too much to hope that the Greeks and Turks of Cyprus should develop fraternal feelings towards each other and common allegiances, which will eventually grow into a conception of common Cypriot ideas, interests and values?

X

APPENDICES

DOCUMENTS AND MAPS

1. UN Security Council Resolutions.
2. Geneva Declaration signed on 30th July, 1974.
3. Proposal of Mr. Denktash submitted at Geneva on the 12th August, 1974.
4. Map showing the effect of proposal of Mr. Denktash (the Attila plan).
5. Translation of Proposal (made in French) by Turkish Foreign Minister on the 12th August, 1974, at Geneva (the Gunes plan).
6. Map showing the effect of proposal of the Turkish Foreign Minister.
7. Proposal of the Greek Cypriot Delegation submitted at Geneva on the 13th August, 1974 (the Clerides plan).
8. Map showing the effects of Turkish aggression and the area of Cyprus occupied by the Turkish troops.
9. Map showing the distribution of Greek and Turkish villages over the island.
10. UN General Assembly Resolution of 2nd November, 1974.

1. SECURITY COUNCIL RESOLUTIONS

Resolution 353 adopted on 20th July, 1974.

The Security Council,

Having considered the report of the Secretary-General at its 1779th meeting about the recent developments in Cyprus,

Having heard the statements made by the President of the Republic of Cyprus and the statements by the Representatives of Cyprus, Turkey, Greece and other member countries,

Having considered at its present meeting further developments in the Island,

Deeply deploring the outbreak of conflict and continuing bloodshed,

Gravely concerned about the situation which led to a serious threat to international peace and security and which created a most explosive situation in the whole Eastern Mediterranean area.

Equally concerned about the necessity to restore the constitutional structure of the Republic of Cyprus established and guaranteed by the International Agreements,

Recalling Security Council Resolution 186 (1964) of 4th March, 1964 and subsequent resolutions of the Security Council on this matter,

Consequent of its primary responsibility for the maintenance of international peace and security in accordance with Article 24 of the Charter of the United Nations.

1. Calls upon all States to respect the sovereignty, independence and territorial integrity of Cyprus;

2. Calls upon all parties to the present fighting as a first step to cease all firing and requests all States to exercise the utmost restraint and to refrain from any action which might further aggravate the situation;

3. Demands an immediate end to foreign military intervention in the Republic of Cyprus that is in contravention of operative paragraph 1;

4. Requests the withdrawal without delay from the Republic of Cyprus of foreign military personnel present otherwise than under the authority of International Agreements including those whose withdrawal was requested by the President of the Republic of Cyprus Archbishop Makarios, in his letter of 2nd July, 1974;

5. Calls upon Greece, Turkey and the United Kingdom of Great Britain and Northern Ireland to enter into negotiations without delay for the restoration of peace in the area and constitutional government in Cyprus and to keep the Secretary-General informed;

6. Calls upon all parties to co-operate fully with UNFICYP to enable it to carry out its mandate;

7. Decides to keep the situation under constant review and asks the Secretary-General to report as appropriate with a view to adopting further measures in order to ensure that peaceful conditions are restored as soon as possible.

Resolution 360 adopted on 16th August, 1974.

The Security Council recalling its resolutions 353 (1974), 354 (1974), 355 (1974), 357 (1974) and 358 (1974).

Noting that all States have declared their respect for the sovereignty, independence and territorial integrity of the Republic of Cyprus.

Gravely concerned at the deterioration of the situation in Cyprus resulting from the further military operations which constituted a most serious threat of peace and security in the eastern Mediterranean area.

Recalls its formal disapproval of the unilateral military actions undertaken against the Republic of Cyprus;

Urges the parties to comply with the provisions of the previous resolutions of the Security Council including those concerning the withdrawal without delay from the Republic of Cyprus of foreign military personnel present otherwise that under the authority of international agreements;

Urges the parties to resume without delay in an atmosphere of constructive cooperation the negotiations called for in resolution 353 (1974), whose outcome should not be impeded or prejudged by the acquisition and advantages resulting of military operations;

Recalls the Secretary-General to report to it as necessary with a view to possible adoption of further measures designed to promote the restoration of peaceful conditions;

Decides to remain permanently ceased of the question and to meet at any time to consider measures which may be required in the light of the developing situation.

2. GENEVA DECLARATION SIGNED ON
30th JULY 1974

1. The Foreign Ministers of Greece, Turkey and the United Kingdom held negotiations in Geneva from 25-30 July 1974. *They recognised the importance of setting in train, as a matter of urgency, measures to adjust and to regularise within a reasonable period of time the situation in the Republic of Cyprus on a lasting basis, having regard to the international agreement signed at Nicosia on 16 August 1960 and to resolution 353 of the Security Council of the United Nations.* They were, however, agreed on the need to decide first on certain immediate measures.

2. The three Foreign Ministers declared that in order to stabilise the situation, the areas in the Republic of Cyprus controlled by opposing armed forces on 30th July 1974 at 22.00 hours Geneva time should not be extended. They called on all forces, including irregular forces, to desist from all offensive or hostile activities.

4. *The three Foreign Ministers, reaffirming that resolution 353* of the Security Council should be implemented in the shortest possible time, agreed that within the framework of a just and lasting solution acceptable to all parties concerned and as peace, security and mutual confidence are established in the Republic of Cyprus, measures should be elaborated which will lead to the timely and phased reduction of the number of armed forces and the amounts of armaments, ammunitions and other war material in the Republic of Cyprus.

5. Deeply conscious of their responsibilities as regards the maintenance of the independence, territorial integrity and security of the Republic of Cyprus, the three Foreign Ministers agreed that negotiations, as provided for in resolution 353 of the Security Council, should be carried on with the least possible delay to secure (a) the restoration of peace in the area, and (b) the re-establishment of constitutional government in Cyprus.

3. THE DENKTASH PROPOSAL

(a) The Republic of Cyprus shall be an independent bi-national State.

(b) The Republic shall be composed of two federated states with full control and autonomy within their respective geographical boundaries.

(c) In determining the competence to be left to the Federal Government, the bi-national nature of the State shall be taken into account and the federal competence shall be exercised accordingly.

(d) The area of the Turkish Cypriot Federated State shall cover 34 per centum of the territory of the Republic falling north of a general line starting from the Limnitis-Lefka area in the west and running towards the east, passing through the Turkish controlled part of Nicosia, including the Turkish part of Famagusta and ending at the port of Famagusta.

3. Pending an agreement on the final Constitutional structure of the Republic, the two autonomous administrations shall take over the full administrative authority within their respective areas as defined above and shall take steps to normalise and stabilise life in the Republic and refrain from acts of violence, harassment and discrimination against each other.

Appendices

4. MAP SHOWING THE EFFECT OF PROPOSAL OF MR. DENKTASH (the Attila Plan).

...... — the proposed line of separation.

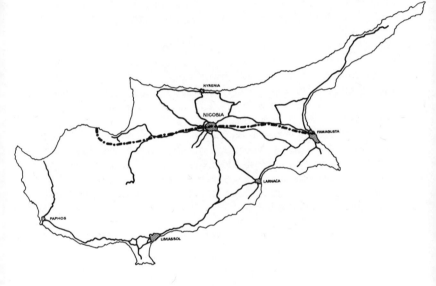

5. TRANSLATION OF TURKISH FOREIGN MINISTER'S PROPOSAL

1. The Republic of Cyprus is a bi-communal and independent state.

2. The Republic will be constituted by one Turkish-Cypriot autonomous zone comprising six districts and by one Greek-Cypriot autonomous zone comprising two districts:

    (a) Greek-Cypriot autonomous zone:
        (i) Main Greek-Cypriot district.
        (ii) Greek-Cypriot district of Karpasia.
    (b) Turkish-Cypriot autonomous zones:
        (i) Main Turkish-Cypriot district the boundaries of which will follow from west to east a line including Panagra - Myrtou - Asomatos - Skylloura - Yerolakkos - Sector of Nicosia controlled by Turks - Moka - Angastina - Yenagra - Maratha - Styllos — "Fresh Water Lake" — Turkish part of Famagusta and to the north-east by a line excluding Galounia, including Komi Kebir, Ayios Efstathios and excluding Gastria;
        (ii) Turkish district of the region of Lefca;
        (iii) Turkish district of the region of Polis;
        (iv) Turkish district of the region of Paphos;
        (v) Turkish district of the region of Larnaca;
        (vi) Turkish district of the region of Karpasia.

The area of the Turkish-Cypriot autonomous zone will be equivalent to nearly 34% of the Republic's territory.

The area and the boundaries of each of the districts other than the main district of the Turkish-Cypriot autonomous zone will be determined at a time and through a procedure to be fixed by the provisions which will be added to the present Declaration.

The main district of the Turkish-Cypriot autonomous zone will be evacuated by units of the Greek armed forces and of the so-called Greek-Cypriot National Guard as well as by Greek irregulars within a time limit which shall in no case exceed 48 hours starting from the date of the signing of the same Declaration. The administration, order and security of this district will also be taken over immediately by the Turkish Cyprus Administration.

3. The Administration of each of the autonomous zones will have entire control of its own area within its geographical boundaries.

4. Free movement between the districts of the same autonomous zone will be secured by the Central Government.

5. There will be determination of the competences of the Central Government of the Republic taking fully into account the bi-communal nature of the State.

6. Until the coming into force of the new constitutional system of the Republic the two existing in practice Greek-Cypriot and Turkish-Cypriot Administrations will adopt jointly the necessary measures with a view to normalising and stabilising life on the territory of the Republic and will abstain from any acts of violence, harassment and discrimination.

12th August, 1974.

6. MAP SHOWING THE EFFECT OF PROPOSAL OF THE TURKISH FOREIGN MINISTER.

•••••• — the proposed boundaries of the suggested Turkish areas of administration.

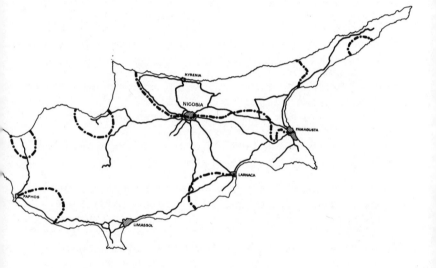

7. PROPOSAL OF MR. CLERIDES AT GENEVA

1. The constitutional order of Cyprus shall retain its bi-communal character based on the co-existence of the Greek and Turkish communities within the framework of a sovereign, independent and integral Republic.

2. This constitutional order shall, through an appropriate revision and the active cooperation and free consent of the two communities, ensure an enhanced feeling of security for both.

3. The co-existence of the two communities shall be achieved in the context of institutional arrangements regarding an agreed allocation of powers and functions between the Central Government having competence over state affairs and the respective autonomous Communal Administrations exercising their powers on all other matters within areas to be established as in paragraph (5) herein below provided.

4. The structure of the Central Government shall continue to be based on the presidential regime.

5. The Greek and Turkish Communal Administrations shall exercise their powers and functions in areas consisting respectively of the purely Greek and Turkish villages and municipalities. For the purposes of communal administration such villages and municipalities may be grouped together by the respective communal authorities. For the same purpose *mixed villages* shall come under the communal authorities of the community to which the majority of their inhabitants belong.

6. Legislative authority over the respective Communal Administrations shall be exercised by the Greek and Turkish members of the House of Representatives constituted in separate Councils for this purpose.

13th August, 1974.

8. MAP SHOWING THE EFFECTS OF TURKISH AGGRESSION AND THE AREA OF CYPRUS OCCUPIED BY THE TURKISH TROOPS.

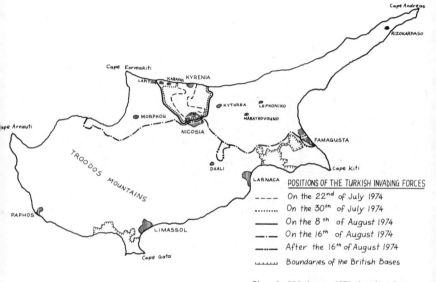

POSITIONS OF THE TURKISH INVADING FORCES

----	On the 22nd of July 1974
....	On the 30th of July 1974
——	On the 8th of August 1974
—.—	On the 16th of August 1974
—..—	After the 16th of August 1974
⊔⊔⊔⊔	Boundaries of the British Bases

Since the 16th August, 1974, there have been additional military operations by the Turkish troops; in consequence of such further operations, more Cyprus territory has come under Turkish occupation and more people have had to abandon their villages and homes.

District	Area occupied (in donums)	% of the total area of Cyprus	% of the total area of the district	Occupied Greek or mixed villages	% of the total No. of Greek or mixed villages
Nicosia	708,340	10.2	37.7	54	10.7
Kyrenia	479,220	6.9	100.0	40	7.0
Famagusta	1,326,497	19.2	89.7	63	12.5
Larnaca	152,368	2.2	18.1	5	1.0
TOTAL	2,666,425	38.5	—	162	32.1

9. MAP SHOWING THE DISTRIBUTION OF GREEK AND TURKISH VILLAGES OVER THE ISLAND.

Greek   •
Turkish ○

PERCENTAGE DISTRIBUTION OF GREEKS AND TURKS OF CYPRUS FROM 1921 TO 1970

Communities	1921	%	1931	%	1946	%	1960	%	1970	%
Greeks, etc.	249,376	80.3	283,721	81.5	369,566	82.1	473,265	81.9	518,617	81.9
Turks	61,339	19.7	64,238	18.5	80,548	17.9	104,350	18.1	114,383	18.1
Total	310,715	100.0	347,959	100.0	450,114	100.0	577,615	100.0	633,000	100.0
	(1)		(1)		(2)		(3)		(4)	

Sources: (1) Report of the Census of 1931 prepared by C. H. Hart-Davis, Nicosia, 1932.

(2) Census of Population and Agriculture, 1946, Report by D. Percival, Nicosia, 1949.

(3) Census of Population and Agriculture, 1960, Government Printing Office, Nicosia, 1962.

(4) Demographic Report for the year 1970, Department of Statistics and Research, Nicosia.

10. THE GENERAL ASSEMBLY RESOLUTION OF THE 2ND NOVEMBER, 1974.

Of considerable interest is the very recent Resolution on Cyprus adopted unanimously by the UN General Assembly on the 2nd of November, 1974. The General Assembly, "gravely concerned about the continuation of the Cyprus crisis, which constitutes a threat to International Peace and Security", and "mindful of the need to solve this crisis without delay by peaceful means, in accordance with the purposes and principles of the UN", (a) called upon all States to respect the Sovereignty, Independence, territorial Integrity and non alignment of the Republic of Cyprus and to refrain from all acts and Interventions directed against it; (b) urged the speedy withdrawal of all foreign armed forces; (c) considered that the Constitutional system of the Republic concerned the Greek Cypriot and Turkish Cypriot Communities; (d) considered that "all the refugees should return to their homes in safety" and called upon the parties concerned to undertake urgent measures to that end, etc.

The Greek Cypriot side immediately welcomed this Resolution as "absolutely satisfactory" and "a moral victory". Indeed the Resolution, urging the swift withdrawal of all foreign troops from Cyprus, calling for the return of the refugees to their homes and placing the responsibility for a constitutional settlement in the hands of the Island's Greek and Turkish Communities, seems to include all those positive elements that, it has been argued above, should determine the framework within which a solution of the Cyprus problem should be sought, and clearly provides a sound basis on which the structure of the Cyprus Republic should be based.

And how has the Turkish Leadership reacted to this Resolution? Mr. Rauf Denktash, the Turkish Cypriot Leader, made it clear that his side does not consider itself bound by any of the provisions of the Resolution which it might regard as prejudicial to its security or to the political settlement it wants. Commenting on the Resolution, Mr. Denktash said that the return of the refugees "is an internal political matter closely connected with a political settlement, and should be treated by us in the light of a political settlement, namely a bi-regional federal State". According to Mr. Denktash, "the creation of a Greek Majority in the Turkish part of Cyprus would be incompatible with the realities of Cyprus". This means in effect that most of the

200,000 refugees who fled from the Turkish occcupied part of the Island will not be allowed to return to their homes. As a result of this reaction, and the apparent indifference of the World Community to Turkey's blatant disregard for the UN Resolution, those provisions of the Resolution which can only be regarded as a victory for the Greek Cypriot cause and a vindication of the Greek Cypriot case — namely the call for the return of all refugees to their homes and the withdrawal of the Turkish invasion force — are already on their way to becoming a dead letter.

One is regretfully led to the conclusion that the UN has once again proved to be a singularly ineffective organ of World Peace, and that International Security based on law is nothing short of a pernicious myth.

XI

NOTES

INTRODUCTION

1. For general works on Cyprus, see Hill's History of Cyprus; Kyriakides' 'Cyprus, Constitutionalism and Crisis Government'; H. D. Purcell's 'Cyprus'; Xydis' 'Cyprus, Conflict and Concilation 1954-1958'; Stephens' 'Cyprus, a place of Arms'; Xydis' 'Cyprus, Reluctant Republic': the relevant Chapter in Macmillan's Memoirs, Vol. 4, 'Riding the Storm'; Dr. Spyridakis' 'A brief History of Cyprus', Revised Edition, Nicosia 1974 (and historical bibliography contained therein). Adams and Cottrell 'Cyprus between East and West'; Tornaritis' 'Cyprus and its Constitution'; the excellent Chapter in De Smith, 'The New Commonwealth and its Constitutions'; P. Terlexis 'Diplomacy and Policy on Cyprus — The Anatomy of a Mistake'; etc. See also the relevant Constitutional documents in 'Cyprus' Cmnd. 1093; Tornaritis' 'Constitutional and Legal Problems of the Republic of Cyprus'. Also, essential for an understanding of the Cyprus problem is the 'Report of the UN Mediator on Cyprus to the Secretary-General' (Dr. Plaza's Report); Ehrlich 'Cyprus 1958-1967' (O.U.P.). For interesting Parliamentary Debates relating to Cyprus and other material, see 'Documents and Speeches on Commonwealth Affairs (1952-1962)', edited by N. Mansergh.

A very full bibliography is provided in Kyriakides' 'Cyprus, Constitutionalism and Crisis Government'.

2. In a paper written by Dr. G. S. Georghallides.

3. H. of C. Deb., vol. 531, coll. 504-11.

4. H. of C. Deb., vol. 550, coll. 387-93, 402-16.

5. H. of L. Deb., vol. 195, col. 251.

6. H. of C. Deb., vol. 547, col. 2034.

7. Ehrlich, p. 21.

8. 13. U.N. GAOR 148 (1958).

For a very good analysis of the interaction of law and politics at this early stage, see Ehrlich, pp 20-35.

9. Ibid.

10. H. of C. Deb., vol. 550, coll. 387-93, 402-16 for speeches by

the Rt. Hon. Aneurin Bevan and the then Prime Minister, the Rt. Hon. Sir Anthony Eden, in the House of Commons, 14 March 1956.

11. H. of C. Deb., vol. 199, coll. 205-10.

This speech by Lord Attlee was given in the House of Lords, on the 25th July 1956.

12. Ibid. Study of The United Nations General Assembly Official Records (UN GAOR) for this period is essential for an understanding of the development of the Cyprus problem. Particularly interesting are the speeches of the Greek and Turkish Foreign Secretaries, Mr. Averoff and Mr. Zorlu.

13. H. of C. Deb., vol. 550, coll. 387-93, 402-16.

14. Ibid.

15. See the speech of Mr. Sarper (Turkey); 11th Session, First Comm. 228.

16. H. of L. Deb., vol. 199, coll. 205-10.

17. Ibid.

18. Ibid.

19. Per Tornaritis, 'The Right of Self Determination with Special Reference to the Republic of Cyprus', p. 8. For further bibliography concerning self determination, see Tornaritis as above.

20. See the speech of Mr. Averoff before the UN, as above.

21. 13 UN GAOR 148 (1958).

22. 13 UN GAOR, 1st Comm. 256 (1958).

23. Ibid.

24. Ehrlich, p. 27.

25. Foley, 'Legacy of Strife', p. 87.

26. 13 UN GAOR, 1st Comm. (1958).

27. Xydis, 'Cyprus, Reluctant Republic'.

28. Xydis, as above.

29. Ehrlich, pp 46-51.

30. Makarios, 'Proposals to amend the Cyprus Constitution'.

31. Ibid.

32. Ibid.

33. See, on the general subject of Treaties, McNair, 'The Law of Treaties'.

See also the General Assembly's 'Declaration of the Prohibition of Military, Political or Economic Coercion in the conclusion of Treaties'. Also, Ehrlich, p. 49.

34. Cyprus, Cmnd. 1093; also, 'Cyprus, the problem in perspective', issued by the P.I.O., Nicosia.

35. See Articles in Cyprus Today, 1964, vol. 11 No. 4, particularly, Tornaritis 'The Constitutional Problem of Cyprus'; Tenekides, 'The Cyprus Problem viewed from the standpoint of International Law'.

36. See Dr. Kuchuk's 'Reply to President's Memorandum', the Turkish side's reply to Makarios's Proposals to amend the Constitution.

37. See Dr. Plaza's approach to self determination in his Report.

38. Ibid.

For recent contributions to the subject of self-determination see: W. Conner, 'Self-Determination: the New Phase', World Politics, Vol. 20, and V. Van Dyke, 'Self-Determination and Minority Rights' International Studies Quarterly (1969). For an understanding of the workings of parliamentary bodies in Greece and Turkey as regards the Cyprus problem, see Th. Couloumbis, 'Greek Political Reaction to American and NATO Influences' (New Haven and London: Yale University Press, 1966); C. H. Dodd, 'Politics and Government in Turkey' (Berkeley and Los Angeles, University of California Press, 1969); and P. Terlexis, 'Diplomacy and Politics of the Cyprus Question' (in Greek). An interesting recent book is 'The Cyprus Question' by Leontios Ierodiakonou, reviewed by Paschalis M. Kitromilides in the American Political Science Review, LXVII, No. 4, p. 1448.

ZÜRICH, ITS AFTERMATH, AND THE UNEASY YEARS

1. All the essential documents can be found in 'Cyprus, Cmnd. 1093'.

2. See the article of Professor Tenekides, as above (footnote 35 of the Introduction); Tornaritis, 'Self Determination', pp 16-22.

2a. See Tenekides, as above.

3. Tornaritis, 'Self Determination', p. 19.

4. See Tenekides, as above.

5. For general evaluations, see De Smith 'The New Commonwealth and its Constitutions', p. 282, to be referred to as De Smith; Friedrich, 'Trends of Federalism in Theory and Practice' (to be referred to as Friedrich), p. 123; Ezejifor, 'Protection of Human rights under the Law', p. 224. Particularly valuable are also Tsatsos, "Observations on the Cyprus Constitution" (In Greek), and Tornaritis, "The birth of the Cyprus Republic and its Form" (In Greek).
Also Papadopoulos, 'Cyprus, Developments and Realities'.

6. De Smith, p. 286; Kyriakides, p. 57.

7. De Smith, p. 286; Kyriakides, p. 63.

8. De Smith, p. 292; Kyriakides p. 68.

9. For a most thorough examination of the 1960 Constitution, see Tornaritis, 'Cyprus and its Constitution'.

10. See De Smith, as above.

11. Kyriakides makes this point well, pp 62-63.

12. Friedrich, p. 125 etc.

13. Kyriakides, p. 77.

14. The Turkish Communal Chamber, 'The Turkish Case: 70:30 and the Greek Tactics'.

15. 'Cyprus, the Problem in Perspective' (P.I.O.); see particularly, the Proposals of Makarios to amend the Constitution.

16. De Smith, p. 285.

17. Friedrich, p. 125.

18. 'Cyprus, The Problem in Perspective', as above. The Proposals of Archbishop Makarios for revising the Constitution can be found in this publication (in summary form).

19. See Kyriakides, p. 83; also, the Turkish Cypriot publication 'The facts about the Separate Majority Right . . . in the House of Representatives' by Halit Ali Riza; also, Dr. Kuchuk, The Turkish Reply to Archbishop Makarios's Proposals.

20. Friedrich, p. 126.

21. In the chapter on 'Division or Unity?'.

22. De Smith, p. 285 etc.
23. President Makarios's Proposals to revise the Constitution.
24. Tornaritis, 'Cyprus and its Constitution', p. 57.
25. Friedrich, p. 127.
26. Friedrich, p. 127.
27. In this I seem to disagree with Ehrlich, p. 38.
28. See Kyriakides, p. 94; and the most valuable paper prepared by Mr. Clerides on this question, 'Outline of the negotiations regarding the Question of Municipalities in the Five Towns' (to be referred to as Clerides).
29. Clerides, p. 1.
30. See Clerides.
31. See the Proposals of Archbishop Makarios and the reply thereto of Dr. Kuchuk.
32. Ehrlich, p. 38. This point is also made by De Smith.
33. Ehrlich, p. 38.
34. See Dr. Kuchuk's 'Reply to the President's Memorandum'.
35. On this see 'The Cyprus problem before the UN' (Nicosia 1965).
36. I am very grateful to Mr. Clerides for giving me permission to see the 'Intercommunal negotiations' files.
37. See later, under 'The Turkish Invasion', where I deal with the principle of necessity.
38. Tornaritis, 'Cyprus and its Constitution', p. 69.
39. Many of the relevant documents can be found in 'Cyprus, the Problem in Perspective'; see also, Tornaritis, as above.
40. Adams and Cottrell 'Cyprus between East and West'; Kyriakides, p. 157 etc.
41. Adams and Cottrell.
42. This letter can be found in 'A Problem in Perspective', p. 33.
43. Adams and Cottrell, p. 29; Kyriakides, p. 159.
44. N. S. Khrushchev speaking to a correspondent of Isvestia on 5th May, 1964.
45. It is clear that the Turkish leadership was throughout aiming at establishing artificial separation between the two Communities. It is nowadays fashionable to speak of the Turkish Community of Cyprus as oppressed and isolated but the truth seems to be different. In fact if the Turks of Cyprus suffered hardship and inconvenience during the period we are discussing, this was mainly due to their leadership. The following order of the Turkish leadership brought to the notice of UNFICYP and the UN Security Council says:

"Turkish Cypriots not in possession of a permit are prohibited to enter the Greek sector.

1. Those who disobey the order with a view to trading with Greek-Cypriots should pay a fine of £25 or be punished with imprisonment.

2. A fine will be imposed on:
   (a) those who converse or enter into negotiations with Greek-Cypriots or accompany any stranger into our sector;
   (b) Those who come into contact with Greek-Cypriots for any official work;
   (c) Those who appear before Greek-Cypriots for any official work;
   (d) Those who visit the Greek-Cypriot hospital for examination or in order to obtain pharmaceuticals...

4. A fine of £25 or other severe punishment and one month's imprisonment or whipping should be imposed on those who enter the Greek-Cypriot sector:
   (a) for promenade;
   (b) for friendly association with Greek-Cypriots;
   (c) for amusement..."

In his reports on Cyprus of 12th December, 1964, and 11th March, 1965, the ex-UN Secretary-General, U Thant, states:

"The situation is complicated by evidence made available to UNFICYP that certain non-normal conditions are being kept in existence by measures applied by the Turkish Community to its own members."

U Thant, Report on Cyprus,
12th December, 1964.

"The Turkish Cypriot policy of self-isolation has led the community in the opposite direction from normality.

The Community leadership discourages the Turkish Cypriot population from engaging in personal, commercial or other contacts with their Greek-Cypriot compatriots, from applying to government offices in administrative matters or from resettling in their home villages if they are refugees".

U Thant, Report on Cyprus,
11th March, 1965.

THE TURKISH INVASION OF CYPRUS

1. Many difficult questions are raised concerning the coup. Did the coup succeed? It is clear that military resistance to it disappeared before the Turkish invasion, but, at the same time, vigorous diplomatic initiatives with the purpose of removing the Cypriot Junta had been embarked upon, particularly by Archbishop Makarios before the UN and the British Government. In this sense, the coup cannot be said to have survived the necessary test of durability. In addition, it had not been recognised by any foreign Government and it was, from the very beginning, quite generally predicted that the Sampson Government could not last for more than a week. Moreover, since the Cyprus operation had obviously been planned in Athens by the Greek Junta, it could well be claimed that what had happened was not so much a coup but foreign military intervention in the affairs of a sovereign country. On the other hand (regarding this last point) one could say that after the military had intervened, civilian Anti-Makarios elements took over, and that, at that point, the character of the operation changed from a military intervention by a foreign country to a political coup. If this was indeed the case and the coup can be said to have succeeded (in that the coup leaders controlled Cyprus' territory, had formed an Administration and had liquidated all internal opposition to the regime) then, since Mr. Clerides assumed power on the 22nd of July as President Makarios' constitutional successor and was universally accepted as the personification of the Constitutional order which the Greek Junta had attempted to overthrow, the conclusion seems to be that Constitutional legitimacy at that point 'revived'. On the other hand, if it is maintained that the coup did not succeed in that it never exhibited those signs of stability necessary before legitimation through revolution can be said to have been achieved (and this is the version I incline to), then the 'coup of the 15th July' was an unsuccessful attempt to assassinate President Makarios and topple his Government, and there was no Governmental hiatus in Constitutional legitimacy.

2. See the address of Archbishop Makarios before the UN General Assembly on the 2nd October, 1974, and the address of the then Greek Minister of Foreign Affairs, Mr. G. Mavros, on 22nd September, 1974.

3. See, particularly, Ian Walker's Report in 'The Sun' on 5th August, 1974; also Frank Thompson's report in the "Daily Mail", on 10th August, 1974. Relevant material can be found in 'The Attila Peacemakers', published by the Public Information Office, Nicosia. There has been a lot of discussion concerning alleged atrocities committed by Greek-Cypriots at the expense of the Turkish-Cypriot population in the southern part of Cyprus immediately after the Turkish invasion. Any such atrocities are, of course, strongly condemned, and it cannot be denied that outrages did take place at the expense of innocent civilians on both sides. Two points however must be made (which, it must be clearly stated, in no way minimise one's abhorrence for such atrocities and crimes). First, it seems legitimate to draw a distinction between the calculated and ruthless policy of genocide, extermination and destruction practised by the Turkish army, and individual crimes and massacres committed by Greeks at the expense of Turks in response to the reports about Turkish atrocities. (This, I repeat, in no way justifies any outrages or crimes nor can it even be presented as an explanation — but it is part of the background and in any evaluation or allocation of responsibility cannot be ignored.) Secondly, as soon as there were reports concerning alleged crimes and, in particular, the mass grave found near Maratha village, Acting President Clerides, on the 2nd September, 1974, immediately expressed his Government's readiness to agree to an independent investigation by the United Nations and the International Red Cross in the presence of an observer of the Government and of the Turkish side. In any case, the Government condemned 'with abhorrence the reported crime regardless of which side is responsible'. Furthermore, the Government challenged the Turkish side to allow an independent investigation, by a commonly accepted committee, of all crimes or acts of violence, atrocities, rapes and looting reported both in the areas controlled by the invasion forces and those controlled by the Government. Both offers were refused by the Turkish side.

4. This subject is excellently dealt with in a Special Study by Jean Pictet 'The need to restore the laws and customs relating to armed conflicts', to be found in The Review of the International

Commission of Jurists, No. 1, p. 22.

5. Under Article 12.4 of the International Covenant on Civil and Political Rights of 1966 'no one shall be arbitrarily deprived of the right to enter his own country'.

6. The refugee problem is dealt with comprehensively by the 'Study Mission Report' prepared for the use of 'The Subcommittee to Investigate problems connected with refugees'; this is a Subcommittee of the Committee on the Judiciary of the US Senate (the Chairman is Edward Kennedy). This report will be referred to as 'the Report'.

7. Much of this information has been taken from a paper issued by the Government of Cyprus, 'The Economic Consequences of the Turkish Invasion'.

8. See Senator Kennedy's Introduction to 'the Report'.

9. On Treaties generally see Oppenheim — Lauterpacht, Lord McNair's 'The Law of Treaties', Kelsen's various works; Tornaritis' 'Constitutional and Legal Problems' p. 12. On the general subject of Intervention by Treaty Right, see Zotiades' 'Intervention by Treaty Right and its Legality in present day International Law'; also see the foreword to such work by D. S. Constantopoulos.

10. See Tornaritis, 'The Right of Self-Determination with Special Reference to the Republic of Cyprus'. Also, the references to this subject in the first two chapters of the present study.

11. A-G of the Republic v Ibrahim (C.L.R. 195) see Kelsen 'General Theory of Law and State'; Hart's 'Concept of law'. On the subject of continuity of Constitutions see Oxford Essays in Jurisprudence, Vol. II and, particularly, the Essays by Dr. Finnis and Mr. Eekelaar.

12. Ibid.

13. per Vassiliades J. p 170

14. per Triantafyllides J.

15. Ibid

16. Ibid p 240

17. for Changeability of Constitutions, see Tornaritis, p 75 of 'Constitutional and Legal Problems'.

18. Indeed, the only way one can reconcile Turkey's invocation of the Treaty of Guarantee as affording justification for the invasion and its claim that the 1960 Constitutional arrangements are no longer of effect is to say that the invasion was embarked upon under such arrangements but resulted in the abrogation of the 1960 Constitutional order. But this is not the way Turkey has

presented its case. The Turkish thesis has been that it was the events following the 1963 disturbances that deprived the Constitution if its validity and not the invasion and its aftermath. It must be further noted that Mr. Denktash, the Turkish Cypriot leader, continues to call himself 'Vice President of the Republic', an office established by the 1960 Constitution. Recently, the Turkish side has not confined itself to claims concerning the invalidity of the previous Constitutional arrangements, but has also declared that the State of Cyprus has disappeared, that Archbishop Makarios is only the leader of the Greek Cypriot Community and cannot represent the Republic of Cyprus etc. Such claims cannot be taken seriously. The UN still recognises Cyprus as a sovereign and independent State and is followed in this by the World Community as a whole. Indeed, if one took such claims seriously, one would have to conclude that such consequences could only be the result of the Turkish invasion since, before such invasion, there could be no question about the independence, sovereignty and indivisibility of the Cyprus Republic. Acceptance of this, would, in its turn, undermine and completely destroy Turkey's alleged justification of the invasion.

19. For an analysis of the Declaration of the Geneva, see Tornaritis, 'Cyprus and Federalism', and Clerides (Lefkos), 'Demands of the Turkish Cypriot Community since 1955'.

20. See the letter of President Johnson to Premier Inonu — Chapter 2.

21 The subject of American involvement is very well dealt with in 'The Report'.

22. America's role in the Cyprus tragedy has been extensively discussed and criticised in Congressional Debates, both in the Senate and the House of Representatives. See, particularly, the speeches of (in the 'Congressional Record'): Senator Kennedy (16th August, 1974); Senate Resolution 386 — 'A resolution expressing the sense of the Senate regarding the Crisis on Cyprus' — and the speech of Senator Tunney (S 15183) who, among other things, stated: 'I was shocked and dismayed at the Turkish actions. They had no justification once the original provocations of the Greek Junta and Sampson coup had been rectified. The way to peaceful negotiation was finally before the parties, but the Turks rejected this path, and chose instead to rely on force. The Turkish side displayed bad faith at the negotiating table and callous disregard for human life in its onslaught'; also, see the speech of Representative Biaggi (H 8677) ('the overall response of

the Department of State to this major international crisis has been both dismal and disappointing'); Senator Kennedy (S 14560) ('Should not our Government give more evidence of concern? What are American policy objectives? What is the substance of our activities? What have we done to restrain Turkish forces?'); Representative Bingham (E 5561), who expressed dismay 'at the shocking manner in which the Government of Turkey has been using brute force, at the cost of innocent lives, to seek to impose its will in Cyprus'; Representative Brademas (H 8679); Representative Sarbanes (H 8681); Representative Eilberg (and the interesting article by Dean Liacouras quoted in this speech) (E 5595); and Senator Eagleton (S 15946). The failures of American diplomacy have also been extensively discussed in the World Press. Particularly interesting are: an article by Anthony Sampson in The Washington Post, 20th August; various editorials in the New York Times, particularly its leading article on the 16th August 'Imperatives for Cyprus' ets. An interesting recent article dealing with Kissinger and American foreign policy by Hans Morgenthau can be found in the Encounter, November 1974.

23. In full, Dr. Kissinger's Proclamation reads as follows: 'US has been playing an active role in negotiations on Cyprus. The President and the Secretary of the State have been in daily touch about them. The Secretary has also been in frequent touch with Prime Minister Ecevit, including four times by telephone during 24 hours; he has been in touch with Mr. Callaghan on telephone, with Prime Minister Karamanlis by letter and with the Cypriot leaders.

US position is as follows: We recognise that the position of the Turkish Community required considerable improvement and protection. We have supported a greater degree of autonomy for them. The parties are negotiating on one or more Turkish autonomous areas. The avenues of diplomacy have not been exhausted and therefore US would consider a resort to military action unjustified. We made it clear to all the parties US would have to act in accordance with the Statement.' (13th August, 1974).

24. This is clearly implied in Secretary Kissinger's August 19 statement on American Policy on Cyprus. The Secretary stated that there was no doubt that the extent of the Turkish zone to be demarcated was negotiable. This, far from being a concession to the Greek Cypriot side, is but acceptance of Turkey's demands on the substantive problem. The American Government, in other

words, has accepted that there should be some kind of geographical federation and accepts the negotiability of only one of the incidents of such solution.

25. Not only was there bias towards Turkey, but there is considerable evidence of 'the cynicism' (the Kennedy Report) with which the US Government has regarded the crisis. In fact, as the study Mission sent by the Refugee Subcommittee reported, evidence available to it, including conversations with American officials, suggested that even humanitarian assistance sent by the American Government for the refugees was being manipulated for policy reasons.

26. Was American foreign policy one of the casualties of Watergate? On this see the very interesting comments of the Kennedy Report which points out that at some of the most crucial moments of the crisis, when decisive action was called for, America was, in effect, without an effectively functioning Government as a result of the dislocation brought about by Watergate.

27. In a very valuable letter to 'The Times'.

28. In letters to 'The Times'.

29. Another interesting aspect of English policy has been that the Foreign Office has not as yet expressed any definite views on the substance of the constitutional problem. Both at Geneva and elsewhere, Mr Callaghan expressed preference for (or commented on the inevitability of) some kind of geographically defined solution, without going into any details. At first, it seemed as if the English Government preferred some kind of 'groupings of villages' solution, or some kind of 'administrative areas' settlement. Lately, however, they seem to have gone beyond this and to have progressed a considerable way in the direction of a 'federal solution', but, as pointed out in the chapter on Regionalism, the essential point which really helps differentiate proposed solutions from each other relates to powers and functions, namely, what Governmental powers should be accorded to the regional or local units to be created? The English Government has remained curiously silent on this point.

30. See the Address of Archbishop Makarios before the UN General Assembly on 1st October, 1974.

31. Ibid.

32. Ibid.

GENERAL STATEMENT OF THE CYPRUS PROBLEM

1. Marshall 'Constitutional Theory'; De Smith 'Constitutional Law'; Wheare 'Modern Constitutions'; De Smith 'The New Commonwealth and its Constitutions'; See footnote 1 of the Introduction.

2. 'Cyprus and Federalism' by Tornaritis, 1974.

3. For defects of Zürich, see chapter 2; the various works of Tornaritis, particularly 'The Right of Self-Determination with Special Reference to the Republic of Cyprus', "Constitutional and Legal Problems in the Republic of Cyprus", particularly pages 7-21; see also the Report of the UN Mediator on Cyprus to the Secretary-General.

4. per Triantafyllides J (as he then was) in A-G of the Republic v Ibrahim (C.L.R. 222).

5. De Smith in his The New Commonwealth, to be referred to as De Smith p. 282.

6. De Smith p. 282.

7. Kyriakides pp 72-103.

8. De Smith p. 285.

9. Idem.

10. The Plaza Report par. 38.

11. The 1963 Makarios proposals can be found in 'Cyprus, the Problem in Perspective', published by the Public Information Office of Cyprus, Appendix I; see also the analysis of Dr Plaza pars 38, 39, 40, 41, 42, 43, 44.

12. This question is dealt with in greater detail later — see 'The protection of the Turkish Minority'.

13. Charles Foley, 'Cyprus, from Rebellion to Civil Strife.'

14. Wheare 'Modern Constitutions', p. 32.
For the general problems of Commonwealth Constitutions, see De Smith. For a brilliant analysis of functions of Constitutions see Bickel, 'The Least Dangerous Branch'; also, the great judgment of Marshall CJ in Marbury v Madison.

15. Bickel 'The Least Dangerous Branch'.

16. Bickel, as above.

CYPRUS AND POLITICAL FEDERATION

1. On the general subject of Federal Government see Wheare 'Federal Government'; also, the Chapter in J. S. Mill, 'Representative Government'; also, see the shorter account in Wheare 'Modern Constitutions' p. 14; Also, R. L. Watts, 'New Federations, Experiments in the Commonwealth'; Livingston, 'Federalism and Constitutional Change'. For the various Federal Constitutions see Amos J. Peaslee's 'Constitutions of the Nations'; The Federal Constitutions mainly studied in the preparation of this Essay are: the Constitutions of America, Canada, Australia, the Federal German Republic, Austria, the Swiss Confederation — and the Regional ones of Italy, Burma etc. On the subject of Commonwealth Constitutions see De Smithp. 253.

2. This definition is Wheare's.

3. See Tornaritis in Constitutional and Legal Problems, p. 23 and Schwarzenberger in Current Legal Problems, 1963 p. 18.

4. Lord Radcliffe: Constitutional Proposals for Cyprus; Cmnd 42.

5. On the general subject of Cyprus' geographical and topographical nature see Tornaritis 'Cyprus and its Constitutions' and the various information pamphlets issued by the Public Information Office of Cyprus. Also, see the Introduction to the present study.

6. H. J. Laski, The New Republic, XCVIII (1939), p. 367.

7. Professor Beloff was able, in 1953, to assert that the Federal solution was enjoying 'a widespread popularity such as it had never known before'. M. Beloff, 'The Federal Solution in its Application to Europe, Asia and Africa', Political Studies, (1953) p. 114.

8. W. S. Livingston, 'Federalism and Constitutional Change' (1956) pp. 1-2. See also Watts, p. 15.

9. The Plaza Report.

10. Tornaritis, 'Constitutional and Legal Problems' p. 22.

11. The opinion of Robert Komer, former American Ambassador to Turkey, was the following: 'The Federal Solution Turkey is calling for would make Cyprus only nominally independent. In reality, it would be partitioned de facto into two quasi-states each protected by its guarantors. Moreover, this uneasy compromise would be pregnant with seeds of further trouble. It might only prove to be another of the temporary patch-up jobs which avert the immediate crisis but perpetuate the problem'.

THE CENTRAL GOVERNMENT

1. I must acknowledge my great indebtedness (in connection with this Chapter and, to a lesser extent, Regionalism) to the 'Intercommunal Talks' files which were made available to me by kind permission of Mr. Clerides. Particularly the present Chapter, namely, the Structuring of the Central Government, owes a lot to the proposals, suggestions and views canvassed in such files. And once more, one must pay tribute to the indefatigable efforts of Mr. Clerides, as Greek Cypriot negotiator at the Intercommunal Discussions, in search of a fair, durable and workable settlement).

2. By the Donoughmore Commission in 1928 (Cmnd. 3131) 1928.

3. Mr. Durga Das Basu (Introduction to the Constitution of India, 2nd Edition p. 398).

4. De Smith, p. 118.

5. 'Constitutional proposals for Cyprus'. Lord Radcliffe's Report Cmnd. 42.

6. Ibid.

7. Ibid. par. 38.

8. See the Proposals of Archbishop Makarios for revising the Constitution.

REGIONALISM

1. On the general subject of Regionalism, see Tornaritis, 'The Concept of Local Government within the framework of a Unitary State'.Dendia, 'Administrative Law', p. 454 seq; Stasinopoulos, 'Lessons of Administrative Law', p. 160 seq; Kyriakopoulos, 'Greek Administrative Law', p. 92 seq. See also statements from Waline, Duguit, Burdeau and Prelot as quoted in Tornaritis 'Local Government' p. 678.

2. On Local Government, see Jennings 'Principles of Local Government Law'; UK Hicks 'Development from Below', Macnalty's 'Local Government'; Sir John Maud's 'Local Government in England and Wales'; Wade's 'Administrative Law' p. 24 seq; Richards' 'The New Local Government System'. Also, relevant Chapters can be found in Hood Phillips 'Constitutional and Administrative Law' and Wade and Phillips 'Constitutional Law'. The standard work in the field is Cross 'Local Government Law'.

3. See the Regionalism of Spain; of Italy — Tornaritis, p. 8.

4. Wheare's 'Modern Constitutions', p. 14 seq.

5. See extracts from Ambrosini, quoted in Tornaritis' 'Local Government', p. 8.

6. Jennings, p. 1; Maud pp 1-8; Richards; Hicks pp 1-25.

7. Jennings pp 5-11; Maud pp 9-30; MacNalty p. 153 seq.

8. Jennings p. 215; Richards p. 46; Wade p. 27.

9. Jennings, p. 1.

10. Richards, p. 34.

11. See Halsbury's Laws of England (3rd Edition), Vol. 24 p. 359; Cross on Local Government; the various recent governmental Reports on the organisation and structure of Local Government in England.

12. MacNalty, p. 67.

13. Hicks, p. 440.

14. See Nedjati's 'Administrative Law'; Tornaritis, 'Local Government', p. 12 seq.

15. For more information on English methods of control see Jennings' last Chapter; Halsbury p. 364.

16. On the difficulties associated with the concept of autonomy, see Tornaritis' 'Cyprus and Federalism', p. 46, note 61.

17. See Wheare 'Federal Government', p. 93.

18. See Wheare 'Federal Government' pp 75-80 etc.

19. Politically self-sufficient cantons should be avoided at all costs."The Guardian" comment on the American proposals for Cyprus (31st July 1964) has lost nothing of its persuasive force: "The idea of Turkish Cypriot cantons, administered by Turkish Cypriots, is impractical, uneconomic and against the eventual interests of the Turkish Cypriots. It would also involve uprooting many Turkish and Greek villagers and would contain the seeds of future communal strife. The rights of a minority can be protected in other ways and the Greek Cypriots are prepared to consider it".

20. It may be that some contradiction (more apparent than real) may be detected if one simply compares the chapters on Cyprus and Political Federation and Regionalism. In the former I seem to reject all federal or geographically defined solutions whereas in the latter I seem prepared to accept what could be called a geographical settlement (or, as I would call it, a 'locality' solution) — as indeed I am. In this sense the chapter on Regionalism is characterised by a realistic acknowledgement that politics is the art of the possible and that world diplomacy, inextricably interwoven with the Cyprus problem, is no impartial tribunal deciding the matter on the accepted principles of logic, fairness and common sense. But this kind of realism does not deviate from principle or, at least, it does not do so significantly for, as I also make clear, any kind of geographically defined settlement must be accompanied by clearly formulated safeguards preserving the unity and integrity of the state.

THE PROTECTION OF THE TURKISH MINORITY

1. Tornaritis, 'Promotion and Protection of Human Rights of National, Ethnic and other minorities, in the Republic of Cyprus', Nicosia 1974. Se Capotorti, special rapporteur, in Study on the rights of persons belonging to ethnic, religious and linguistic minorities, E/CN/Sub 2/L 582. See, also, the excellent memorandum (to be referred to as the Memorandum) submitted to the Sub Commission on Prevention of Discrimination and Protection of Minorities by the Secretary-General. This memorandum attempts to present, in an organised fashion, the principal elements which must be taken into consideration in any attempt to define or clarify minorities. Also, De Smith, p. 106. Especially useful, is chapter X of 'The Politics and Dynamics of Human Rights' by Moses Moskowitz. Of particular interest are the three lectures given under the auspices of the Minority Rights Group. (1st lecture: 'What Rights should Minorities have?' by Conor Cruise O'Brien; 3rd lecture: 'The Roots of Prejudice', by Professor Marie Jahoda; and the 2nd lecture 'The Integration of Minorities', by Prof. Edmund Leach. This 2nd lecture proved particularly useful.) Very interesting comments can also be found in Ben Whitaker's Essay on Minorities, first published in the New Internationalist in June 1973.

2. Dr. Plaza's Report.

3. See the Turkish case as presented both before Dr. Plaza and elsewhere.

4. The Memorandum.

5. This is basically Dr. Plaza's approach in his Mediator's Report.

6. The Memorandum.

7. Ibid.

8. Particularly interesting are the debates in the Political Committee of the 20th General Assembly Session in 1965 concerning the Cyprus question. As Moskowitz observes at p. 268, such debates 'revealed a strong bias against the very idea of minorities'. Minorities, of course, should be strictly protected, but 'the principle of separate development', almost all agreed, could only lead to disaster. Particularly interesting are the comments of the Representative of Equador (A/C. 1/PV.1410; pp 26-27); of the Representative of Nepal (A/C 1/PV. 1410; p. 37). The Indian Representative spoke in the same vein, and warned against the dangers attending the erosion of the unity and integrity of the

State, particularly in the case of many States of America, Asia, Latin America which 'are multi-racial, multi-religious and multi-lingual'. (A/C. 1/PV. 1411. p. 6). Speaking for African nations, the representative of Kenya declared that his country believed 'that all sovereign states should be supported in their endeavours to function democratically', and the Representative of Uganda could not 'seriously endorse the idea that any country (could) correctly speak of two separate Communities or speak of the division of Cyprus into two separate entities' (A/C. 1/PV. 1413, p. 3).

9. See Dr. Plaza's Recommendations in his Report.
10. De Smith, p. 134.
11. De Smith, p. 136.
12. Dr. Plaza's Report, pp 25-28.
13. See the speech of the then Foreign Minister of the Republic, Mr. Kyprianou, before the General Assembly of the UN on the 14th October, 1965.
14. See the Minorities article of Ben Whitaker mentioned above.

DIVISION OR UNITY?

1. For a stimulating book on a not very different subject, see S. V. Cowen 'The Foundations of Freedom'.

2. The three Minority Rights Group lectures mentioned in footnote 1 of the Protection of the Turkish Minority have proved very useful in this chapter as well.

3. Ralf Dahrendorf.

4. Roy Jenkins. See Ben Whitaker's lecture on Minorities.

5. Mr. Clerides is reported to have said this in the Guardian of the 16th August 1974.

6. Tagore.

7. Tagore.

8. The Plaza Report, par. 26.

9. Watts, 'New Federations, Experiments in the Commonwealth' (O.U.P.) pp 15-16 etc.

XII

POSTSCRIPTUM

Since the above was written, there have been some developments which cannot go unnoticed. I will first discuss various issues relating to the substantive problem and then briefly advert to recent English foreign policy on Cyprus.

Negotiations have begun (or are continuing) between the Representatives of the two Communities; such Discussions at first were confined to humanitarian issues but have since then expanded by the inclusion in the agenda of substantive constitutional problems. It was argued above that the Greek Cypriot side should not negotiate unless some elementary conditions were first satisfied, and it was stated in no uncertain terms that the return of the refugees to their homes and the withdrawal of at least some of the Turkish troops were such conditions. This point, it is true, was mainly developed in connection with the holding of full talks on Cyprus in the framework of the Treaty of Guarantee and it could, therefore, be argued that even though what were above put forward as necessary prerequisites to genuine negotiations have been ignored, still, the fact that responsibility for a settlement has, as it were, come to devolve mainly upon the two Communities is a positive development and one to be welcomed. This may be so, but one cannot ignore the fact that negotiations for a resolution of the substantive problem are taking place against a background whose main characteristics are continued (and patently illegal) occupation of a great part of Cyprus territory, a perpetuation of the refugee problem and cynical disregard for U.N. Resolutions, a background, one need not add, hardly conducive to free negotiations or bona fide attempts to reach a workable and fair settlement. Consequently the very fact that negotiations expressly directed towards a resolution of the political and constitutional problem have been embarked upon cannot but be considered as yet another concession on the part of the Greek Cypriot side.

Furthermore, there was recently an important announcement concerning the Intercommunal talks, namely that one of the subjects being discussed is the question of "the powers of the Central Government within a Federal State". Two questions present themselves with regard to this development. First, how does this qualify what was said above and, particularly, the Chapters on Political Federation and Regionalism? And, secondly, how should this particular question be answered, i.e. what powers should be accorded to the Central Government of the Republic of Cyprus given the fact that some Federal framework of Government has become inevitable?

1. Federal Government comes in a considerable variety of forms and a great number of institutional variations is possible. Three characteristics of government seem to be inevitably associated with federal experiments and would thus be almost certainly reflected in any new institutional arrangements that were to be adopted within the framework apparently agreed upon — such are (i) the existence of two different levels of government, the central and the regional or local, (ii) the fact that powers, functions and authority are assigned to the two levels of government on a coordinate and normally independent basis and have to be exercised within the statutorily defined and allotted ambits of activity and without encroachments on the respective and exclusive spheres of competence and (iii) the fact that both central and regional powers derive directly from the Constitution which is supreme law per excellence, in the sense that neither the federal institutions nor the component parts of the federation can exercise either unrestricted power in repealing or amending the Constitution or unilateral authority in modifying the relationship between the constituent units thereby set up.

Within such broad outlines, however, there is no set pattern to be followed by the negotiators. Arrangements must be set up that will conform to the realities of the island, and, in particular, subjects such as the manner in which authority will be distributed, the actual shape of the functions which will be assigned to the two tiers of government, the degree to which the two levels of government are independent or interdependent, etc. must surely command the most meticulous attention and thorough treatment. What cannot be emphasized strongly enough, however, is that the proposed federation for Cyprus must not be based on a strictly defined biregional settlement but on a multiregional one. The fact that some kind of federal framework has been agreed upon does not foreclose consideration of many questions regarding the specification and implementation of such a federal framework, including the crucial issue of the geographical basis for, or geographical units of, such federation in the circumstances of Cyprus. The arguments why insistence on a genuine multiregional settlement and implacable opposition to bizonal solutions cannot abate whatever the temporary realities of local power have been canvassed above and will not be here repeated. Yet, despite the force of such considerations and the almost universal condemnation to which both partition and biregional settlements involving compulsory population movements have been subjected, Turkey continues to insist on a biregional federation based on geographical separation as 'the only realistic solution', to quote Mr. Esenbel, the Turkish Foreign Secretary. Mr. Esenbel, in a recent statement of his, emphasized his side's rejection of a cantonal solution and stressed that the Greeks should understand 'that there is no possibility of turning the clock back'. Mr. Esenbel added that the question of the borders of the Turkish-held area would be discussed only when the Greek side accepted the bizonal federal system. 'Once this is accepted, Turkey will agree to discuss modifications of the present borders . . . the borders are negotiable, but, first, the bizonal system must be accepted'. In case the intercommunal talks failed, Mr. Esenbel said, 'the present de facto situation will continue and the Turkish sector will be consolidated. Therefore the questions now discussed will become facts'. Moreover, recent actions and statements on the part of both the U.S. and British Governments seem to indicate that they both regard a bizonal federal system as inevitable and as something that the Greek Cypriot Community should come to terms with, despite the fact that, as explained above, it is difficult to envisage the recognition of a substantial area of Cyprus as an area of Turkish Administration without a severe compulsory population movement; as a result, the choice offered Cyprus by Turkey and the Great Powers at present seems confined to whether the fait accompli, in all essential respects, should be accepted and legitimated, some minor and as yet undefined concessions on the part of Turkey to follow upon such acceptance and legitimation, or whether the Greek Cypriots should forgo compromise and endure behind barricades as an increasingly Athens-orientated fortress of embitterment, dedicated only to the recapture of the lost homelands. Either way, whether, that is, the Turkish demands are acceded to or the present stalemate continues, a strictly defined bizonal federation (which is both what we have at present and what we would forever

be pledging ourselves to were we to bow before Turkish pressure)
'would not be a short, sharp, cruel solution to the problem. It
would not be a quick slice of the knife . . . dealing with the
problems cruelly and effectively . . . rather it would leave a
running sore which would last for decades' (Lord Bethell in a
speech before the House of Lords on November 5). Already, as the
recent demonstrations and marches indicate, the Greek Cypriot
people, frustrated and bitter at the world's apparent indifference to
the plight of Cyprus and utterly disillusioned over the de facto
partitioning of the island have taken to violent methods for
venting their anger and voicing their desperation. To say that
'familiar hysteria in the streets solves nothing and contributes
nothing' (leading editorial of the Guardian on 20th January, 1975)
is to miss the point, and both ignores the reasons for, and
disregards the dangers of, such bitterness. It was argued above that
unless a fair settlement was reached and effective action taken
against Turkish aggression, the situation would develop all the
ingredients of the Palestinian and other such disputes — 'the
refugees, the hasty partition, the solution imposed from outside,
the hundreds of thousands of displaced persons feeling that they
have nothing to lose, their bitterness festering as the decades pass'.
(Lord Bethell in the above mentioned House of Lords speech).
Clearly, such argument and such prediction were not
misconceived.

2. Which powers should be given to the Central Government
in the proposed Federation? This raises two distinct issues: First,
the form in which legistlative authority should be distributed and,
secondly, the question of which specific legislative powers and
responsibilities should be allocated to the two governmental tiers
to be recognized.

(a) There are three general patterns of distribution of
legislative powers. First, there might be a single legislative list of
regional powers, all residual powers to remain vested in the
Central Authority; secondly, there could be a Central
Government list, all residuary powers to be assigned to the States
or regions; finally, there might be two legislative lists (i.e. a list of
Central Powers and a list of local ones) or, and more usually, there
could be three legislative lists, namely, lists of central, regional or
local and concurrent powers. It should be noticed that even if it is
decided that residual powers will belong to the Centre, a three-list
division of legislative authority may be necessary or desirable as
the use of three catagories of power may somehow allay regional

fears about the actual scope of central power. What scheme of distribution should be adopted for Cyprus? In the Chapter on Regionalism I suggested that the preferable solution would be to enumerate regional powers and expressly declare in the Constitution that all other governmental powers remain vested in the Central institutions and authorities of the Republic, the main reason behind the suggestion that such a scheme be adopted having been the desire to emphasize that the governmental system to be established should be not so much a federal one as one based on the decentralization of authority within an integral state. Such a course no longer seems feasible and, indeed, the statement that what was being discussed was the subject of the powers of the Central Government within a Federal State clearly indicates that, whatever else might emerge from the negotiations currently being held, the powers of the Central Government will be enumerated in the new Constitution. This makes all the more necessary that: (a) there should be two additional lists, one of regional and one of concurrent ones; (b) residual powers should stay with the Central Government; and (c) appropriate devices and mechanisms should be adopted for the purposes of co-ordinating the exercise of governmental powers and ensuring that constitutional flexibility in a rapidly developing world is retained.

(b) Allocation of powers and responsibilities should be based on the following considerations: Whatever concerns the people of Cyprus as a whole rather than the inhabitants of particular regions or localities should be placed under central control, or, to put it differently, whenever it can be seen that matters are interregional ones, or that the needs of the people in given areas of governmental activity are similar and are not dependent either on locality or community, then such matters or areas of legislative activity must be entrusted to the Central Government; powers should be assigned to the authorities best able to administer them; fragmentation of integral and interrelated functions should be avoided; and attribution of functions and responsibilities should not lose sight of the considerable advantages that nowadays almost inevitably flow from central control.

With such considerations in mind, the legislative list of the Central Government should, inter alia, certainly include the following subjects:

External affairs (including Treaty Implementation, citizenship and aliens, immigration and emigration;

Defence (even though if the island is demilitarised, some

different solution may be given here);
Public order, police, prisons;
Law and procedure;
Machinery of government;
Finance (Foreign exchange, Currency and Coinage, Foreign Loans, Taxes, Banking);
Trade, Commerce and Industry (External trade, Interregional trade, Insurance, Weights and Measures, Industries);
Shipping, Navigation, Ports;
Communications and transport (Roads, Air, Posts and telecommunications);
Utilities and Natural Resources (Water and Electricity);
Social Services (Social Welfare Services, Workmen's Compensation, Social Security, Unemployment relief).

As already observed, these should be a concurrent list and it should be provided that when the laws of the General Government upon matters in the concurrent field conflict with the laws of the regional government in that field, then the regional laws must give way to the general laws to the extent of their repugnancy. Concurrent subjects should be the following:

Industrial activity; Banking; Corporations and Companies; Planning; Labour and Social Services; Agriculture; Tourism.
The list of regional powers should be the one given in the chapter on Regionalism.

But, it must be repeated, the fundamental point is whether Turkey will continue insisting upon a strictly defined bizonal system or whether her negotiating position will become more realistic. Regrettably, there appears little chance of the latter. Indeed, the Turkish position has lately hardened as a result of the U.S. Congress's very recent decision (4th February) to cut off military aid to Turkey. The Turkish Government immediately announced that it was suspending talks with the Americans on agreements relating to the basic military pacts between Turkey and the U.S. under which the U.S. maintains in Turkey a force of about 7000 military personnel and technicians, several air bases and numerous sophisticated monitoring installations. Turkey's National Security Council in its turn accused Congress of committing a very grave mistake and "indulging in an experiment of pressure on Turkey" and the caretaker Prime Minister, Mr. Sadi Irmak, said that the Turkish Government would review its relations with the U.S. and NATO. "Turkey is determined to protect the legitimate rights of Turkish Cypriots under all circumstances until the end", he said. Furthermore, since the ban on military aid went into effect, the Turkish authorities have cancelled a meeting which was to have taken place in Brussels between Dr. Kissinger and the Greek and Turkish Foreign Secretaries. Such Turkish reactions to the Congressional ruling to halt U.S. arms shipments to Turkey have clearly caused acute worry to the American Administration. A statement issued by the White House but clearly bearing the stamp of Dr. Kissinger's views said that the suspension of military aid to Turkey was likely "to impede the negotiation of a just Cyprus settlement" and "could have far reaching and damaging effects on the security, and hence the political stability, of all the countries of the region; moreover, the ban would "adversely affect not only Western security but (also) the strategic situation in the Middle East" and might "jeopardise the system on which (American) relations in Eastern Mediterranean have been based for 28 years". The Congressional ruling, in line with what was suggested in the third chapter of this study, is to be welcomed. Such decision not only amounts to the exertion of overdue pressure both on Turkey and the American Government to show greater flexibility in the negotiations relating to Cyprus but can also be seen as important recognition that political legitimation should not be extended to Turkey's attempts to present the other parties with a fait accompli. Indeed, consistently with what was above suggested to be a distinct bias in American policy towards Turkey, President Ford has already called on Congress to authorise a resumption of arms sales to Turkey but congressional leaders have made it clear that they will not act unless there is progress in Cyprus and Turkey makes major concessions and, here, one should repeat that progress can only be said to have been made if the Turkish side abandons its insistence on a strictly defined bizonal federation and declares its readiness to negotiate on the basis of an outline solution which would neither necessitate dislocating compulsory population movements nor result in the virtual carving up of the state. Far from any such indication, Mr. Denktash said on the 4th February that he was in favour of declaring an independent Turkish Cypriot State "as the future copartner of a confederated Republic of Cyprus" and expressed doubts whether the continuation of his talks with Mr. Clerides would serve any useful purpose.

Every strand of the Cyprus problem now appears to lie hopelessly tangled — complication is daily added to complication, external involvement intensifies and the knots seem to be growing daily, enmeshing the Eastern Mediterranean, Middle Eastern security and NATO's weakest flank. Congress has at last halted military aid to Turkey but Ankara's position has hardened and the American Administration does not seem to be embarking on any worthwhile initiatives for breaking the stalemate; Turkey has refused to attend the Brussels discussions and Dr. Kissinger's long delayed initiative has come to a standstill before even getting off the ground; Great Britain has disqualified itself from playing a useful negotiating role in the future (see below), NATO is limping from crisis to crisis and the Eastern block, clearly enjoying fishing in troubled Mediterranean waters and causing as much discomfort as it can to the NATO allies, still studiously avoids alienating either Greece or Turkey and, despite hopes entertained by the Greek Cypriot Community relating to possible Soviet intervention in the island, hopes born of desperation rather than logic, is unlikely at the moment — a time of apparent strain between Washington and Ankara — to jump in on the Greek side. In the island itself, the Intercommunal discussions seem to be grinding to a painful halt under the weight of unacceptable and unrealistic Turkish demands, Mr. Denktash threatens all with a unilateral Proclamation of independence as an intermediate stage to the establishment of a confederation and, meanwhile, a de facto Turkish state is being built in the north of the island whilst 200,000 Greek Cypriots are still languishing in the refugee camps. Things have seldom looked so bleak. What is to be done? I can only repeat what I have said in my analysis of the essence of the Cyprus problem in the IV Chapter. The core of the problem lies in Cyprus itself. If there can be some form of agreement on the shape of a Constitutional settlement (and the recommendations put forward above are thought to provide such a settlement), then the manifold distorting complications might disappear. the numerous extraneous coils and disfigurations might easily fall into place. And, at present. there is simply no meeting point on any such settlement — and there will be none if Turkish demands on a de facto partitioning of the island are not abandoned. If such insistence continues, the prospects for an agreed settlement appear to be nil. Indeed if the choice offered by Turkey is whether the Greek Cypriot Community should accept a solution under which there would be 100,000 refugees and virtual abdication of State authority over a substantial sector of the island or accept no solution at all and allow the present disastrous stalemate to continue, following the second alternative whatever the consequences (and the consequences are bound to be disastrous) appears to be the only defensible course. For, there surely comes a point when concession and realism are no longer the answer, and when courage, however futile, and perseverance in the face of adversity, however destructive, are preferable to temporary relief or transient illusory benefits.

Lincoln College, Oxford. 10th February, 1975

RECENT ENGLISH POLICY ON CYPRUS

The view was expressed above that British inactivity in the face of Cyprus' vicious dismemberment was

(1) in clear violation of the Treaty of Guarantee under which Britain guaranteed Cyprus' independence and sovereignty and

(2) regrettable politically. Yet, the present writer was reluctant to accuse British foreign policy of appeasement or lack of principle because, at that time, the British attitude was, perhaps, unavoidable given Britain's weakened military position and clear American pressure to desist from any dynamic action against Turkey. This assessment must now be reconsidered and the charges of appeasement and giving in to pressure are now thought to be both accurate and fair judgments on the recent performance of the Foreign Office.

As repeatedly observed above, Mr. Callaghan, both at Geneva and elsewhere, was very critical of Turkish policy and aggression, attempted to persuade Turkey to make 'concessions' to the Greek Cypriot side so that meaningful negotiations could resume and a fair settlement become possible and, consistently with Britain's position as a guarantor, refused to take any action that would either help (or give the impression of extending help and/or recognition to) Turkish attempts to create a fait accompli, namely a biregional State with almost complete population separation. In line with such policy, Mr. Callaghan adamantly refused to help the Turkish Government transfer Turkish Cypriots ordinarily resident in the South of the Island to the occupied North as it could be readily seen that such action would

(a) make a fair and workable political settlement more difficult,

(b) help in illegally changing the demographic pattern of the island and,

(c) undermine Britain's position as a guarantor pledged to protect the island's sovereignty and independent status. Despite such early insistence on principle and the hopes entertained by many that the British Government would stand steadfast and firm in its resolution to do nothing that would jeopardize chances of a settlement and its own legal and moral authority in the matter, the Foreign Office, by its recent action in doing what it had for so long said that it would not do, has gone back on its pledges, betrayed its position and duties as a guarantor and has substantially and actively helped the Turks (and the Americans) to proceed further along the road to achieving their long cherished dream of partitioning Cyprus (or imposing upon the Cypriot people some strictly defined geographical solution amounting to de facto partition).

The specific problem until recently confronting the Foreign Office was created in the wake of the Turkish invasion when about 10,000 Turkish Cypriots living around Limassol crowded into the British base. In September, the Turkish Cypriot Administration suggested to the British Government that the refugees should be sent to the Turkish mainland (without disguising their eventual intention to transfer such refugees to the northern part of the island and settle them in the homes of Greek Cypriots), but the British Government indicated that nothing could be done until a full settlement of the refugee problem was reached (which meant that 200,000 Greek Cypriot refugees should also be able to return home) or a political solution emerged from the negotiations between Mr. Clerides and Mr. Denktash. It was also pointed out to the Turkish Cypriots that there was nothing to stop the 'refugees' from leaving the Akrotiri area, and, in fact, the Government of the Republic on many occasions made it clear that it was prepared to extend every guarantee and safeguard concerning the safe return of the above mentioned Turkish Cypriots to their homes, including international supervision. Meanwhile (and there is convincing evidence of this) the Turkish leadership was

(1) doing everything possible to prevent the 'refugees' from returning to their homes by, among other things, promising them bigger and better homes in the north and telling them that there were land and houses there for the taking, and

(2) attempting internationally to represent Britain as detaining the 10,000 Turkish Cypriots against their will, something that was patently not true since it was the 10,000 'refugees' who had gone into the base voluntarily. On the 14th January, four months after the original request and after turning such request down time and time again, Britain gave in to Turkish pressure, by agreeing to the transfer of the refugees to Turkey mainland and from there to the occupied north of Cyprus. Predictably, there were immediate angry reactions in the Greek Cypriot Community, such anger and frustration eventually manifesting themselves in riots and demonstrations against Britain.

The British Government's decision to allow the airlift of these 9,000 Turkish Cypriots from the base at Akrotiri to Turkey mainland and, from there, to the occupied northern area of Cyprus must be dealt with (a) legally and (b) politically.

Legally, there can be little doubt that Great Britain, in yielding to Turkish pressure and, in effect, helping the 'refugees' resettle in the North of the island and, in the process, take over the properties of Greek Cypriots situated there, is in violation both of the International Agreements setting up the Republic of Cyprus and guaranteeing its sovereignty and continued Independence and the recent UN Resolutions dealing with the Cyprus problem.

(a) The Sovereign Bases in Cyprus were created by the Treaty of Establishment and the preamble to the Treaty makes it clear that it was intended to create such military bases in order to give effect to the Declaration made by the Government of the UK on the 17th February, 1959, in which the Government of the UK made it clear that the Akrotiri — Episkopi — Paramali and Dhekekia — Pergamos — Ayios Nicolaos — Xylophagou areas would be retained under full British Sovereignty to be used as military bases and clearly recognised that the rights being conferred on the UK government by the Republic of Cyprus were being conferred for this purpose only. Moreover, Her Majesty's Government solemnly declared that the main purpose of the proposed administration of the sovereign areas was their effective use as military bases and, as a result promised,

> (1) not to develop such areas for other than military purposes,
> (2) not to impair the economic, commercial, or industrial unity or life of the island,
> (3) not to establish commercial or civilian seaports or airports etc. (Declaration by Her Majesty's Government regarding the Administration of the Sovereign Base Areas. This appears in Appendix D to the Treaty of Establishment).

It is immediately clear that in this case the Sovereign Base areas were not used as military bases but for the transportation of civilian passengers; that, in effect, the Sovereign Base Areas were used as civilian airports, and that, by such use of the Bases, in consequence of which a substantial number of Turkish Cypriots were enabled to move and settle in another part of the island against the clearly expressed wishes of the Government of the Republic, neither the economic or commercial prospects of Cyprus nor its industrial unity have been promoted; and again, it is abundantly clear that the UK authorities, by the above mentioned use of the airport facilities of the Bases, have neither shown due regard "for the interests of the Republic of Cyprus and of its citizens, including in particular the usual rights of private property" (Section 9 (2) of Annex B, Treaty of Establishment) nor observed the pledge for "full co-operation with the Republic of Cyprus" (Declaration by Her Majesty's Government, as above; also, under the above mentioned Declaration — such a Declaration itself being an International Agreement — the British Government declared that "the laws applicable to the Cypriot population of the Sovereign Base areas will be as far as possible the same as the laws of the Republic" (par 3(2)). As the learned Attorney General of the Republic, Mr. Tornaritis, has pointed out, various laws of the Republic impose various restrictions upon travel (passports etc.), and, obviously, the exit of such people from the Republic no less than their resettlement in the homes of Greek Cypriots in the North was in clear contravention of Cypriot Law).

(b) Britain's aid to Turkey in this matter manifestly contravenes the Treaty of Guarantee. Under this Treaty, the UK guaranteed the independence, territorial integrity and security of the Republic and also undertook "to prohibit any ... activity aimed at promoting, directly or indirectly, either Union of Cyprus with any other State or partition of the Island". Since there is no doubt that the 'refugees' have already settled in the northern part of the island, since Turkey's proposed intention was always known to Britain and since such development directly promotes partition of the island contrary to the aforesaid provision of Act II of the Treaty of Guarantee or, at least, an equally destructive fait accompli (namely, separation of the two Communities within defined and fixed geographical boundaries), the British Government's action offends against the Treaty and its obligations thereunder.

(c) Moreover, such action of the British Government also offends against the Resolutions of the Sec. Council and the General Assembly calling upon all States to respect the sovereignty, independence and territorial integrity of the Republic of Cyprus. In fact, Britain's assistance to Turkey in this matter cannot be described otherwise than as an act of intervention against the Republic (such acts and interventions being directly prohibited by the above mentioned UN Resolutions).

Politically, the decision of the British Government is strongly to be condemned. It appears that powerful American pressures behind the scenes may have been the key factor in persuading the Foreign Office and Mr. Callaghan that the time for resolute stands on principle was gone and that it was time for 'realism', even though such realism meant betrayal of solemn international obligations. British officials insist that the decision to allow the Turkish Cypriots' transfer to Turkey and provide the Base facilities for this purpose was made not in response to Turkish pressure, but purely for humanitarian reasons "because of the hardship suffered by the refugees living under canvas in severe winter weather" (The Times). Two points can be made about such invocation of humanitarian motives: The weather was and is no better for the 200,000 Greek Cypriot refugees whom the Turkish authorities have refused to allow to return to their homes, and as a result, if people object to refugees being used as political pawns (not that the Turkish Cypriots were so treated since, as already observed, they were always free to return to their homes) one's attitude in this matter should not be one sided; and, secondly, how does one explain Britain's sudden change of policy in this matter, particularly when such reversal of policy was preceded in point of time by severe Turkish pressure coupled with threats otherwise than as submission, abdication of responsibility and appeasement? Furthermore, if this decision was taken as part of any kind of deal under which the Turkish Government in its turn would make some concessions to the Greek Cypriots, not only has there been no indication of this but also the Turkish Foreign Secretary is recently reported to have said that 'no gestures' can be made as, apparently, any gestures to be made on the part of the Turkish side must await a political settlement and agreement on the framework of a bizonal federation. At the very least, England could have acceded to Turkey's request for a transfer but insisted on watertight guarantees relating to such Turkish Cypriots remaining in Turkey and not illegally coming back to Cyprus. This surely would not only have been within Great Britain's rights as a guarantor but should also have been seen as the performance of an existing obligation.

What seems to have happened is that the British Government has come to regard a bizonal federation as inevitable and has given up all hope of pressurizing or influencing Turkey *prior to full satisfaction of Turkish substantive demands*. If British policy proceeded upon the hope or expectation of important Turkish concessions following upon the transfer of the 'refugees' to the north, such expectation has been disappointed; at the same time, the British action has cast doubt upon continued existence of the sovereign bases and has effectively incapacitated Great Britain from any constructive negotiating role in the future.

Britain, in fact, has become an active co-partner to Turkey in the destruction of Cyprus' Independence and Mr. Callaghan's decision, clearly contrary both to International law and the institutional framework of the Republic, does not help either the people of Cyprus or Great Britain's moral position in the world.

INDEX

Index   221